SMALL GROUPS FOR BIG READERS

10 QUESTIONS ANSWERED ABOUT CORE READING INSTRUCTION IN THE K–5 CLASSROOM

TAYLAR B. **WENZEL**

ANALEXIS **KENNEDY**

DENA D. **SLANDA**

MELISSA R. **CARLI**

Solution Tree | Press

Copyright © 2025 by Solution Tree Press

Materials appearing here are copyrighted. With one exception, all rights are reserved. Readers may reproduce only those pages marked "Reproducible." Otherwise, no part of this book may be reproduced or transmitted in any form or by any means (electronic, photocopying, recording, or otherwise) without prior written permission of the publisher.

AI outputs featured in figures 5.2, 5.7, 8.10, and 8.12 generated with the assistance of ChatGPT and Copilot. Cover images created with Adobe Firefly.

555 North Morton Street
Bloomington, IN 47404
800.733.6786 (toll free) / 812.336.7700
FAX: 812.336.7790

email: info@SolutionTree.com
SolutionTree.com

Visit **go.SolutionTree.com/literacy** to download the free reproducibles in this book.

Printed in the United States of America

Library of Congress Cataloging-in-Publication Data

Names: Wenzel, Taylar (Taylar B.), 1981- author. | Kennedy, Analexis, author. | Slanda, Dena, 1977- author. | Carli, Melissa R., author.
Title: Small groups for big readers : ten questions answered about core reading instruction in the K-5 classroom / Taylar B. Wenzel, Analexis Kennedy, Dena Slanda, and Melissa R. Carli.
Description: Bloomington, IN : Solution Tree Press, [2025] | Includes bibliographical references and index.
Identifiers: LCCN 2024039616 (print) | LCCN 2024039617 (ebook) | ISBN 9781960574565 (paperback) | ISBN 9781960574572 (ebook)
Subjects: LCSH: Reading (Elementary) | Group reading. | Group work in education.
Classification: LCC LB1573 .W397 2025 (print) | LCC LB1573 (ebook) | DDC 372.4--dc23/eng/20241120
LC record available at https://lccn.loc.gov/2024039616
LC ebook record available at https://lccn.loc.gov/2024039617

Solution Tree
Jeffrey C. Jones, CEO
Edmund M. Ackerman, President

Solution Tree Press
President and Publisher: Douglas M. Rife
Associate Publishers: Todd Brakke and Kendra Slayton
Editorial Director: Laurel Hecker
Art Director: Rian Anderson
Copy Chief: Jessi Finn
Production Editor: Madonna Evans
Copy Editor: Anne Marie Watkins
Proofreader: Sarah Ludwig
Text and Cover Designer: Fabiana Cochran
Acquisitions Editors: Carol Collins and Hilary Goff
Content Development Specialist: Amy Rubenstein
Associate Editors: Sarah Ludwig and Elijah Oates
Editorial Assistant: Madison Chartier

ACKNOWLEDGMENTS

Thank you to every educator we have met, those we have not, and those who have yet to enter the field. From each teacher we have encountered, we have gained valuable insight into practices that make an impact for readers. When you foster the skill and joy of reading within your students, you open their world to increased access and opportunity. We've witnessed this transformation firsthand in our own children, whose confidence in and love for reading has flourished thanks to the knowledge and passion of amazing teachers like you, who have dedicated their hearts to this incredible profession.

—*Taylar, Ana, Dena, and Melissa*

We extend special appreciation to Collaborative Classroom and Orange County Public Schools as thought partners who have contributed to our impact as authors and educators. We would also like to thank Mickey Kennedy for serving as our video editor.

Solution Tree Press would like to thank the following reviewers:

Lindsey Bingley
Literacy and Numeracy Lead
Foothills Academy Society
Calgary, Alberta, Canada

Becca Bouchard
Educator
Calgary, Alberta, Canada

Jennifer Rasmussen
Literacy Specialist and
Instructional Service Director
CESA 4
West Salem, Wisconsin

Christie Shealy
Director of Testing and
Accountability
Anderson School District One
Williamston, South Carolina

Rachel Swearengin
Fifth-Grade Teacher
Manchester Park Elementary School
Lenexa, Kansas

Kim Timmerman
Principal
ADM Middle School
Adel, Iowa

Visit **go.SolutionTree.com/literacy** to download
the free reproducibles in this book.

TABLE OF CONTENTS

About the Authors ix

Introduction 1
    Literacy Instruction Matters 3
    Things to Consider as You Read 3
    About This Book 7

Chapter 1: What Do I Know About My
Students as Readers? 17
    An Asset-Based Lens 19
    The Active View of Reading Model 20
    Data Sources and Student Reader Profiles 24
    The ABC Reader Profile Framework 25
    Summary 32

Chapter 2: How Does Differentiating Small-Group
Instruction Promote Access and Equity? 35
    Differentiated Reading Instruction 36
    Differentiated Instruction in the Classroom 43
    Differentiated Instruction Within MTSS 43
    Summary 47

Chapter 3: How Do I Connect to Whole-Group Instruction?. 49
    Interleaved Practice 52
    The Gradual Release Model. 55
    Knowledge of Curriculum Standards. 57
    Alignment and Coherence From Whole Group to Small Group 59
    Summary. 62

Chapter 4: How Do I Plan for Small-Group Instruction?. . 65
    Intentional Planning 67
    Lesson Structures and Instructional Routines to Support Readers . . . 72
    Logistics for Organizing, Managing, and Preparing Materials 86
    Teacher Content Knowledge. 88
    Summary. 91

Chapter 5: How Do I Select and Evaluate Text? 93
    Text Definition 94
    Text Selection 95
    Text Alignment to Lesson Purpose 99
    Text Considerations 102
    Text Accessibility 103
    Artificial Intelligence for Text Creation. 105
    Representation in Texts 106
    Summary. 106

Chapter 6: How Do I Engage My Readers During Small-Group Instruction? 109
    Teacher Facilitation and Student Engagement. 110
    Engagement Strategies in Action 119
    Summary. 135

Chapter 7: How Do I Monitor and Respond to My Students as Readers? 137
Monitoring and Responding to Readers. 138
Responding to Readers on the Spot 142
Leveraging Observations as Opportunities for Future Instruction....147
Summary.........147

Chapter 8: How Does Writing Connect to My Small-Group Instruction?.........149
The Reading and Writing Connection 150
Writing Instruction in Small-Group Lessons.........152
Writing to Support Word Recognition.........152
Writing Samples for Understanding Word Recognition Skills 154
Writing to Enhance Reading Comprehension.........158
Writing Opportunities in and Beyond the Small-Group Lesson......158
Writing Samples for Understanding Your Readers' Comprehension ..161
Summary.........165

Chapter 9: How Do I Build My Readers' Knowledge? 167
The Role of Knowledge Building in Literacy Instruction 168
Common Strategies to Gauge Readers' Background Knowledge 172
Connections to Whole-Group Topics.........176
Text Sets.........176
Summary.........177

Chapter 10: What Are the Rest of My Students Doing While I'm Teaching a Small Group?.........179
Considerations for the Rest of the Class 180
The Literacy Block.........181
Authentic, Aligned Tasks With Accountability 184
Student Grouping.........189
Structure in Independent Practice.........190
Summary.........195

Epilogue 197

   Extend Your Reflections 198

   Expand Your Professional Community and Commitment 198

Appendix: Leading the Learning Action Guide 201

   Chapter 1: What Do I Know About My Students as Readers?. 204

   Chapter 2: How Does Differentiating Small-Group Instruction
      Promote Access and Equity? 207

   Chapter 3: How Do I Connect to Whole-Group Instruction? 209

   Chapter 4: How Do I Plan for Small-Group Instruction?. 211

   Chapter 5: How Do I Select and Evaluate Text? 213

   Chapter 6: How Do I Engage My Readers During
      Small-Group Instruction? 215

   Chapter 7: How Do I Monitor and Respond to
      My Students as Readers? 217

   Chapter 8: How Does Writing Connect to
      My Small-Group Instruction? 220

   Chapter 9: How Do I Build My Readers' Knowledge? 221

   Chapter 10: What Are the Rest of My Students Doing
      While I'm Teaching a Small Group? 224

   Summary. 226

References and Resources 227

Index 243

ABOUT THE AUTHORS

Taylar B. Wenzel, EdD, is a faculty member in the College of Community Innovation and Education at the University of Central Florida. She teaches undergraduate and graduate courses in elementary and reading education and supports preservice and practicing teachers in the field. Her research has focused on the role of students' cognitive and metacognitive strategy use across reading and mathematics contexts, job-embedded professional learning, and the use of artificial intelligence in education. Wenzel's classroom experience includes work as a public-school teacher and instructional coach.

Wenzel is the cofounder of the UCF Reading Clinic, a collaboration with other faculty members through which undergraduate and graduate students provide instruction and intervention to K–8 students in the Central Florida area. She is also the faculty lead of the UCF Downtown Saturday Reading Camp, a community-based reading program offered in partnership with the City of Orlando. As a leader in higher education practices, she serves as a team member of the Evidence Advocacy Center's Institutes of Higher Education and Educator Preparation Programs.

Wenzel regularly presents her work at regional, national, and international conferences, as well as in invited keynote addresses. She advises numerous school districts and education agencies and has published articles, book chapters, and professional development handbooks.

Wenzel earned bachelor's and master's degrees in elementary education from the University of Florida and a doctorate in curriculum and instruction from the University of Central Florida.

To learn more about Wenzel's work, follow @taylar_wenzel on X, formerly known as Twitter.

Analexis Kennedy, EdD, is a reading faculty member in the College of Community Innovation and Education at the University of Central Florida, where she teaches literacy courses to undergraduate and graduate students. She spent fifteen years working with K–12 students, teachers, and administrators as a classroom teacher, literacy coach, district reading specialist, and state professional development coordinator. Her research focuses on literacy coaching, professional and adult learning, literacy strategies, and best practices in K–12.

Kennedy is a member of the International Literacy Association, ASCD, and the Florida Literacy Association. She has been recognized as First Year Teacher of the Year, Teacher of the Year, and a National Board Certified Teacher. She presents regularly in state, national, and international conferences, and some of her most cherished work is when she works alongside teachers and students in classrooms across the country.

Kennedy earned a bachelor's degree in elementary education from Florida International University, a master's degree in reading and literacy education from Florida International University, an education specialist degree in curriculum and instruction and literacy from the University of Central Florida, and a doctorate in curriculum and instruction from the University of Central Florida.

To learn more about Kennedy's work, follow @anakenn on X, formerly known as Twitter.

About the Authors

Dena D. Slanda, PhD, is a senior technical assistance consultant with the American Institutes for Research (AIR), where she leads large-scale projects to deliver tools, training, and a diverse range of services to state agencies, districts, schools, educator preparation programs, and other education organizations. She coleads technical assistance for the Lead IDEA Center, supports state literacy plan development for the Comprehensive Literacy State Development (CLSD) National Literacy Center, and manages special projects for the Center on Great Teachers and Leaders. Prior to joining AIR, Slanda was faculty at the University of Central Florida, where she served as co-principal investigator of several federally-funded personnel preparation grants from the Office of Special Education Programs at the U.S. Department of Education and taught undergraduate and graduate courses. Her passion for advancing literacy development was evidenced in her work as a middle school teacher, where she taught intensive reading and STEM.

Slanda has a remarkable practitioner's and researcher's perspective in the field of special education, including a focus in inclusive practices, culturally inclusive pedagogies and practices, literacy, and multitiered system of supports (MTSS). Her professional activities have included serving as the president of the Florida Association of Teacher Educators and the Florida Council for Exceptional Children and chair of the College of Community Innovation and Education Alumni Association.

Slanda is an accomplished advocate, researcher, presenter, professional development leader, and author of several books and peer-reviewed journal articles in the field of education and special education. She received a master's degree in exceptional student education and a doctorate in education with an emphasis in exceptional education from University of Central Florida.

To learn more about Slanda's work, follow @DrDenaSlanda on X, formerly known as Twitter.

Melissa R. Carli, MEd, is a project manager for several federally-funded projects at the University of Central Florida. Through these projects, Carli supports teachers as they build their professional knowledge to support all learners.

In her former role, Carli was a curriculum program specialist, where she collaborated with schools and teachers to assist them in preparing for and implementing effective instruction. Her focus was on providing teachers with the tools and knowledge necessary to help their students think critically about the content they encounter. Carli taught at both the elementary and middle school levels and has served as both mathematics coach and department chair.

Carli is a coauthor of *Making Sense of Mathematics for Teaching the Small Group*, a book in the *Making Sense of Mathematics for Teaching* series. She has presented her work at local and state conferences, including the National Council of Teachers of Mathematics (NCTM), on using effective instructional practices in mathematics. She is a member of the Florida Council of Teachers of Mathematics and NCTM.

She earned both bachelor's and master's degrees in education from the University of Florida, as well as a master's degree in educational leadership.

To learn more about Carli's work, follow @MCarliLovesMath on X, formerly known as Twitter.

To book Taylar B. Wenzel, Analexis Kennedy, Dena D. Slanda, or Melissa R. Carli for professional development, contact pd@SolutionTree.com.

INTRODUCTION

Competence precedes confidence, Zaretta Hammond (2015) states in her book *Culturally Responsive Teaching and the Brain*. Students are more likely to feel confident when they have demonstrated proficiency of skills and knowledge in a supportive, risk-free environment (Hammond, 2015). This seems to be especially true for literacy, and we suspect that if you're reading this book, you likely agree. In our work in classrooms, we've seen firsthand how readers' motivation grows when they become proficient in both decoding and deeply understanding text. To become increasingly skilled and strategic readers, students must have access to high-quality literacy instruction, which we know you strive to achieve each day (International Literacy Association [ILA], 2020). Readers have the right to knowledgeable, skilled, and qualified literacy educators—that's you—who have integrated support systems to strengthen their teaching and learning practices. In writing this book, we hope to become part of your integrated support system.

Small-group reading instruction offers a powerful context that can significantly impact your students' achievement and passion for reading (Gersten, Newman-Gonchar, Haymond, & Dimino, 2017; Neitzel et al., 2021; Wanzek et al., 2016). Russell Gersten, Rebecca Newman-Gonchar, Kelly S. Haymond, and Joseph Dimino (2017) find that small-group instruction allows for targeted, individualized support, enabling teachers to focus on specific skills and needs. Small-group settings have also been found to promote greater student engagement and participation, providing opportunities for more personalized feedback and interaction (Wanzek et al., 2016). These findings are further supported by recent research that shows small-group instruction not only boosts academic achievement but also cultivates a passion for reading by creating a supportive and motivating learning environment (Haelermans, 2022). When students can connect with texts that are both meaningful and appropriately challenging, they are more likely to develop a positive attitude toward reading and a lasting interest in literacy.

In our work supporting teachers, we often hear about the difficult decisions involved in planning for and implementing small-group instruction. We believe this is because schools and teachers know the value that individualized instruction and feedback provide for each of our readers, especially those with diverse learning needs. In an effort to maximize that value, we sometimes see that this knowledge increases the pressure around the practice of small-group instruction. Even though small-group instruction seems like such a simple concept, the multitude of choices—including logistics, content, grouping, text selection, delivery, and much more—make the practice of running small groups complex. We know small-group instruction is about our readers and supporting them the best we can; however, small-group instruction is also about us, the teachers. When an instructional practice feels effective and rewarding, then we are happy to focus our energy and time on it—competence precedes confidence. Small-group instruction empowers us as teachers to learn more about our students and where they are as readers so that we can lean into their strengths to help them become strong readers.

Our goal is to strengthen your self-efficacy around small-group reading instruction by building on your current knowledge of literacy practices. Just as students' competence precedes their confidence in reading, we know the same can be true for educators. To feel confident in our instructional decision making, we must also feel assured that our instructional choices are grounded in research and that they positively impact our readers' achievement. That said, we know you have many decisions to make when it comes to planning for what happens inside and outside of small-group reading lessons. You may feel more confident about some decisions than others. To honor your unique professional learning needs, we organized this book in a way that lets you prioritize your areas of focus. We are honored that you have chosen this book to recharge your instructional expertise, and it is our intent to partner with you as you read through the ideas, explanations, and examples we are eager to share.

Literacy Instruction Matters

As an author team, our experiences range from serving as classroom teachers, instructional coaches, and curriculum specialists to supporting preservice and in-service teachers within higher-education contexts. Each of us began in the classroom and took various journeys within the education profession, which is why we found it important to bring each of our voices into this critical resource guide. We collaborate closely with teachers and teacher teams across the United States to strengthen our instructional pedagogy. Being able to collectively step into thousands of classrooms around the United States allows us clarity on both the effective instructional practices that improve reader achievement as well as the obstacles teachers face every day.

In addition to our work with practitioners, we also have experience supporting school districts as they strive to build communities of learners within their schools. These collaborations focus on planning and facilitating professional learning as well as developing curriculum and pedagogical resources. Learning with and from teachers in this process has provided us with unique insight into how to best support our readers. We have gained a lens on how to enable access and equity within our classrooms by supporting *all* readers. This lens serves as an important part of our writing as we consider all readers through the various aspects of literacy development.

No matter what roles we hold, our efforts align most with practitioners who give their all to develop their students as readers. We have created this book with our shared goal of providing every reader with the instructional literacy opportunities they deserve.

Things to Consider as You Read

As we wrote this book, we identified underlying assumptions we knew would be important to share with you before you started reading to offer context and share insight into our thinking. We outlined them in the following sections to invite you into our discussions and considerations as an author team.

STUDENTS AS READERS

In an effort to put students' reading experiences at the forefront of this book, we often refer to students as *readers*. When we share about students within a reading lesson or discuss how they engage in text, we refer to them as *readers*. When we step back and look at the big picture of our classroom or classroom practices, we refer to them as *students*. With this distinction, we hope to focus our lens on readers' identities and experiences in literacy instruction.

In the title of this book, we use the term *big readers* to represent the multidimensional strengths that we aspire to develop within the readers in our classrooms. In the elementary classroom, the *big readers* we envision are:

- Skilled in decoding to support word recognition of connected text; they apply their phonics knowledge and print awareness by persistently tackling increasingly complex texts.
- Expressive in their reading; they are aware of the structure of text and use it to make meaning as they are reading the passage.
- Curious and eager to learn about words, ideas, stories, and information in text; they consider their relationship with the author and look for ways to appreciate and learn from what the author has portrayed.
- Analytical of what they read; they ask questions beyond what is clearly stated and consider other texts and media when developing conclusions.
- Reflective of their own understanding as they read; they slow down and reread as necessary for full comprehension.
- Able to use various strategies; they employ techniques such as summarization, visualization, and the use of questioning to think about their reading and learning from the text.

The experiences readers encounter within the small group can have a *big* impact on their reading proficiency and identity.

CORE INSTRUCTION WITHIN TIERED SUPPORTS

You likely support a wide range of readers within your grade level. In doing so, you ensure your readers have access to grade-level curriculum by leveraging their strengths and meeting their individual needs. Multitiered system of supports (MTSS) is a proactive, equity-focused framework designed to support all students (Little, Slanda, & Cramer, 2025). MTSS is designed to identify strengths and address the needs of students who require additional support. Tier 1—the core instruction within the three-tiered MTSS framework—should include differentiated instruction for all students. Tiers 2 and 3 are designed to provide individualized and intensified intervention for students who require additional support beyond core instruction.

A common question we explore in our work with teachers is, "How do we plan and deliver strong core instruction in Tier 1 to reduce the likelihood of a disproportionate number of readers needing Tier 2 intervention?" In an aim to consider this question, this book focuses on core instruction and how small-group reading instruction can be strengthened by differentiating learning for readers within Tier 1. Throughout the book, we discuss alignment within and across tiers of instruction in consideration of reading intervention, and in chapter 2 (page 35), we dive into MTSS—but our primary focus is on building strong core instruction in Tier 1.

ACCESS AND EQUITY FOR ALL READERS

Accessible and equitable literacy instruction must be central to the literacy block as you design differentiated small-group instruction to meet the needs of *all* readers. Readers enter our classrooms with unique funds of knowledge shaped by their experiences in the world around them. Understanding readers' cultural and social capital allows us to leverage their strengths to meet their needs. Instructional design should be highly individualized and allow teachers to remove barriers and promote equitable access to learning. For some readers, this may look like explicitly building background knowledge, while for others, it may require additional opportunities to practice new learning. By matching teaching strategies and approaches with students' diverse learning needs, we recognize that not all students need the same support.

As teachers, we can offer assurance and consistency in our instructional decision making that leverage accessible and equitable literacy instruction in our classrooms. This includes ensuring all students have the phonics skills necessary to accurately decode text with automaticity, providing all readers with access to text and choice for reading experiences, and promoting intellectual curiosity about text (versus a pedagogy of compliance; Hammond, 2001). In this context, consistency refers to the intentional implementation of effective teaching practices for all students, ensuring that these assurances are not sporadic or limited to certain groups.

We are reassured by the fact that these examples, among other equitable literacy teaching practices, can be implemented by teachers at the classroom level. Rather than waiting for top-down implementation of literacy shifts, you can identify assurances and create consistency to prioritize access and equity for all readers. With this in mind, the practices and examples we share in this book are intended to help you identify opportunities for consistency and potential shifts in your instruction. If we want to build strong readers, we must create a classroom culture that empowers students, affirms their identities and strengths, and recognizes their data-informed opportunities for growth. In this book, we strive to affirm what you already know to be strong teaching practices and to empower you as you seek to achieve equitable outcomes for all.

EVIDENCE-BASED PRACTICES AND PROGRAMS

In our field, it's imperative to implement evidence-based practices or programs that ensure high-quality literacy instruction. An evidence-based practice or program is based on outcomes from rigorous research that show the practice or program worked. In this book, we invite you to learn about evidence-based practices through our efforts to translate research into practice.

We also acknowledge that you may have varying levels of autonomy in the selection of curriculum materials and the development and implementation of lesson plans for small-group instruction. For example, perhaps your district adopted an evidence-based program and expects it to be taught with fidelity. Regardless of your district's or school's selection of curriculum materials, we believe the evidence-based practices in this book can support you. We know that teachers can deliver intentional and impactful lessons when they understand the *why* behind steps in a lesson. We hope this consideration helps frame your reading about evidence-based practices, regardless of the curriculum materials you use for small-group reading instruction.

VIDEOS AND ARTIFACTS AS SHARED LEARNING EXPERIENCES

Although this book does not have all the answers about small-group reading instruction, we hope that its chapters can be used as a launchpad to dig deeper into instructional practices by sharing our work with teams of teachers and educational leaders. With this in mind, we use video files throughout this book to encourage shared learning experiences. We provide video segments of individual readers, small-group lessons, and teacher interviews to demonstrate practices, springboard discussion, and help form next steps. Videos are filmed in kindergarten through fifth-grade classrooms and explore a variety of reader types, reader behaviors, teacher practices, and routines. We do not consider these videos to be model videos without potential for improvement. Rather, they serve as shared experiences from which we can reflect with you and highlight our own wonderings based on real instruction in action. We also know that most of the work and thinking you do cannot be captured with video. In some cases, when video is not the preferred medium to create a shared vision, we provide planning tools and sample lessons for you to examine, apply, or adapt within your own learning communities. The videos are presented as QR codes that you can easily access from your phone. You can also go to **go.SolutionTree.com/literacy** to access these videos.

About This Book

We designed this book in a question-and-answer format so that you—or you and your team—can prioritize your reading in a way that works best for you. Each chapter title focuses on one predominant question within the context of small-group reading instruction.

To support you in prioritizing the chapters that align with your professional learning needs, we describe each chapter's content here.

- **Chapter 1: What Do I Know About My Students as Readers?** Forming small groups begins with getting to know the students in your classroom. Collecting, analyzing, and interpreting reading data allows teachers to make informed grouping and instructional decisions to improve outcomes for *all* students. This chapter introduces the Asset-Based Continuum (ABC) Reader Profile Framework tool, which we reference throughout subsequent chapters with reader examples.

- **Chapter 2: How Does Differentiating Small-Group Instruction Promote Access and Equity?** Small-group instruction provides teachers with the opportunity to individualize supports to meet the needs of *all* students. Access and equity are central to the literacy block as teachers build inclusive classrooms designed to meet the needs of all students. This chapter explores how data-informed differentiation within small-group instruction supports all students. Additionally, it covers considerations for flexible grouping and meeting frequency.

- **Chapter 3: How Do I Connect to Whole-Group Instruction?** Understanding how small-group instruction connects to and extends from whole-group instruction helps teachers keep both the content and students in mind when planning for their literacy block. Using the lens of the gradual release of responsibility framework, this chapter encourages teachers to think about how small-group instruction is situated within the literacy block as a form of differentiation for whole-group instruction, curriculum standards, and decision making. This chapter includes resources to align instruction with curriculum standards and strategies for meeting readers where they are while also providing access to grade-level content.

- **Chapter 4: How Do I Plan for Small-Group Instruction?** Planning for small-group instruction requires deep content knowledge, an understanding of students as readers, and mastery of various evidence-based instructional practices. In this chapter, we share lesson structures and evidence-based routines to promote efficiency and effectiveness. In addition, we provide considerations and tips for organizing and managing materials for small-group lessons.

- **Chapter 5: How Do I Select and Evaluate Text?** A deep understanding of instructional text is critical when planning for small-group instruction. Whether using an adopted curriculum or selecting text on their own, teachers' multifaceted understanding of a text's complexity impacts instructional opportunities and decision making. This chapter offers a protocol for evaluating instructional text, including quantitative and qualitative aspects such as text structure, language features, syntax, and more. This protocol prompts teachers to consider their readers' characteristics, such as their background knowledge of the topic and level of interest.

- **Chapter 6: How Do I Engage My Readers During Small-Group Instruction?** This chapter offers facilitation strategies to ensure readers are the ones doing the heavy lifting during small-group lessons. Content is framed around the role of the teacher and students within the small group. This chapter discusses when the teacher should facilitate and when they should provide explicit instruction. Additionally, it explains how building and maintaining predictable routines with clear, consistent expectations helps students (and teachers) feel comfortable.

- **Chapter 7: How Do I Monitor and Respond to My Students as Readers?** Monitoring and responding to students during small-group instruction looks different than during whole-group instruction. This chapter focuses on the ways teachers can monitor and respond to readers as they engage with text. Anchored in the ABC Reader Profile Framework, we provide recommendations for observing students' reading behaviors and determining when and how to respond with intention. We share both immediate, on-the-spot responses and responses to plan into subsequent small-group and whole-group lessons and extended practice opportunities.

- **Chapter 8: How Does Writing Connect to My Small-Group Instruction?** Rich literacy instruction includes opportunities for writing development through explicit instruction and purposeful tasks. This approach includes supporting early readers' development of encoding skills, which equips them to build word knowledge, communicate their thinking, and deepen their comprehension through written response. Extending writing tasks beyond small-group instruction for collaborative and independent practice also strengthens students' literacy skills. This chapter provides concrete ideas to integrate writing opportunities both within small-group instruction and as extensions beyond lessons.

- **Chapter 9: How Do I Build My Readers' Knowledge?** Knowledge building is an essential condition for reading comprehension. Knowledge on a variety of topics makes it easier for readers to read text, understand their reading, and retain information. Instruction grounded in knowledge building facilitates interdisciplinary connections. This chapter shares how small-group instruction affords the opportunity to determine a student's background knowledge; identify rich, quality texts and resources that support knowledge building; and plan instruction that focuses on both literacy and knowledge.

- **Chapter 10: What Are the Rest of My Students Doing While I'm Teaching a Small Group?** Students spend a significant amount of time engaged in literacy learning outside of small-group instruction. Depending on the classroom, this time may be organized as centers or stations, collaborative practice, or independent work. Regardless of the organizational structure, this time provides a valuable opportunity for students to practice and apply their learning through meaningful, authentic literacy tasks. This chapter helps teachers identify content and tasks to support literacy learning for the rest of the class while they pull small groups. Sample organizational structures and considerations are also a focus.

- **Appendix: Leading the Learning Action Guide**—The "Leading the Learning Action Guide" is designed to support teacher leaders, instructional coaches, administrators, and those leading professional learning on small-group reading instruction. This action guide contains videos that spotlight teaching strategies and reflection questions organized by chapter topic. You can use these videos to make practices come to life, aid discussions on focus areas for your school or district, and create a space for wonderings. The action guide offers additional videos not part of the text. You will also find resources to dig deeper into a particular focus area.

In addition to the question-and-answer format of the book, you will find predictable chapter features to support your journey to using small groups to support big readers. These features include:

- An opening vignette to situate you within the chapter's focus question
- Guiding questions to launch you into the chapter
- Emphasis on why each chapter topic is important and suggestions for research
- Embedded QR code videos that demonstrate practices, highlight teacher voices, or show readers in action
- Expand Your Toolbox sections to assist you in building your professional resources to support instruction
- Reflections that serve as a bridge from your reading to your classroom practice and suggestions to support you as you recharge your small-group reading instruction

The following are some suggestions for reading this book.

CHOOSE YOUR OWN PROFESSIONAL LEARNING ADVENTURE

We encourage you to read the book in order, but you may select a chapter sequence guided by your personal wonderings and professional learning needs. Whichever order you choose, we highly recommend starting with chapter 1; it will help you place your students at the forefront of your thinking as you consider what you know about them as readers and how you know it. The remaining chapters will build on this understanding with various lenses to strengthen your instructional practices around small-group reading lessons. Within each chapter, you will find notes that share where more information on a particular idea can be found in another chapter. These notes may guide you as you choose your own adventure on the spot for personalized professional learning throughout this book.

USE THE SMALL-GROUP READING IMPLEMENTATION QUICK-GUIDE

We created the Small-Group Reading Implementation Quick-Guide (figure I.1) as a reference tool to guide you before, during, and after planning for small-group lessons. This tool includes questions that are intended to support your instructional decision making while also streamlining the process for planning and teaching multiple small-group lessons each day. Each category of the quick-guide, and the accompanying example questions, is aligned with the chapters in this book that offer supportive content for that aspect of lesson implementation. Use these questions to guide your lesson planning. If you find that you need instructional support with a certain question, we've also referenced the chapter where that content is addressed to help guide your thinking.

	Create Data-Informed Groups (Chapters 1, 2, 3)
Reliable assessment data	• What do I notice about my students as readers? What data-informed evidence supports what I know about my students? • What additional informal reading assessments might I use to know more about students as readers? • How can I use the ABC Reader Profile Framework to interpret and integrate multiple assessment sources?
Data to form groups	• How will I use data points to make grouping decisions? • What is the data-informed instructional focus area for each group of readers (comprehension, fluency, or word recognition and decoding)? • Which readers have similar data-informed goals? How might students be grouped flexibly for instruction?
Instructional organization	• How will I use organizing tools to plan for when I will meet with each group and what the lesson focus will be?
Differentiated instruction	• What are some important considerations as I work to meet the needs of all students, including students with high-intensity needs, students with disabilities, and students who are multilingual?
	Prepare for the Lesson (Chapters 3, 4, 5, 9)
Text selection and materials	• How might I connect to whole-group instruction, including text selection considerations, if my students are reading below grade-level benchmarks? • How will I ensure access to text for all students, including those who are building foundational skills? • How will I select text to implement knowledge-building practices in small-group lessons?
Timing and frequency	• How much time will I spend with each group based on their instructional focus? • How many days per week will I meet with each group?
Lesson routines	• What evidence-based instructional routines support the instructional focus for each group? • If using an adopted curriculum with lesson plans provided, which evidence-based routines are embedded in the lesson plan structures? • How can I employ predictable routines to promote equity, efficiency, and engagement during instruction?

FIGURE I.1: The small-group reading implementation quick-guide.

continued ▶

	Teach the Lesson (Chapters 6, 7, 8, 9)
Engagement strategies	• How do my engagement strategies align with the instructional focus of the lesson (comprehension and metacognition, building foundational skills)? • How might my understanding of teacher-student roles impact student engagement opportunities in my lessons?
Text reading considerations	• Do the opportunities and time allotted for student practice and application match the actual time spent on practice and application during lesson facilitation? • How am I planning for students to read text (independently aloud, independently silently, chorally, prompted for decoding and high-frequency words) based on readers' proficiency and lesson goals? • How am I chunking the text, when needed, for a single day's lesson?
Monitoring and responding to readers	• How will I monitor students' text reading progress to guide my instruction? • What will I listen for to respond to my readers with on-the-spot scaffolds? • What are ways I can adjust my instruction to respond to students within and beyond a single small-group lesson?
Student ownership	• Do my students have ample opportunities for applied practice and ownership during small-group instruction?
Embedded writing	• How does the content of my small group serve as a springboard for writing for a variety of purposes? • How might small-group instruction serve as a scaffold for daily writing practice opportunities?
	Adjust After the Lesson (Chapters 1, 2, 3)
Flexible grouping	• How might you group students for small-group instruction to create learning opportunities that allow you to observe and gather data about their learning?
Learning goals	• When should I move to a new learning goal? • How does the interleaved practice approach impact my selection of learning goals? • How might texts be used within and across small-group lessons to meet learning goals?
	Extend the Lesson (Chapter 10)
Organization	• How might I organize the rest of the class while I meet with small groups? • How might I plan for and convey clear expectations for student learning? • How might the intended learning goals for activities and tasks help me to determine whether students should work individually or collaboratively during extended practice?
Connect to small group and whole group	• How do I plan for extended practice opportunities that connect to small group? To whole group? • How might I use consistent lesson materials (including texts) to offer authentic extended practice for readers?

Visit **go.SolutionTree.com/literacy** *for a free reproducible version of this figure.*

LAUNCH A BOOK STUDY WITH COLLEAGUES

In developing the chapter topics for this book, we chose to focus on the top ten questions teachers typically ask us to address the depth and breadth of knowledge that supports effective small-group instruction. We also recognize that, in most districts, a school year is typically ten months. With this alignment, we offer the idea that this book can serve as a useful book study for you and your colleagues, with one chapter reading and discussion scheduled per month.

In this approach, you and your colleagues can decide together how to navigate the sequence of book chapters. You might also want to use the chapter videos, vignettes, and reflections as anchors for your monthly book study discussions.

REFLECT ON YOUR LEARNING

Since we intend for you to navigate this book with a *choose your own adventure* approach, we provide a tool for considering priority topics—or chapters—to guide your own professional learning. This tool can also be used as a note-taking guide along your journey. Figure I.2 outlines the small-group reading practices following the book's chapter order.

Small-Group Reading Practice	My Strengths	My Opportunities for Growth	My Wonderings
Knowing students as readers (Chapter 1)			
Differentiating small-group instruction to promote access and equity (Chapter 2)			
Connecting to whole-group instruction (Chapter 3)			
Planning for small-group instruction (Chapter 4)			
Selecting and evaluating text (Chapter 5)			
Engaging readers during small-group instruction (Chapter 6)			
Monitoring and responding to students as readers (Chapter 7)			
Connecting writing to small-group instruction (Chapter 8)			
Building readers' knowledge (Chapter 9)			
Planning and organizing beyond the small group (Chapter 10)			

FIGURE I.2: Self-assessment of small-group reading practices.

*Visit **go.SolutionTree.com/literacy** for a free reproducible version of this figure.*

We also offer a tool for your personalized goal setting and action planning as you consider small-group reading instruction in your classroom. Figure I.3 can help guide your thinking about a long-term goal, three aligned minigoals, and three actionable tasks. This process enables you to track your progress and recognize incremental success as you work toward the implementation of your long-term goal.

Teacher Reflection Tool

As you consider your professional learning goals while reading this book, identify your personal strengths in planning and teaching small-group instruction and your opportunities for growth.

Based on your identified opportunities for growth, develop a goal that you would like to work on this school year. Once you have determined your goal, identify incremental minigoals that will help you get there. Break these down into actionable tasks that you will carry out in your classroom.

Strengths	Opportunities for Growth

Long-Term Goal

Three Minigoals		Three Actionable Tasks	
1		1	
2		2	
3		3	

FIGURE I.3: Teacher reflection tool.

*Visit **go.SolutionTree.com/literacy** for a free reproducible version of this figure.*

As we close this introduction, we invite you to embark on a journey of professional growth in small-group reading instruction. By affirming and building upon your existing knowledge, we aim to bolster your self-efficacy and confidence in making impactful instructional decisions. Just as students' competence precedes their confidence in reading, we believe the same holds true for educators. In the chapters that follow, you'll have the flexibility to prioritize your areas of focus, allowing you to tailor your learning experience to your specific goals and challenges.

We are truly honored that you've chosen this book to reinvigorate your instructional expertise. As we move forward, consider us your partners in this endeavor. We're eager to share the ideas, explanations, and examples in the coming chapters to inspire, inform, and empower you in your noble pursuit of nurturing confident, capable readers. Let's turn the page together and explore the impactful world of small-group reading instruction.

CHAPTER 1
WHAT DO I KNOW ABOUT MY STUDENTS AS READERS?

Forming small groups begins with knowing the students in your classroom—both as people and as readers. Teachers can use informal reading assessments and observational data to identify readers' strengths and target specific areas for supplemental and focused support during small-group instruction. However, synthesizing multiple data sources to identify instructional learning goals isn't always as easy as it may seem. Obstacles such as contradictory data points, data that quickly become outdated as instructional weeks and months pass, and the navigation of complex data can make it challenging to gain insight into each reader's strengths and needs. This chapter introduces an asset-based approach to assist you to collect, analyze, and interpret reading data so you can make informed decisions that improve outcomes for *all* readers.

Understanding students as readers is key to planning and implementing effective and engaging lessons. By knowing students' reading preferences, interests, strengths, and areas for growth, teachers can tailor instruction to meet their individual needs (Guthrie et al., 2004). Each student brings a diverse reading background with cultural and linguistic strengths into the classroom, and understanding those backgrounds enables teachers to differentiate instruction through the text they select, the resources they provide, and their areas of focus. Knowing students as readers empowers teachers to create dynamic and responsive lessons that build not only students' reading abilities and knowledge but their love for reading, especially when the emphasis is on their reading strengths.

As you read this chapter, consider your students. The following questions may also help frame your thinking.

- What do I notice about my students as readers? What data-informed evidence supports what I know about my students?
- How might I frame the characteristics of my students as readers through an asset-based lens?
- How might I interpret and integrate multiple assessment sources to have a clear understanding of each student's reading profile?
- How does the broader scope of reading development across the grades impact my perspective of the reading skills and behaviors that my students will develop at their grade level?

Consider the example of Adler, a second-grade reader, and watch the accompanying video.

MEET THE READER: ADLER

> Adler is a second-grade reader who is motivated and eager to read a variety of picture books across genres. Leading with curiosity to learn more about characters and topics in texts, he takes reading risks when he encounters unknown words. He embraces opportunities to talk about his reading experiences and shares retellings about what he read. At times, Adler's persistence and stamina for decoding outweigh his self-monitoring. This is evident when he continues to read with fervor despite mispronouncing words or using inconsistent phrasing that conveys a possible lack of understanding of the text. He readily applies reading skills taught during whole-group and small-group instruction and seeks opportunities to read silently and aloud, either to himself, his classmates, or his teacher.

PRIMARY READER SNAPSHOT: ADLER

What do you notice about Adler as a reader? Specifically, what observations help you make inferences about his strengths in decoding, fluency, comprehension, and metacognition?

Based on the video, what additional reading tasks and opportunities would you like to see Adler tackle as a reader?

We'll revisit these ideas and questions at the end of the chapter to identify ways to support instructional practices for small-group lesson planning in your classroom.

An Asset-Based Lens

What do you know about your students as readers? This open-ended question is one of the first questions we ask in our work with teachers because it puts the focus on our readers from the very beginning of our professional learning experiences together. Answers to this question are often varied. Sometimes, we hear teachers share trends about their class as readers overall, and sometimes we hear about data patterns among readers, almost as a precursor to how instructional groups might be formed. Other times, we hear about individual reader data, where teachers articulate which students are reading on, above, or below grade level.

As we begin to explore and strengthen our instructional practices around small-group reading in this book, we invite you to consider the same question: What do you know about your students as readers, and how do you know it? Consider whether your responses are framed in an asset-based or deficit-based approach.

- The *asset-based approach* promotes identifying and leveraging readers' strengths, including knowledge and skills, that readers bring to a unique situation or content area. This approach recognizes that readers each hold distinct talents and experiences that lead to their success (Flint & Jaggers, 2021).
- The *deficit-based approach* tends to recognize and address the noticed weaknesses, including missing knowledge and skills, that readers may have. This approach tends to view readers through the lens of what they lack and the challenges they face, which can result in limited expectations for their performance (Valencia, 2010).

While we are often drawn to notice our readers' instructional needs, reframing our observations through an asset-based lens can have a powerful impact on both our own instructional planning and our students' self-perceptions as readers. This approach allows us to identify what our students are currently able to do independently while planning instruction and selecting text or instructional materials that will support a learning trajectory to advance their reading skills and processes. An asset-based lens also enables us to share reading strengths with students directly. In doing so, our students learn more about themselves as readers and can have an active role in understanding and developing the skills they are working toward, which strengthens their reading processes and experiences with text (Förster & Souvignier, 2014).

The Active View of Reading Model

To maximize the benefit of using an asset-based approach, teachers need to have a strong understanding of the multidimensionality of the reading process. We find it helpful to use a conceptual framework of the reading process to ensure that we have a complete picture of our students' reading strengths and identities. The Active View of Reading model (Duke & Cartwright, 2021), shown in table 1.1, portrays the many reading processes that work in tandem during proficient text reading. The Active View of Reading model expands on the simple view of reading (Gough & Tunmer, 1986) and Scarborough's reading rope (Scarborough, 2001).

Nell K. Duke and Kelly B. Cartwright (2021) posit three important advances from the earlier models. The Active View of Reading recognizes the importance of active self-regulation for successful reading. Second, it expands on the relationship between word recognition and language comprehension and, third, presents how the two are not separate but rather overlapping processes. This is an important distinction as we think about our students as readers.

TABLE 1.1: The Active View of Reading

Word Recognition		
Phonological Awareness	The awareness of sounds that serves as the foundation to reading and spelling. *Phonological awareness* is the umbrella term that includes being able to hear the number of words in a sentence, rhyme, alliteration, and onset and rime, and includes *phonemic awareness*, which focuses on the sounds in individual words.	**Examples:** The girl ran the race. (5 words) /r/ /un/, /s/ /un/, /f/ /un/ (onset and rime) /r/ /u/ /n/ = run (phoneme blending) sun = /s/ /u/ /n/ (phoneme segmenting)
Alphabetic Principle	The relationship between letters and sounds.	**Examples:** /ă/ = a /b/ = b /ch/ = ch
Phonics Knowledge	The ability to understand the relationship between phonemes and graphemes and the patterns that support decoding. Students use this knowledge to read (decode) words in print. Phonics exists within a systematic scope and sequence.	**Examples:** CVC = short vowel sound CVe = long *e* is silent, and the vowel is typically long Digraphs = /ch/, /sh/, /th/

Decoding Skills	The ability to understand the relationship between letters and sounds and translate print into speech. *Encoding* is the ability to turn speech into print.	**Example:** Word: sunset A reader can recognize this is a compound word made up of two CVC words (sun-set). They read the words from print or hear the word *sunset* and are able to spell it while applying the relationship between sound and print to written form.
Recognition of Words by Sight	The ability to identify words by sight. There are high-frequency words that are temporarily irregular or permanently irregular. These words appear with high frequency in text and are taught explicitly, regardless of where students are in the phonics scope and sequence. Some of these words eventually become decodable once students have learned the pattern, while others will remain permanently irregular.	**Examples:** Permanently irregular high-frequency words: where, there, was, said Temporarily irregular high-frequency words: here, when, with, words
Bridging Processes		
Print Concepts	The ability to understand how print is organized and how it works. Concepts associated with print concepts are directionality (reading left to right and top to bottom), spaces between words, punctuation, and the connection between graphics and text.	**Examples:** Pointing to the first word in a sentence Pointing to punctuation Reading to the end of the line and sweeping back to the first word in the next line
Reading Fluency	The ability to read accurately at the appropriate rate and with expression (prosody).	**Examples:** Natural phrasing (as indicated by phrase-cued marks) and inflection at punctuation The boy / went over the hill / to see the sunset. (inflection for period)
Vocabulary Knowledge	The knowledge of words that are part of a person's receptive and expressive language. Understanding a word's connotation (implied meaning) and denotation (dictionary meaning) is also related to a person's vocabulary knowledge.	**Example:** The word *cheap* has a denotation of inexpensive but a connotation that is negative.

continued ▶

Bridging Processes		
Morphological Awareness	The awareness of word parts or morphemes (smallest units of meaning), which includes the inflectional endings, prefixes, suffixes, bases or roots, and derivation of words.	**Example:** Word: transportable trans = across port = to carry able = able to transportable = able to be transported across
Grapho-phonological-Semantic Cognitive Flexibility	The ability to simultaneously decode and apply meaning to printed words.	**Example:** A reader sees the word *transportable* and recognizes the meaning of the word's parts while being able to read (decode) the word.
Language Comprehension		
Cultural and Other Content Knowledge	*Cultural knowledge* means that you know about the characteristics, history, values, beliefs, and behaviors of your own cultural group or that of another ethnic or cultural group. *Content knowledge* means that you know about specific topics in a particular discipline.	**Examples:** Cultural knowledge: Understanding child-rearing practices in different cultures or religious traditions Content knowledge: Knowing about the greenhouse effect (science) or about historical figures of the Renaissance and their contributions (social studies)
Reading-Specific Background Knowledge	The knowledge about texts. This includes genre, text structures, and text features.	**Example:** A reader identifies which text structure is most commonly used in different disciplines or how text features enhance the way authors communicate information.
Verbal Reasoning	The ability to make inferences and understand literary devices, such as metaphors and analogies. Verbal reasoning must be figured out, and it taps into a reader's background knowledge.	**Example:** A reader identifies character traits based on the author's description of a character's actions and relationships.
Language Structure	The knowledge about the way a language works to make meaning. A reader's ability to use syntax to communicate effectively and anticipate what comes next when reading text.	**Example:** The subject comes before the predicate. In English, the adjective typically comes before the noun it is describing.

Theory of Mind	This type of knowledge is related to affective knowledge (see page 171 in chapter 9) and is a reader's ability to make connections with a character's feelings, emotions, and motives.	**Example:** A reader can understand how it feels when a loved pet passes only if they've had a similar experience.
Active Self-Regulation		
Motivation and Engagement	The goals, values, beliefs, and dispositions that inspire behavior.	**Example:** A reader chooses a book that interests them from a teacher's curated list of books.
Executive Function Skills	The management part of the brain. This is the ability to regulate emotions, organize, plan, set goals, and filter out distractions while staying focused on the task.	**Example:** A reader immerses themselves in a text and manages any distracting outside noise.
Strategy Use	A reader's ability to be metacognitively aware to use different methods to aid comprehension. The reader is also able to identify when and where to use strategies that are helpful for word recognition, vocabulary, or comprehension.	**Examples:** Self-monitoring strategies Summarizing Asking questions Using context clues

Source: Adapted from Duke & Cartwright, 2021; ILA, n.d.

Education professor and researcher Scott G. Paris (2005) discusses the difference between constrained skills (phonological awareness, alphabetic principle, and phonics knowledge) that can be mastered and unconstrained skills (vocabulary, background knowledge, and comprehension) that evolve and change and are not mastered. For example, recognizing and decoding the consonant digraph /ch/ as the initial sound words—such as *chat*, *chapter*, and *charitable*—is an example of a constrained skill that can be mastered. As you can see from these examples, the mastery of word recognition and decoding of /ch/ as a phonics pattern applies no matter the length or complexity of the word.

Alternatively, identifying the structure of a text or text excerpt and understanding how the author uses that structure to communicate events, ideas, concepts, or information is an example of an unconstrained skill. In this example, you can likely imagine how a reader may successfully demonstrate this learning goal with one text but struggle to do so with another, depending on the literary elements the author employed or the complexity of the text excerpt. This example highlights a meaning-based skill that readers will develop over time through repeated encounters with various authors and texts.

In our work with teachers, we often hear the familiar adage, "In K–2, students are learning to read, and in third grade and beyond, they are reading to learn."

We understand that this statement stems from the knowledge that constrained skills should be mastered in the primary grades and facilitate the continued work with unconstrained skills. Although we appreciate the intent of this, word recognition isn't something that must be mastered prior to language comprehension instruction; in other words, teachers shouldn't minimize language comprehension instruction in the early grades in the belief that students need to master word recognition first. Constrained skills are the primary focus in the earlier grades; however, it is imperative that educators equally prioritize and infuse language comprehension components (unconstrained skills) alongside word recognition skills to develop our students as readers. In this model, Duke and Cartwright (2021) describe the overlap as bridging processes to place the reader at the center of the model to further expand on the relationship between both constructs. Additionally, they discuss how reading difficulties may be a result of processes beyond language comprehension and word recognition.

Data Sources and Student Reader Profiles

Reflect on your answers to the questions at the beginning of this chapter about what you know about your students as readers. Think about the data sources that informed your responses. Do they reflect a holistic view of your students as readers? Are they based on assessments that were mandated by your district or school or on your informal classroom observations? While many teachers have access to reading assessment data to support instructional planning, synthesizing and integrating data from multiple sources often leaves teachers with more questions and curiosities than answers. While this may seem problematic, this context is actually a powerful opportunity to build assessment literacy and personalize the process of using data to inform instruction. When you categorize and sort data in a way that creates a complete picture of each reader, you can then find an instructional pathway that builds on readers' strengths.

Consider the analogy of sports trading cards for how the various data sources can generate this picture. As teachers, we have seen firsthand how many students love to collect trading cards that showcase their favorite teams and players. From getting a highly sought-after card to organizing and displaying cards to show others, we notice similar behaviors among collectors that highlight their pride and excitement.

Let's take a minute to think about a feature that makes trading cards so exciting for their owners: the statistics. Highlighted by year, each card contains a carefully selected photo of the player to pair with the player's strengths for the season. Although players experience challenges and setbacks during individual games in a season, the challenges are not included on a trading card. While the cardholder may remember watching a difficulty during a game firsthand, the format of the trading card draws attention to what that player has done well during the season—a reminder of the accomplishments of an athlete who had the privilege of playing in a competitive league, likely due to their work ethic and persistent effort toward self-improvement in the game.

You have likely caught on to where we are going with this analogy as you compare an asset-based approach for your students as readers to the idea of a statistics-packed trading card. By viewing students' reading skills and behaviors as a current snapshot of their statistics—their data—in the "game" of reading development, you have an opportunity to identify and celebrate their strengths. This approach will help you make instructional decisions for grouping readers, determine instructional focus areas, and select texts and materials that align with your instructional goals and reader data. We use the term *instructional focus area* to describe a broader decision-making focus for reading instruction, which can be a helpful first step to determine more specific instructional goals. This strengths-based approach inherently offers the opportunity to compile supportive reading behaviors, which can be encouraging for readers and for teachers when tracking progress over time.

The ABC Reader Profile Framework

Just as we can view the strengths of athletes within various components of the game, we can view our readers' strengths through the various components of reading. The Asset-Based Continuum Reader Profile Framework (figure 1.1, page 26) —which we refer to as the *ABC Reader Profile Framework* from here forward— provides a model to consider your students' individual strengths as readers in the key areas of decoding, fluency (with consideration of additional bridging processes), comprehension, and self-regulation. This framework isn't intended to replace reading assessments that help teachers learn more about their readers. Rather, it offers a way to consider existing data and identify readers' high-level strengths.

You will notice that each area of reading depicted by column presents a continuum of reading. For each specific area of reading, consider how the reader's assessment data align to the characteristics of reading development within that particular area. The continuum in each column likely spans beyond your individual grade level (below or above), as it is intended to offer a broad view of reading development across elementary grade-level expectations. The framework here can be used either as a reference or as a tool to check student levels and process and take notes.

	Pre-Alphabetic	Partial Alphabetic	Full Alphabetic	Consolidated Alphabetic	Automatic
Decoding	☐ Readers use cues such as pictures, context cues, and guessing strategies. ☐ Readers notice semantic rather than phonological relationships. ☐ Readers' connections are more arbitrary than systematic.	☐ Readers use emerging grapheme–phoneme connections, such as the first letter sound. ☐ Readers' connections are incomplete, and they use known phonetic cues to guide their decoding attempts.	☐ Readers attend to every letter in every word as they convert graphemes into phonological representations. ☐ Readers have working knowledge of most letter-sound correspondences and decode sequentially, though slowly.	☐ Readers use chunks to decode. They recognize multiletter patterns instantly (such as consonant blends, vowel teams, affixes, and so on) and use syllables and morphemes as chunks to support decoding. ☐ Readers teach themselves new connections as orthographic mapping further develops.	☐ Readers quickly and effortlessly decode, and most words are sight words. ☐ Readers use decoding processes that are highly automatic when they encounter unknown words. ☐ Readers have a variety of strategies at their disposal, especially when reading technical words.

Reader Goals:

	Word by Word	Local Grouping	Phrase and Clause	Sentence Prosody	Passage Expression
Fluency and Bridging Processes	☐ Readers focus on individual words or sounds. ☐ Less than one-quarter of the words are read aloud with appropriate expression.	☐ Readers focus on local word groups and may be mostly arrhythmic or monotone. ☐ More than one-quarter and less than one-half of words are read aloud with appropriate expression.	☐ Readers express the structure or meaning of words, phrases, clauses, and a few sentences. Intonation may reinforce rhythmic grouping, or reading may be monotone. ☐ More than half of the words are read aloud with appropriate expression.	☐ Readers express text, sentence structure, and meaning. ☐ Readers may be inconsistent but not monotone. Reading rate is at least fifty-five words per minute. ☐ More than three-quarters of the words are read aloud with appropriate expression.	☐ Readers convey elements as if reading for a listener and are expressive throughout. ☐ Readers consistently express the structure and meaning of sentences, paragraphs, and passages. Their reading rate is at least eighty words per minute.

Additional bridging processes to consider along this continuum include concepts of print, vocabulary knowledge, morphological awareness, and graphophonological-semantic cognitive flexibility.

Reader Goals:

CHAPTER 1: What Do I Know About My Students as Readers?

Comprehension

	Literal Comprehension	Inferential Comprehension	Evaluative Comprehension	Reorganization Comprehension	Appreciative Comprehension
	☐ Readers understand a text, including facts, ideas, vocabulary, events, and stated information. ☐ Readers can provide direct and explicit answers to questions extracted from a text.	☐ Readers make valid inferences from the information found in text. ☐ Readers understand the facts, even if they aren't explicitly stated in the reading material. Inferences made include generalizations, comparisons, assumptions, predictions, and so on.	☐ Readers analyze an author's intent, opinion, language, and style of text presentation. ☐ Readers evaluate the appropriateness of an author's devices and then make inferences based on the fact or idea implied in text.	☐ Readers use information gained from various parts of the text and rearrange it into new patterns that integrate the information into an idea for further understanding. ☐ Readers apply creativity or curiosity as they analyze, digest, and evaluate text to identify a unique view of a situation or event.	☐ Readers recognize the purpose, perspective, and philosophy of the author by understanding the deeper meaning of the text. ☐ Readers reflect and respond emotionally to the text while making connections. This requires a literal and inferential understanding, which is then used to evaluate and reflect.

Reader Goals:

Self-Regulation and Metacognition

	Initial Awareness and Control	Emerging Awareness and Control	Developing Awareness and Control	Skilled Awareness and Control	Independent Awareness and Control
	☐ Readers begin reading a text at the first word, paragraph, or page. ☐ Readers read slowly and carefully for all texts and purposes. ☐ Readers think about their understanding of text during or after reading.	☐ Readers think about what they know before they read. ☐ Readers slow down and pay closer attention to text when it becomes difficult. ☐ Readers employ a strategy to think about texts as they read (such as summarizing, visualizing, or asking questions).	☐ Readers preview the text before reading to anticipate content and determine a purpose for reading. ☐ Readers stop to think about what they're reading from time to time, regardless of text difficulty. ☐ Readers employ multiple strategies to think about text as they read (such as summarizing, visualizing, or asking questions).	☐ Readers preview the text before reading to anticipate content while noting the text's organization and structure to support their purpose for reading. ☐ Readers adjust reading speed to try to get back on track if they lose concentration or to deepen understanding. ☐ Readers employ multiple strategies to think about their reading (such as summarizing, visualizing, or asking questions) and seek opportunities to discuss their reading with others to check for understanding.	☐ Readers preview the text before reading by noting its organization and structure and making inferences about how to prioritize content in alignment with reading purpose. ☐ Readers adjust rate, reread, and refocus flexibly according to text, purpose, and difficulty. ☐ Readers flexibly employ multiple strategies to think about their reading (such as summarizing, visualizing, or asking questions), seek opportunities to discuss their understanding, and use additional resources to connect, repair, or extend their learning.

Reader Goals:

Source: Ehri, 1995; Lastiri, 2022; Mokhtari & Reichard, 2002; White et al., 2021.

FIGURE 1.1: The ABC Reader Profile Framework.

Visit go.SolutionTree.com/literacy for a free reproducible version of this figure.

The ABC Reader Profile Framework includes space for you to indicate which characteristics you observe based on informal reading assessment data. It is important to note that this framework is not an assessment itself but rather an organizer to capture observations and reading data to have a holistic snapshot of a reader's current strengths and a trajectory for future growth, even beyond a single grade level. In the following section, we show how to use the framework to record observations of reading behaviors in action with a video example. If reading assessment data are not available in one or more of the areas depicted in this framework, you might consider administering an informal reading assessment to inform your observations.

While we encourage you to use the framework as often as you see fit, we anticipate you using this organizer three times per year (at the beginning, middle, and end of the year, perhaps) to track reading progress and growth. Remember, though—this framework spans multiple stages of reading development that correlate to multiple grade levels of growth, so it is appropriate for progress from one stage to the next to appear slow in some instances when it is tracked within a single semester or school year, especially for the categories that track unconstrained skills. We don't want you to feel discouraged if this is the case. At the same time, using this holistic, asset-based view of reading progress can help you and your colleagues document the progression of reading development over time, informed by the multiple data points that you already have accessible.

OBSERVATIONAL READING DATA BUILD A READER PROFILE

Let's look at a student example to see how to implement the framework. The following video shows Mikayla as she reads from the text she and her peers have been reading during small-group instruction. In this video, Mikayla also shares about what she just read.

Figure 1.2 is a possible interpretation of Mikayla's ABC Reader Profile. Consider how you might interpret Mikayla's video. Since we have only a short clip and not multiple data sources to consider, it would make sense for our responses to vary.

CHAPTER 1: What Do I Know About My Students as Readers?

Decoding

Pre-Alphabetic	Partial Alphabetic	Full Alphabetic	Consolidated Alphabetic	Automatic
☐ Readers use cues such as pictures, context cues, and guessing strategies. ☐ Readers notice semantic rather than phonological relationships. ☐ Readers' connections are more arbitrary than systematic.	☐ Readers use emerging grapheme-phoneme connections, such as the first letter sound. ☐ Readers' connections are incomplete, and they use known phonetic cues to guide their decoding attempts.	☐ Readers attend to every letter in every word as they convert graphemes into phonological representations. ☐ Readers have working knowledge of most letter-sound correspondences and decode sequentially, though slowly.	☐ Readers use chunks to decode. They recognize multiletter patterns instantly (such as consonant blends, vowel teams, affixes, and so on) and use syllables and morphemes as chunks to support decoding. ☐ Readers teach themselves new connections as orthographic mapping further develops.	☑ Readers quickly and effortlessly decode, and most words are sight words. ☑ Readers use decoding processes that are highly automatic when they encounter unknown words. ☑ Readers have a variety of strategies at their disposal, especially when reading technical words.

Reader Goals:
Met year-long goal for decoding (reads most words quickly and effortlessly, uses a variety of strategies for unknown words). Future goal of fluency and comprehension.

Fluency and Bridging Processes

Word by Word	Local Grouping	Phrase and Clause	Sentence Prosody	Passage Expression
☐ Readers focus on individual words or sounds. ☐ Less than one-quarter of the words are read aloud with appropriate expression.	☐ Readers focus on local word groups and may be mostly arrhythmic or monotone. ☐ More than one-quarter and less than one-half of words are read aloud with appropriate expression.	☐ Readers express the structure or meaning of words, phrases, clauses, and a few sentences. Intonation may reinforce rhythmic grouping, or reading may be monotone. ☐ More than half of the words are read aloud with appropriate expression.	☑ Readers express text, sentence structure, and meaning. ☑ Readers may be inconsistent but not monotone. Reading rate is at least fifty-five words per minute. ☑ More than three-quarters of the words are read aloud with appropriate expression.	☐ Readers convey elements as if reading for a listener and are expressive throughout. ☐ Readers consistently express the structure and meaning of sentences, paragraphs, and passages. Their reading rate is at least eighty words per minute.

Additional bridging processes to consider along this continuum include concepts of print, vocabulary knowledge, morphological awareness, and graphophonological-semantic cognitive flexibility.

Reader Goals:
Reads with some expression. Future goal is to increase her expression to match the tone of the text.

Source: Ehri, 1995; Lastiri, 2022; Mokhtari & Reichard, 2002; White et al., 2021.

FIGURE 1.2: Sample ABC Reader Profile for Mikayla.

continued ▶

SMALL GROUPS FOR BIG READERS

Comprehension

	Literal Comprehension	Inferential Comprehension	Evaluative Comprehension	Reorganization Comprehension	Appreciative Comprehension
	☑ Readers understand a text, including facts, ideas, vocabulary, events, and stated information.	☐ Readers make valid inferences from the information found in text.	☐ Readers analyze an author's intent, opinion, language, and style of text presentation.	☐ Readers use information gained from various parts of the text and rearrange it into new patterns that integrate the information into an idea for further understanding.	☐ Readers recognize the purpose, perspective, and philosophy of the author by understanding the deeper meaning of the text.
	☑ Readers can provide direct and explicit answers to questions extracted from a text.	☐ Readers understand the facts, even if they aren't explicitly stated in the reading material.	☐ Readers evaluate the appropriateness of an author's devices and then make inferences based on the fact or idea implied in text.	☐ Readers apply creativity or curiosity as they analyze, digest, and evaluate text to identify a unique view of a situation or event.	☐ Readers reflect and respond emotionally to the text while making connections. This requires a literal and inferential understanding, which is then used to evaluate and reflect.
		☐ Inferences made include generalizations, comparisons, assumptions, predictions, and so on.			

Reader Goals: *States what occurred explicitly in the text. Future goal is to create valid inferences from information found in the text to gain deeper meaning.*

Self-Regulation and Metacognition

	Initial Awareness and Control	Emerging Awareness and Control	Developing Awareness and Control	Skilled Awareness and Control	Independent Awareness and Control
	☑ Readers begin reading a text at the first word, paragraph, or page.	☐ Readers think about what they know before they read.	☐ Readers preview the text before reading to anticipate content and determine a purpose for reading.	☐ Readers preview the text before reading to anticipate content while noting the text's organization and structure to support their purpose for reading.	☐ Readers preview the text before reading by noting its organization and structure and making inferences about how to prioritize content in alignment with reading purpose.
	☐ Readers read slowly and carefully for all texts and purposes.	☑ Readers slow down and pay closer attention to text when it becomes difficult.	☐ Readers stop to think about what they're reading from time to time, regardless of text difficulty.	☐ Readers adjust reading speed to try to get back on track if they lose concentration or to deepen understanding.	☐ Readers adjust rate, reread, and refocus flexibly according to text, purpose, and difficulty.
	☐ Readers think about their understanding of text during or after reading.	☑ Readers employ a strategy to think about texts as they read (such as summarizing, visualizing, or asking questions).	☐ Readers employ multiple strategies to think about text as they read (such as summarizing, visualizing, or asking questions).	☐ Readers employ multiple strategies to think about their reading (such as summarizing, visualizing, or asking questions) and seek opportunities to discuss their reading with others to check for understanding.	☐ Readers flexibly employ multiple strategies to think about their reading (such as summarizing, visualizing, or asking questions), seek opportunities to discuss their understanding, and use additional resources to connect, repair, or extend their learning.

Reader Goals: *Slows down to make sense of text; summarizes what she read. Future goal to review text prior to reading to determine a purpose for reading, and employ multiple strategies to think about the text.*

THE ABC READER PROFILE FRAMEWORK IN ACTION

We created the ABC Reader Profile Framework with the primary goal to help teachers build clear profiles of their students as readers. We recognize that this framework could also be helpful for teachers to use in a variety of instructional contexts.

- **Individual reader:** Teachers can use this framework to identify specific areas of focus within the reading process and guide their instructional planning for an individual reader.
- **Student reflection and goal setting:** Teachers empower students to take ownership of their learning when they involve them in discussions about their identities as readers that highlight their strengths and identify opportunities for growth. This framework provides students with a visual to see the multidimensional nature of reading as a process, which can help them refine their own reflections and perceptions of themselves as readers. Rather than having a self-identified ("I'm an OK reader") or general label to describe their reading ability, students can identify specific skills where they excel. Knowing this information helps students when they read and enables them to leverage their strengths while working to strengthen other areas.
- **Grouping decisions:** Teachers can use this framework as a quick grouping resource to identify which readers might benefit from instruction of the same focus. To learn more about planning for each group of readers, see chapter 4 (page 65).
- **Collaborative team discussions:** Professional teams can utilize this tool to engage in data-based discussions, since it offers a powerful framework for teams to track reader progress toward proficiency and benchmarks by grade. Teams can use this framework to discuss reader profiles on a high level within each classroom in a grade level. Additionally, using this framework as a checkpoint throughout the school year provides teams with a tool to highlight reader growth and development.
- **Vertical team discussions:** Teachers can develop a broader picture of readers' progress and development across the elementary grades by using this framework as a tool to promote dialogue among teachers at different grade levels. Although the framework does not change from one grade to the next, curriculum standard expectations and discussions about which texts are considered on grade level become more advanced and nuanced. The framework serves as a starting point to launch conversations about how reading expectations and instruction develop from one grade level to the next, with an aim to offer coherence for readers throughout their elementary reading experiences.

- **Communication tool among reading instruction providers:** In some schools, readers are taught by more than one teacher throughout the school year. Additional school staff—such as interventionists, paraprofessionals, literacy coaches, and media specialists or librarians—may also be planning lessons and supporting reading instruction in various contexts. The framework can be used as a consistent, common tool to communicate current strengths and goals among instructional providers.
- **Parent or caregiver communication:** Teachers can struggle to communicate reading assessment data to parents, as there is a dual need to share student-specific outcome data while also building parents' and caregivers' assessment literacy. Teachers can anchor their discussions about data within this framework to help build a parent's knowledge of their child's reader profile. This educative stance not only helps parents and caregivers learn about their child's reading assessment data but helps them understand the processes that work simultaneously during reading experiences, which can help them support their child at home.

Summary

When creating small groups, we first think of the individual readers who will comprise that group. As we consider each reader, we can use an asset-based approach to collect, analyze, and interpret literacy data to shape our instructional decisions. The ABC Reader Profile Framework (page 25) serves as a tool for building each student's reader profile. It is a way for teachers to identify student strengths and target areas to support students during small-group instruction. Use the following tools and reflection prompts to recharge your small-group instruction through an asset-based approach.

LAUNCH YOUR REFLECTION

Let's reconnect with Adler, the second-grade reader we met at the beginning of this chapter (page 18). Now that you've read this chapter, revisit your reflections for the following questions.

- What do you notice about Adler as a reader? Specifically, what observations help you make inferences about his strengths in decoding, fluency, comprehension, and metacognition?
- Based on the short video of Adler, what additional reading tasks and opportunities would you like to see Adler tackle as a reader?

RECHARGE YOUR SMALL-GROUP READING INSTRUCTION

The following are some questions you can use to apply the chapter concepts to your own classroom context.

- How will I reframe observations of my students to focus on their strengths as readers?
- How might I use the ABC Reader Profile Framework to help group students and determine learning goals for small-group reading instruction?
- How might the ABC Reader Profile Framework and tools help me interpret and integrate multiple assessment sources to characterize profiles of my students as readers?
- How might the ABC Reader Profile Framework help me communicate about my readers' collective and individual strengths and learning goals with various stakeholders—colleagues, school leaders, and parents and caregivers?
- How does understanding the broader scope of reading development across the grade levels influence which reading skills and behaviors I will develop at my grade level?

EXPAND YOUR TOOLBOX

To continue your learning, see the "Leading the Learning Action Guide" in the appendix (page 201) to support you and your colleagues. In the action guide for this chapter, you'll find videos that spotlight teaching strategies as well as differentiated professional learning activities you can try out with your team. Additional tools that support this chapter topic can be accessed online (visit **go.SolutionTree.com /literacy**).

CHAPTER 2

HOW DOES DIFFERENTIATING SMALL-GROUP INSTRUCTION PROMOTE ACCESS AND EQUITY?

Small-group instruction gives teachers the opportunity to individualize support to meet the needs of all readers. Through intentional grouping based on data-informed decisions, teachers can provide targeted instruction and intervention for students with high intensity needs, provide specially designed instruction for students with disabilities, or implement best practices for students who are multilingual. Access and equity are central to the literacy block as teachers build an inclusive classroom designed to meet the needs of *all* students. In this chapter, we will first define *differentiation*, then explore the role of data-informed decision making in the process of differentiation, and finally determine how differentiation in small groups can support all students.

As you read this chapter, consider your own experiences with differentiation during small-group instruction. The following questions may also help frame your thinking as you read.

- What is differentiated instruction, and how do I implement it during small-group instruction?
- What does differentiated instruction look like within a MTSS framework?

- What strategies for grouping students maximize the benefits of differentiated instruction?
- How do I meet the needs of students with diverse learning characteristics?

We will revisit these ideas and questions at the end of the chapter to identify and plan for differentiation strategies that you want to try with your own students.

Consider the following example of Mr. Moore.

MEET THE TEACHER: MR. MOORE

> Mr. Moore is a second-grade teacher for students with diverse learning needs. At the beginning of the year, Mr. Moore administers a screening diagnostic to assess students in oral language acquisition, phonological awareness, phonics, vocabulary, fluency, and comprehension. After reviewing the data, Mr. Moore is able to determine the types of supports students require as they work in small groups. As the school year progresses, Mr. Moore continues to gather data on his students' learning preferences and monitor their progress, then he adjusts his instruction and intervention accordingly. Mr. Moore tries to remain responsive to individual student needs while grouping students in ways that effectively leverage their cultural and linguistic strengths to address areas of instructional opportunity.

How would you advise Mr. Moore on meeting individual student needs while planning for small-group instruction? Using assessment data, how can Mr. Moore differentiate instruction within a small group?

Differentiated Reading Instruction

Readers enter school with a wide range of academic skills and abilities known as *learner diversity*. Learner diversity continues to grow and impact students as they matriculate through their K–12 school experience. Some students are quick to master grade-level standards, while others require additional support and time to achieve mastery. The amount of time or strategies that promote literacy skill achievement is dependent on a student's background knowledge, previous skill acquisition, and learning preferences. Further, we know students experience gaps in opportunity prior to entering school and during their school experiences. These variations in opportunity create a wide range of differences in literacy knowledge and skills and stem from unequal access to experiences, resources, and opportunities. These disparities can often result in misconceptions about academic ability and lead to discrepancies in student achievement and outcomes (Wint, Opara, Gordon, & Brooms, 2022).

To help close the opportunity gap and tend to individual learners' needs, styles, cultural values, and interests, educators can differentiate instruction (Kise, 2007, 2021). Differentiating instruction is the practice of adjusting instruction to meet individual student learning needs. Carol Ann Tomlinson and Jane M. Jarvis (2009) describe *differentiation* as "proactively planning to achieve optimal fit between curriculum and instruction and students' readiness, interest, and learning profile" (p. 599).

Since the mid-20th century, educators have asked, "How can the teacher best meet—and most wisely use—the wide range of differences in [student] abilities, interests, and development . . . ?" (Washburne, 1953, p. 138). After reviewing decades of research to find the answer, Rhonda S. Bondie, Christine Dahnke, and Akane Zusho (2019) find that small-group instruction and intervention is the best way to differentiate and meet individual student needs. To differentiate effectively, teachers need to know (1) the reader's current level of performance and (2) the goal or desired outcome for instruction (Hattie, 2012). Knowing just these two items gives teachers the power to differentiate and makes differentiation doable (Kise, 2021).

DESIGNING EQUITY-CENTERED, DIFFERENTIATED LITERACY BLOCKS

Differentiation is not individualization, but rather a way to respond to learner diversity. When you differentiate instruction, you are actively matching a student's learning preference with the appropriate teaching strategy, materials, curriculum goals, and method for displaying learning (Onyishi & Sefotho, 2020). Ultimately, the goal of differentiation is to remove potential barriers to student learning. There are many ways you can achieve this goal. Differentiation can be realized through one or more of the following tactics (Bondie et al., 2019; Grimes & Stevens, 2009; Jenkins, Schiller, Blackorby, Thayer, & Tilly, 2013; Ladson-Billings, 2009; Tomlinson, 2001).

- Adjusting content
- Adjusting process
- Adjusting product
- Adjusting the learning environment
- Using student grouping structures
- Including student voice and choice
- Connecting to students' cultural capital

When you use one or more of these differentiation strategies simultaneously, your students will benefit not only academically but socially, emotionally, and behaviorally. When you differentiate instruction, you recognize that students have multiple ways of taking in information and equally as many ways of presenting their learning. Differentiation occurs using grade-level text. Differentiation is not modification of the curriculum but a way to support readers to meet grade-level standards, as shown in table 2.1.

TABLE 2.1: Domains of Differentiation Across Grade-Level Text

Differentiation Domain	Description	Example
Content	*Content* is what students learn. Students can engage with varied grade-level text or diverse topics. Students appreciate engaging with content that interests them.	Text: Students may engage with different texts on the same topic. To learn more about selecting texts, see chapter 5 (page 93). Topic: Students are working on skills that are aligned with their area of need.
Process	*Process* is how students learn. The way students engage with the content may vary. Tailoring the process to make it meaningful and applicable to each student can enhance the learning experience.	Students may receive the information best through concept mapping, manipulatives, technology-based programs, project-based learning, repeated reading, and so on.
Product	*Product* is how students make their learning visible. The way students express their learning could differ. Presenting multiple opportunities for practice, giving detailed feedback, and providing students time to reflect on how their learning applies to the real world are essential for mastery.	Students show their learning through essays, plays, singing, brochures, PowerPoint presentations, oral presentations, and so on.

DIFFERENTIATING WITH UNIVERSAL DESIGN FOR LEARNING

Universal Design for Learning (UDL) is a framework for differentiating instruction and improving student outcomes by integrating the science of learning. The goal of UDL is to proactively reduce barriers to learning (CAST, 2024). The three UDL principles are (1) engagement, (2) representation, and (3) action and expression. These three principles provide students with choice, inviting them to learn in meaningful, inclusive, and accessible ways (CAST, 2024). The learning environment is flexible and responsive, allowing students to learn and demonstrate their learning in a variety of ways. When used in small-group instruction, UDL empowers both teachers and students while leveraging students' strengths, as shown in table 2.2.

TABLE 2.2: Universal Design for Learning and Small-Group Instruction

UDL Principle	Description	Small-Group Benefits
Engagement	Students engage with their learning environment in different ways. Students are motivated to learn in different ways. Teachers can sustain engagement through collaboration.	Working in small groups can: • Deepen engagement • Motivate students
Representation	Students interact with information differently. Students comprehend information when presented through different means. Teachers can present information in multiple ways in small groups.	Working in small groups can allow interactions between teacher and students or between students and students that: • Activate prior knowledge • Help highlight patterns, relationships, or big ideas • Clarify information
Action and Expression	Students appreciate choice in how they represent their knowledge. Students approach their tasks differently, so being able to show their learning in ways that are meaningful to them is important. Teachers can consider student strengths when deciding how a student should represent their learning, when appropriate.	Working in small groups allows teachers to gauge student learning easily. Students can engage in goal setting. Teachers can allow for variation in response modes. Teachers optimize their ability to monitor progress.

Differentiation begins with knowing your readers. It is building relationships, gathering assessment data, and engaging in instruction to develop strong and confident readers. Through various types of assessments, you can analyze the data to make informed instructional decisions. By coupling strong pedagogical knowledge of the reading process with student data, you can engage in data-based decision making, small-group formation, and differentiated instruction. You can begin to match resources and materials with your students' strengths and needs. For more information on compiling student data, refer to chapter 1 (page 17).

The following is a video snapshot of a lesson that highlights matching resources with students' strengths and needs.

PRIMARY LESSON: DECODING

USING DATA

Student data should be used to drive instructional decisions about content, process, product, learning environment, and student grouping. As you adjust—or differentiate—instruction in response to assessment data, student performance and achievement should increase. Therefore, you should consider the various types of data you can collect that can positively influence student performance. You can use these data to determine short-term and long-term goals as well as make on-the-spot decisions.

In order to determine data-informed instructional focus areas for small-group instruction, teachers must have access to current, reliable, informative data about students' reading skills and behaviors. As discussed in chapter 1 (page 17), synthesizing multiple data points can sometimes be confusing, but it's critical to have these data to inform your instructional planning. The following list offers ideas of potential data sources.

- **Curriculum-based measures of assessment:** For example, classroom assessments based on whole-group instruction, Tier 1 literacy instruction, or previous small-group instruction, which may include unit assessments, curriculum progress-monitoring tools, common formative and summative assessments developed by school or district teams, and mastery assessments
- **Open-access informal reading assessments:** For example, the Phonological Awareness Screening Test (PAST; Kilpatrick, 2016), Listening to Reading–Watching While Writing Protocol (LTR-WWWP; Duke, Ward, & Klingelhofer, 2020), reading attitude and metacognitive surveys, and oral reading fluency probes
- **District-purchased and -adopted screener and diagnostic assessments:** For example, DIBELS (Dynamic Indicators of Basic Early Literacy Skills; University of Oregon, n.d.), i-Ready Diagnostic (Curriculum Associates, 2011), and Amira (formerly Istation) Reading (Amira Learning, n.d.)
- **Observational notes from instruction:** For example, skills checklists and trackers, anecdotal lesson notes from small-group lessons, or individual reading conferences and observations

The following is a video snapshot of a lesson that demonstrates a teacher capturing informal assessment data and using them to inform instruction.

PRIMARY LESSON:
SUPPORTING INDEPENDENT
READING-GRADE 1

You can use data from classroom assessments to differentiate instruction, increase intervention supports, make grouping decisions, and engage in multiple other instructional approaches. This process is continual and cyclical in nature. You are repeatedly identifying, analyzing, and using assessment data throughout the data-informed decision-making process. Vicki Park and Amanda Datnow (2017) warn that the use of data to drive instruction can be both promising and problematic. You can use data to reflect on your teaching practices and make instructional changes, but we caution that data can be used to perpetuate beliefs about a student's abilities, leading to narrow definitions of differentiation of instruction that are based solely on grouping.

USING FLEXIBLE GROUPING

Differentiation is not individualized instruction. You differentiate instruction to meet the needs of small groups of readers (IRIS Center, n.d.). Differentiation is maximized when you respond to learner diversity through cooperative learning structures to develop and advance literacy achievement. However, we caution that cooperative learning groups aren't meant to be used to track readers. Gayle Gregory, Martha Kaufeldt, and Mike Mattos (2016) stress that differentiation isn't *ability grouping*—the practice of placing readers in small groups based on their perceived ability. Research evidence spanning decades indicates that ability grouping equates to student tracking, which is a controversial practice that isn't beneficial or equitable (Hattie, 2009; Park & Datnow, 2017). Tracking students can look like placing students in high, middle, or low achievement groups. Likely a result of high-stakes testing, ability grouping has grown in popularity. For example, one study found that for fourth-grade students, ability grouping grew from 28 percent in 1998 to 71 percent by 2009 (Park & Datnow, 2017).

Conversely, differentiation involves the practice of flexible grouping, which is responsive to students' needs, readiness, and interests and provides multiple opportunities to engage with classmates of various readiness levels (Gregory et al., 2016). In various readiness-level groups, or heterogeneous groups, students interact with the content or presentation of the curriculum. Mixed-level grouping optimizes student learning through student interaction and engagement.

Flexible grouping is a data-informed strategy that can utilize heterogeneous or homogeneous group structures. *Heterogeneous groups* include students with different learning abilities or even different learning needs. In a heterogeneous group, each reader brings unique strengths to the group. *Homogeneous groups* include readers who have similar strengths or needs who are grouped together for those similarities. Flexible groups are temporary and fluid, changing based on data and need (for example, the skill focus changes or the goal changes). These changes may occur over weeks of instruction. You can determine groups based on an identified goal or skill rather than reader ability alone. Since grouping is not based on ability alone or text level, readers do not feel singled out. Flexible grouping is an asset-based and culturally responsive practice, where all readers in the group feel valued. Research suggests that groups are most effective with no more than three to six students meeting at once (Conradi Smith, Amendum, & Williams, 2022).

Based on the schedule in your literacy block, you will likely not be able to meet with every group of readers every day. Determining how frequently you meet with each group will be an important consideration. Additionally, you may need to weigh other meeting pattern factors such as the following.

- If not meeting daily, which groups would be served best to meet on subsequent days for continuity of instruction, compared to those who may meet every other day with collaborative or independent extended practice opportunities on the days that they do not meet with you?
- If not meeting daily, which groups might benefit from meeting with the teacher at the beginning of the week, or even as the first group for the day, to offer clarity on how their extended practice (for the day and across the week) should connect to the small-group instruction provided?
- If meeting daily, how might you focus on different data-informed learning goals to ensure readers have comprehensive opportunities in areas of reading (for example, readers aren't limited to only phonics instruction five days a week without opportunities to engage in lessons that focus on comprehension)?

Figure 2.1 shows how you might start to plan for each group in a week-long view. In this example, the teacher has started to map out small-group meeting frequencies and focus areas for the week.

	Monday	Tuesday	Wednesday	Thursday	Friday
Group 1	Foundational skills	Foundational skills	Foundational skills	Comprehension	Comprehension
Group 2	Fluency	Fluency	Comprehension	Comprehension	Comprehension
Group 3					

FIGURE 2.1: Sample tool to organize flexible grouping and learning needs.

Differentiated Instruction in the Classroom

The following are five guidelines to begin differentiating instruction in your classroom.

1. **Start slowly:** Implement one differentiation domain (content, process, or product) at a time as you build your confidence and skill. For example, you can focus on differentiating content first by having students choose their books or writing topics.
2. **Use existing data:** Use data or assessments that you already collected to make decisions about goals, needs, and flexible grouping. For example, rather than identifying and administering a new assessment, you can use the oral reading fluency assessment data you already have to make instructional decisions.
3. **Evaluate the outcomes:** Once you implement the practice, gather data on the implementation and evaluate the outcome. For example, use progress-monitoring assessments to examine how students are responding to instruction. This is a powerful way to not only monitor student progress but reflect on how differentiation strategies influence on their progress.
4. **Refine and adjust:** Determine if there is an opportunity to refine and adjust implementation. For example, you can use data—including progress monitoring—to tailor your differentiation strategy to align with students' strengths and needs.
5. **Add domains:** Once you feel that you have mastered a domain, you can begin to add domains or increase the skills of focus for the same domain. For example, if you feel confident in your ability to differentiate content, consider differentiating process. This gradual approach will build your efficacy while creating strong and confident readers.

Differentiated Instruction Within MTSS

As we discussed in the introduction (page 1), MTSS is a framework to support students, and differentiated instruction is at the core of the framework. Tier 1 within the three-tiered MTSS framework should include differentiated instruction, while Tiers 2 and 3 are designed to provide intensified, individualized intervention to students who require additional support beyond core instruction.

Differentiated instruction is a proactive, equity-driven approach designed to meet the needs of all students. Differentiating literacy instruction within an MTSS framework ensures that high-quality, research-backed instruction and intervention are provided based on readers' individual strengths and needs. MTSS emphasizes equity and aims to improve educational opportunities and outcomes for all students. By integrating practices that promote and support readers' academic growth, you can make data-informed decisions to improve reader outcomes (Jackson, 2021). MTSS employs evidence-based literacy practices that aim to proactively prevent learning problems by addressing the needs of struggling readers through its intensifying intervention structure (Miciak et al., 2018). *Evidence-based literacy practices* are research-based methods that consider students' data-based needs to provide systematic and explicit reading and writing instruction (Reading Rockets, n.d.b).

MTSS includes:

- Evidence-based practices at all tiers
- Data-informed decision-making process
- Individualized and targeted literacy interventions (Lemons, Vaughn, Wexler, Kearns, & Sinclair, 2018)

Ideally, MTSS provides and matches high-quality instructional practices and curricular resources to readers' strengths and needs (Leonard, Coyne, Oldham, Burns, & Gillis, 2019).

The MTSS framework includes three tiers of support. Within the first tier, all students are provided with high-quality literacy instruction. For effective Tier 1 instruction, ensure you have established a learning-friendly environment, implemented a well-rounded literacy curriculum that meets the students' and classroom's needs, and applied instructional strategies suited to student learning requirements (Slanda, Pike, Herbert, Wells, & Pelt, 2022). If implemented with fidelity, Tier 1 instruction should meet the literacy needs of most students (about 85 percent). Strong and responsive core instruction in Tier 1 can be delivered whole group and by differentiating in small groups.

Despite your efforts, there may be some students who need additional support beyond Tier 1 to achieve grade-level standards. These students should receive supplemental instruction and intervention from their classroom teachers or other grade-level teachers in Tier 2. Tier 2 provides additional guidance, reinforcement, and more frequent progress monitoring for students in a small-group setting (Kramer, Sonju, Mattos, & Buffum, 2021). Teachers deliver intervention at Tier 2 to supplement Tier 1 instruction and to individualize student learning. In Tier 2, teachers can use small groups to intensify instruction and provide intervention for a targeted skill. These small groups occur in addition to the small-group instruction in Tier 1.

Tier 3 is the strongest intervention level, providing customized, one-on-one instruction, and an intervention specialist or other form of specialist typically provides it (Rogers, Smith, Buffum, & Mattos, 2020). This stage involves rigorous progress monitoring, systematic implementation of varied interventions, and continued data collection to gauge the effectiveness of instruction and interventions. Even though this intervention level is highly specialized, it supplements—not replaces—the core curriculum and is delivered one on one. In this way, students who need additional support continue to benefit from core small-group instruction in Tier 1 and targeted skill instruction in Tier 2 while receiving individualized intervention in Tier 3.

Here's a video snapshot of a lesson that highlights an intervention provided in a one-on-one setting.

PRIMARY READING CONFERENCE: LIAM

Students who struggle despite Tier 3 intervention may be evaluated for special education. Once eligibility is determined, students with disabilities continue to receive specially designed instruction within the tiered system of supports.

PROVIDING INTERVENTION

Meeting grade-level standards and achieving mastery of the reading process persistently pose a challenge for numerous students (Fien, Chard, & Baker, 2021). Students who struggle with reading skills will continue to struggle if they do not receive targeted and immediate intervention and support. Research finds that supporting readers in a small group through targeted supplemental instruction and intervention leads to improved literacy development (Phillips et al., 2021). Therefore, providing intervention and support in small groups within an MTSS framework is critical for your readers' success.

It's important to keep in mind that not all readers who struggle have a language impairment or other reading-based disability—they may simply require supplemental instruction and intervention that teachers can deliver in a small-group setting. What's most important is that teachers provide intervention at the first sign of struggle. Using a data-informed approach, you can address the specific reader skillset that needs intervention. You can use data to determine individual needs as well as identify patterns across groups of readers. Providing intervention to readers who have similar skill-based learning goals in a small-group setting allows you to efficiently and effectively deliver explicit and systematic intervention.

Supplying reading intervention in small groups has been shown to improve foundational reading skills, especially when readers struggle with code-based reading skills (Al Otaiba, McMaster, Wanzek, & Zaru, 2023).

PROVIDING ENRICHMENT

Providing enrichment through small groups and within the MTSS framework is important for building and sustaining student literacy achievement. There has been a steady decline in students' interest and engagement in reading, thereby impacting reading competency across the grade levels (Reis, McCoach, Little, Muller, & Kaniskan, 2011). As students move through grade levels, reading engagement wanes further. Research suggests there may be a "mismatch between the needs of students who read at different levels and the instructional opportunities provided to them" (Reis et al., 2011, p. 463). Therefore, differentiated instruction and enrichment that meet the needs of students with high reading ability are necessary to sustain their engagement and interest. To learn more about engaging readers within the small group, see chapter 6 (page 109).

Fostering enjoyment in reading is as important as providing intervention. Providing enrichment through small groups can include the following.

- Supplying access to a broad range of books in a print-rich environment
- Teaching metacognitive skills that support reading tasks
- Engaging readers in enriching discussions about text
- Incorporating choice through UDL strategies

Providing enriching experiences with text increases fluency and comprehension.

MEETING THE NEEDS OF STUDENTS WITH DISABILITIES

In accordance with U.S. federal mandates, students with disabilities must have the same access to the curriculum and the same opportunities to master standards as their peers without disabilities. To provide access and opportunity, student grouping should be inclusive and never based on disability. In other words, teachers should not develop small groups based on a disability category or group all students with disabilities together. Students with disabilities have a wide range of abilities and needs—just like any student—and their grouping should be individualized and responsive. The same strategies for grouping apply to all students, including students with disabilities. Teachers should provide accommodation to ensure all students have access to the curriculum when working in small groups.

MEETING THE NEEDS OF MULTILINGUAL STUDENTS

Just as with students with disabilities, multilingual students should have the same access to the curriculum and the same opportunities as all students to develop their reading skills. Effective strategies for fostering literacy in multilingual students include creating a multilingual space within the classroom, implementing UDL principles for instruction and intervention, and paying particular attention to multilingual-learner small grouping. It's important to consider small-group configurations that will benefit multilingual students as well as the opportunities available for literacy development during small group.

Although they have good intentions, teachers frequently tend to cluster multilingual students together, thinking that this is an efficient approach to grouping. Often, they group students who share the same primary languages and pair newly-arrived students with those who have been in North America for a longer time to serve as translators—or they give students the freedom to choose their own groups, assuming that they will make suitable decisions based on their educational requirements (Christison, Krulatz, & Sevinç, 2021). However, these grouping strategies are not effective for multilingual students, especially those with high-intensity literacy needs. Instead, to meet the needs of your multilingual students, use data and the same grouping strategies for all of your students.

Summary

Teachers can provide differentiated support for each reader through small-group instruction. You can achieve this differentiated support through intentional grouping that uses data to inform your flexible groups. Within groups, teachers can tailor their instruction, intervention, and enrichment by implementing best practices for students with diverse learning needs. Small-group instruction enables access and equity to be at the core of literacy instruction. The following reflection provides a way for you to integrate the topics shared in this chapter with your own classroom experiences as you recharge your small-group instruction.

LAUNCH YOUR REFLECTION

Let's reconnect with Mr. Moore, the teacher we met at the beginning of this chapter (page 36). Now that you've read this chapter, consider the following questions.

- What would be some equitable and inclusive ways Mr. Moore can differentiate small-group configurations and instruction?
- What are some first steps Mr. Moore can take?

RECHARGE YOUR SMALL-GROUP READING INSTRUCTION

The following are some questions you can use to apply the chapter concepts to your own classroom context.

- How can I use small groups to promote access and equity for all my readers?
- How might I group students for instruction? How can I use organizing tools to plan for when I will meet with each group and what the lesson goals will be?
- What are some important considerations as I work to meet the needs of all students, including students with high-intensity needs, students with disabilities, and students who are multilingual?

EXPAND YOUR TOOLBOX

To continue your learning, see the "Leading the Learning Action Guide" (page 201) to support you and your colleagues. In the action guide for this chapter, you'll find in-action videos that spotlight teaching strategies as well as differentiated professional learning activities you can try out with your team. Additional tools that support this chapter topic can be accessed online (visit **go.SolutionTree.com/literacy**).

CHAPTER 3
HOW DO I CONNECT TO WHOLE-GROUP INSTRUCTION?

Small-group instruction should be aligned to both curriculum standards and data-informed instructional goals for students. Understanding how small-group instruction connects to and extends from whole-group instruction helps teachers keep both the content and students in mind when identifying areas of focus for small-group instruction. Ensuring that all students have access to grade-level expectations also supports equitable instruction. This chapter enables teachers to think about how small-group instruction is situated within the literacy block as a form of differentiation for whole-group instruction, curriculum standards, and decision making related to the gradual release of learning. This chapter also includes resources for aligning instruction with curriculum standards and meeting students where they are as readers.

As you read, consider if and how your small-group learning goals and whole-group learning goals are aligned. The following questions may also help frame your thinking as you read.

- Should the focus for a small-group lesson be aligned to whole-group instruction (core instruction and aligned curriculum standards) or data-informed instructional goals that may align with standards

taught earlier in the school year or even in earlier grade levels? Is it possible to combine both of these ideas as dual goals?
- How can I avoid simply reteaching whole-group instruction during small-group lessons?
- How might I connect to whole-group instruction, including text selection considerations, if my students are reading below grade-level benchmarks?

Consider the following example of Dr. Harris.

MEET THE PRINCIPAL: DR. HARRIS

> Dr. Harris has been the principal of Enterprise Elementary for eleven years. She strives to engage in professional learning alongside teachers and sees her role as an instructional leader as one to empower teachers and families to promote the learning of all students at Enterprise Elementary. In supporting the instructional coach and teachers to strengthen small-group reading instruction, Dr. Harris has become aware of a persistent obstacle that teachers are discussing as they plan in collaborative teams: Although teachers aim to form student groups and identify learning goals for small-group reading instruction, they are not sure if or how their instructional focus areas should align to their whole-group learning goals. Teachers are not sure if they should base their lessons, text selection, and questioning on standards-based curriculum or if they should prioritize specific data points from assessments to drive these instructional decisions. To assist teachers with navigating this obstacle, Dr. Harris prompts them to consider how they might accomplish both goals: to use data-informed decision making as their initial lens for small-group lesson planning and to look for opportunities to connect to the standards-driven curriculum of whole-group instruction. When talking about this theoretically, teachers agree that it makes sense. However, when they try to put it into practice, they feel stuck. Dr. Harris is looking for ways to offer concrete examples for teachers at her school so they can feel confident about their small-group instructional practices.

Do the challenges that the teachers are sharing with Dr. Harris resonate with you? How have you navigated instructional decision making for small-group reading lessons when considering both data-informed goals and curriculum standards? If you were a teacher at Enterprise Elementary, how could Dr. Harris help you feel unstuck?

We'll revisit these ideas and questions at the end of the chapter to identify ways to connect small-group instruction to whole-group instructional goals at your grade level.

Regardless of individual reader profiles and data-informed instructional needs, providing readers with effective, evidence-based grade-level core instruction is non-negotiable as an equitable teaching practice. Every reader has the right to access grade-level text in alignment with on-level curriculum standards, although the scaffolding needed to access grade-level text may vary from one reader to the next (Mattos et al., 2025).

In some educational spaces, we have encountered a persistent misconception that reading experiences must be offered in a lock-step approach through which readers gain access to increasingly complex text only when they have demonstrated mastery of foundational skills. If this were the case—if we did not provide opportunities to strengthen readers' language comprehension until *after* they mastered foundational skills—by the time they focused on comprehension, they would have lost the opportunity to build understanding of text as part of their reading process. Instead, foundational skills can be developed within context and as a part of work with other skills.

In the following video, an instructional coach shares the bigger picture of how foundational skills fit within small-group reading instruction. She describes how many teachers at her school shared the misconception that foundational skills had to be mastered before readers could engage in rich comprehension tasks.

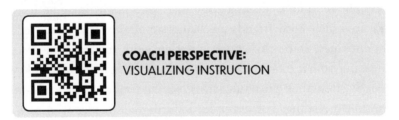

COACH PERSPECTIVE:
VISUALIZING INSTRUCTION

Additionally, with text complexity increasing from year to year, waiting to focus on comprehension could result in readers having to make sense of complex grade-level text without previous practice using less sophisticated text. In this approach, it can be easy to understand how students who are reading below grade-level expectations may have difficulty meeting grade-level standards of rigor, if for no other reason than the clock of the academic school year runs out before they can advance to on-grade-level reading experiences and opportunities. If this sounds familiar, it may be helpful to build a deeper understanding about how varied practice experiences can help readers develop not only from where they are but beyond their current level of proficiency.

Interleaved Practice

The concept of *blocked practice* is one in which focused instruction and application practice are centered around a single topic, skill, or concept before advancing to a more complex topic. By contrast, *interleaved practice* incorporates different topics or skills into practice and application tasks.

By using interleaved practice, teachers can support readers to integrate and apply the skills that they are learning in different instructional contexts (whole group, small group, and intervention) as they read.

In the following video of a first-grade lesson, readers are reviewing inflected endings as they demonstrate interleaved practice decoding words with various inflected endings.

PRIMARY LESSON: DECODING REVIEW

So, rather than representing the relationship between word recognition and language comprehension as a running relay race, one might imagine it as a three-legged race in which both strands are being simultaneously developed. Though you might anticipate some challenges as readers work toward both decoding and making meaning from text—similar to a three-legged race that feels clunky—readers simultaneously strengthen processes across reading strands as they advance toward proficient, skilled reading. For example, a third-grade reader who receives additional support within Tier 2 intervention for decoding and fluency can practice and apply those concepts to reading multisyllabic words in grade-level text, while also applying recently learned knowledge of commonly used prefixes and suffixes when decoding the same words.

We are not implying that the third grader who is working to build early foundational skills will be able to accurately and fluently read and comprehend a sophisticated passage due to a single interleaved practice opportunity. Instead, this reader will better comprehend grade-level text during whole-group instruction over time when they concurrently receive Tier 1 whole-group instruction, Tier 1 small-group instruction, and Tier 2 intervention instruction across the day and are prompted to practice and apply their learning across contexts. The following anecdote presents an example of interleaved practice in action.

We were fortunate to have the opportunity to learn from David Coleman, a literacy researcher and curriculum designer who presented on the topic of text complexity at a professional conference. During his talk, he shared a video game analogy with participants, which offered a helpful frame for thinking about text. To start, he described how, in the world of gaming development, there is a *boss figure*—the character or object that game users must defeat at each level. Game developers work carefully to develop boss figures who present a myriad of challenges that result in certain defeat of a gamer's character after multiple attempts. After all, who would want to play a video game that is so easy that you could beat a level—or even the entire game—on your first try? Not any students we know!

Instead, gamers appreciate the challenges the boss figure presents, and with each round of failure, they attempt to develop a strategy or uncover a tip that will help them in their next attempt. With an alluring enough boss figure, gamers become persistent and motivated to tackle the challenge repeatedly until they ultimately succeed at defeating the boss, thereby conquering a level or the entire game (Coleman & Money, 2020). You may already be anticipating the analogy here. After providing this gaming background, Coleman posed this question to our group: "How can we apply what we know about a gamer's motivation, persistence, and competencies to unlock the challenge of a boss figure so that students use the same approach when they read a 'boss' text?"

We suspect you can imagine a time when a reader in your classroom encountered a challenging text and demonstrated a cognitive (or perhaps even physical) retreat. Such a response is understandable. Imagine how you might feel reading an article from a medical journal or a few pages of tax code (assuming you haven't spent time in either of those fields). Initial feelings of overwhelm when faced with a boss text make sense. We argue that it's what comes after the initial text encounter that matters most, however. How can we equip our readers with the skills, competencies, stamina, and motivation to chip away at a boss text in the same way that they would tackle a boss in a video game? This is where interleaved practice comes back into the picture. We support readers in tackling boss texts when we provide interleaved practice opportunities for them to build specific competencies and skills at their point of need (whether part of differentiated core instruction or through reading intervention) and when we offer guided applications of those skills with grade-level text.

Table 3.1 (page 54) offers examples of interleaved practice within a grade-level text at both the primary and intermediate levels.

TABLE 3.1: Examples of Interleaved Practice Within a Grade-Level Text

Data-Informed Reader Focus	Application Opportunities With Boss Text
Primary Examples	
Vowel digraphs (/sh/), high-frequency words, decoding	Word hunt in which students use two different colors to highlight words with vowel digraph patterns and known high-frequency words within a text they are reading
	Word hunt similar to the preceding example, but with a third color added for students to highlight words with the sound-spelling pattern being taught in whole-group instruction, aligned with grade-level standards
	Chunking of text passage for decoding practice (chunking could be as simple as cutting the text into phrases, sentences, or smaller "strips" to reduce overwhelm and cognitive load)
	Discussion (pair or group) of meaning of chunked text passages (retelling or summary)
	Reassembly of chunked passages (physically putting parts back together)
	Text analysis and discussion (pair or group) with emphasis on what is being taught in whole-group comprehension instruction, aligned with grade-level standards
Intermediate Examples	
Single-syllable vowel digraphs, decoding, oral reading fluency	Two-color word hunt for (a) multisyllabic words with vowel digraph pattern and (b) unknown, challenging multisyllabic words that impede comprehension during first reading
	Word-attack strategies for challenging multisyllabic words identified in the previous step (applying grade-level expectations, including morphology instruction)
	Chunking of text passage for decoding practice (for example, by paragraph, by section, by page)
	Discussion (pair or group) of meaning of chunked text passages (retelling or summary)
	Reassembly of chunked passages (physically putting parts back together or discussing how the different parts connect and why the author organized the text this way for us as readers)
	Text analysis and discussion (pair or group) with emphasis on what is being taught in whole-group comprehension instruction, aligned with grade-level standards

Figure 3.1 offers a visual of a text-attack protocol developed by a collaborative team within a professional learning community as a concrete example of interleaved practice in action.

> **Text-Attack Process** 
>
> **Carefully *Read the Passage*:**
> - #(1, 2, 3, 4, and so on) Paragraph and stanzas
> - ⬭ Unknown words and phrases
>
> **After Reading, *Stop and Think*:**
> - What was the passage mainly or mostly about?
> - Why did the author write this passage?
>   + To give information about . . .
>   + To tell a story about . . .
>   + To convince or persuade me . . .
>
> **Now, *Time to Answer Questions*:**
>
> | Highlight | • Clue words in the question
• Answers and details within the passage |
> |---|---|
>
> ---
>
> **Test-Taking Strategies**
> - Find clue words in the question.
> - Read every answer choice.
> - ~~Eliminate~~ wrong answers.
> - Choose the best answer.
> - Flag and go back.

Source: © 2023 by Moline Elementary, Riverview Gardens School District. Used with permission.

FIGURE 3.1: Text-attack process poster.

The Gradual Release Model

Douglas Fisher and Nancy Frey (2008) assert that teaching should lead to deep learning that students can successfully apply to new challenges as they think critically and creatively and grow in confidence, knowledge, and skill—an approach referred to as the *gradual release of responsibility*. The gradual release of responsibility (GRR) instructional framework includes four components: (1) focused instruction, (2) guided instruction, (3) collaborative learning, and (4) independent learning (Fisher & Frey, 2008). Table 3.2 (page 56) illustrates each of these instructional components with a literacy example.

We encourage teachers to keep this big picture in mind as readers develop skills that will serve as a means to the end of proficient reading. Helping readers to not only demonstrate skills but understand and express how those skills help them as a reader is one concrete way to reframe standards-specific learning toward a larger goal of developing skilled readers. As teachers, it is worth our effort to create opportunities for readers to express ownership of their reading processes and identities.

TABLE 3.2: Components of the Gradual Release of Responsibility Framework

GRR Component	Component Description	Component Example From Literacy Lessons
Focused instruction	Teacher establishes the purpose of the lesson and provides modeling that includes examples of the thinking and language to be successful.	**Text Structures** *Text structure* is the way the authors organize information in a text. • What is the author trying to tell me in each section of the text? • How does this section of the text connect to the others? • How is the author organizing each part of the text?
Guided instruction	Teacher provides instructional scaffolds such as questions, prompts, and cues to facilitate reader understanding while releasing responsibility to the readers.	**Argumentative Text** • States the author's claim and gives facts and information • May include text features **Purpose for Reading** Identify how text structures help us to better understand the text. *Note:* While this example is embedded in whole-group instruction, the teacher could use a different text in a small-group lesson with the same lesson goal to provide more targeted instructional scaffolds.
Collaborative learning	Students work in collaborative groups to consolidate their understanding through tasks that use academic language. Each reader has individual accountability for their own contribution.	**Placemat Consensus** Student One Response My Answer: A Student Two Response My Answer: C Student Three Response My Answer: B Student Four Response My Answer: A Our Answer: C Our Consensus: Directions: Each person in the group will think independently about the question and record their answer in their own section of the chart. The group will discuss the question and come to consensus on the answer. This is written in the center of the placemat. Each group will share their responses in a whole-group discussion with the class.

| Independent learning | Students apply their learning and knowledge to new situations with independence. | **Write to Respond:** Your Turn! This text uses the cause-and-effect text structure. Cause and effect explains the relationship between events. Explain how this text structure was used in the passage. |

Source: Fisher & Frey, 2008.

The gradual release model (Pearson & Gallagher, 1983) can support teachers as they plan for day-to-day experiences that link whole-group and small-group lessons.

Although there are numerous grade-level standards students work toward each academic year, the primary goal of literacy instruction is to advance the automaticity and depth of our students' reading skills. Grade-level standards and benchmarks serve as guideposts for both teachers and students as readers progress toward this goal. Although assessing proficiency in specific skills and concepts aids in measuring progress, it is crucial to place these skills within a wider, authentic reading context.

Knowledge of Curriculum Standards

As teachers differentiate small-group instruction to meet the needs of readers, they can use their knowledge of curriculum standards to offer interleaved practice during reading and discussion. Often, by integrating curriculum standards into small-group lessons, teachers can demonstrate their deep, nuanced understanding of grade-level standards. For example, a teacher may include an encoding task that links readers' data-determined phonics needs to the recent phonics concept taught during whole-group instruction. Similarly, readers may be receiving intervention to build foundational skills, but the teacher can offer strategic scaffolds and prompts that help readers make connections in service of grade level–aligned tasks during differentiated small-group lessons. For example, students who are learning about compound words in core instruction but receiving intervention in consonant-vowel-consonant (CVC) words could practice spelling words through dictation like *catnip* and *sunlit*.

Instructional approaches that can assist teachers in leveraging their knowledge of curriculum standards during small-group lessons include those outlined in table 3.3 (page 58).

To identify opportunities for interleaved practice for your students, consider the following recommendations.

TABLE 3.3: Instructional Approaches to Leverage Curriculum Standards

Instructional Approaches	Small-Group Lesson Examples
Look for opportunities to connect to current standards.	In a small-group lesson where readers are being taught about the consonant digraph /th/ and reading a decodable text with this phonics pattern (words like *them* and *Thad*), teachers can connect to whole-group morphology instruction, where readers are learning about inflected endings and suffixes to extend word reading using "challenge words" (like *thunderous*).
Look for opportunities to connect trailing standards.	During a small-group lesson focused on nonfiction text structure and its role in enhancing comprehension, teachers can prompt readers to first identify the central idea of the text before delving into its structure. This approach ensures that all students understand the author's intended message. In this case, the central idea is a trailing standard from a previous unit that the teacher is embedding as a scaffolding question prior to focusing on the primary goals of identifying text structure and determining how the text structure helps readers to better understand the text.
Consider prerequisite knowledge.	In a small-group lesson where readers analyze how a character changes throughout a literary text, the teacher listens carefully for readers' knowledge of and reference to characters (main and supporting), key events and details, problem and solution, and other fiction story elements to support readers in identifying how and why the character changes. In this case, the teacher is drawing on knowledge of the previous grade level's curriculum standards that align to the learning goal with the understanding that the previous grade level's expectations serve as intended prerequisite skills to demonstrate proficiency for this lesson's learning goal. Curriculum standards that are formatted to highlight vertical alignment can support teachers to readily make connections and observations during both planning and instruction.

- Clearly identify the learning goals for core reading instruction for a current unit (or week of instruction).
- Clearly pinpoint the current learning goals for students receiving intervention.
- Look for opportunities that align the goals in intervention and core instruction. You might also consider where each goal lies on a reading continuum to brainstorm ways to integrate each one into your instruction.
- Consider instruction or practice opportunities where students can apply their learning across lessons and interventions in authentic reading contexts.
- Ensure that students who are receiving intervention are also engaging with core instruction with meaningful practice opportunities.

Alignment and Coherence From Whole Group to Small Group

Most elementary teachers are responsible for planning learning experiences for their readers that span all content areas across the school day (although we acknowledge that some of you may be in departmentalized settings where your content-area responsibility is slightly narrower). In considering the literacy block alone, teachers typically plan for whole-group lessons (or lessons with various instructional focus areas), small-group lessons, and independent or collaborative work through centers, stations, or independent tasks. These contexts present a significant demand on teachers' instructional planning time by requiring teachers to synthesize both reader-specific and group-level data with grade-level curriculum standards. Figure 3.2 provides visuals of a literacy block at the first-grade level.

120-Minute Literacy Block: First Grade				
The following are recommendations for the 120-minute literacy block. The 30-minute slot for writing is designated based on evidence-based best practices to connect concepts and skills taught in reading. This time does not have to be consecutively taught with reading, but it does need to be taught for at least 30 minutes daily.				
Recommended Time (Daily)	**Instructional Setting**	**Literacy Components**	**Focus**	**Recommended Instructional Resources**
10 minutes	Whole group	Phonological awareness	To develop the ability to identify and manipulate individual sounds in speech	• Heggerty Phonemic Awareness • Model video: Heggerty
15 minutes	Whole group	Phonics	To develop the acquisition of letter-sound correspondences and their application to read and spell words	• Curriculum Resource Materials (CRMs) • Multisensory kits • Model video: Foundation Routines
45 minutes	Small group	Phonological awareness Phonics Comprehension Fluency Writing Oral language	To provide time devoted to individualized instruction that targets foundational skills, comprehension, vocabulary, fluency, and writing in response to text	• Multisensory kits • Being a Reader • Raz-Plus • Wonders Decodable Readers • Wonders Leveled Readers • Scholastic Bookroom • Model videos

Source: © 2023 by Orange County Public Schools. Used with permission.

FIGURE 3.2: Example first-grade 120-minute literacy block model. continued ▶

Recommended Time (Daily)	Instructional Setting	Literacy Components	Focus	Recommended Instructional Resources
20 minutes	Whole group	Comprehension Vocabulary Oral language	To provide time devoted to reading aloud meaningful literature and independently reading to foster comprehension skills through model and vocabulary-rich conversations	• Curriculum Resource Materials (CRMs)
30 minutes	Whole group or small group	Writing or encoding	To create a bridge between students' understanding of phonological and phonics skills and utilizing written expression (according to developmentally appropriate practices) to convey meaning	• Curriculum Resource Materials (CRMs)

Figure 3.3 provides visuals of the literacy block at the fourth- and fifth-grade level. Chunking the instructional block by literacy component or learning goal and instructional setting can help teachers ensure that they are consistently providing comprehensive reading instruction.

120-Minute Literacy Block: Fourth and Fifth Grade

The following are recommendations for the 120-minute literacy block. Florida state statutes dictate that the 90-minute reading block be consecutive time spent. The 30-minute slot for writing is designated based on evidence-based best practices to connect concepts and skills taught in reading. This time does not have to be consecutively taught with reading, but it does need to be for at least 30 minutes daily.

Recommended Time (Daily)	Instructional Setting	Literacy Components	Focus	Recommended Instructional Resources
30–45 minutes	Whole group	Teacher read aloud Phonics & word analysis Fluency Comprehension Vocabulary Oral language Writing integration	To provide time devoted to reading meaningful literature and independently reading to foster comprehension skills through modeling and vocabulary-rich conversations	• Curriculum Resource Materials (CRMs)

45–60 minutes	Small group	Phonics & word analysis Fluency Comprehension Vocabulary Writing integration	To provide time devoted to individualized instruction that targets foundational skills, comprehension, vocabulary, fluency, and writing in response to text	• Raz-Plus • BEST questioning dashboard • Wonders Leveled Readers • Wonders differentiated passages • Scholastic Bookroom • Model videos
30 minutes	Whole group or small group	Writing	To create a bridge between students' understanding of phonics skills and utilizing written expression (according to developmentally appropriate practices) to convey meaning	• Curriculum Resource Materials (CRMs)

Source: © 2023 by Orange County Public Schools. Used with permission.

FIGURE 3.3: Fourth- and fifth-grade 120-minute literacy block model.

Visual representations such as the literacy block models in figures 3.2 (page 59) and 3.3 can help you conceptualize the planning and organization necessary to coordinate multiple contexts of literacy instruction. At the same time, it is important to think about how your lesson experiences are aligned to learning goals based on curriculum standards. It is also important to consider how lessons offer instructional coherence, which explains how each component of our readers' academic experiences is connected and carefully designed to advance grade-level learning (TNTP, 2022). Instructional coherence is critical for teachers and readers. It allows readers to identify how extra support during small-group lessons and through extended learning opportunities (such as centers, stations, and independent work) benefits them as they work to enhance their proficiency and build skill. The following visualization activity prompts you to check your instructional block for coherence through the lens of readers in your classroom.

1. Pick a single day of reading instruction you recently taught or will teach.
2. Pick three of your readers to consider for this visualization activity.
3. With your day of instruction in mind, visualize what the reading block will look like for each of the three readers. Ask yourself the following questions.
    a. Are the connections between the learning goals in whole-group instruction and independent or collaborative practice clear? Are they clear and apparent for your three readers?

b. Do the readers have opportunities to practice reading skills and concepts in authentic contexts?

c. Can the readers see connections between what they are learning in small-group instruction and whole-group instruction?

d. If the learning goals for each setting are different, can the readers understand how the goals work together to help them build skills as a reader?

e. Can the readers tell you in their own words how their learning experiences help them become stronger readers?

f. Can the readers tell you in their own words how their learning connects to previous learning?

g. Are the reading tasks authentic and meaningful for readers, or are they disjointed assignments that they must submit according to the teacher's directions?

To learn more about developing extended learning opportunities, see chapter 10 (page 179).

Summary

Planning for alignment and coherence between small-group reading lessons and whole-group instruction offers important connections for students as readers. Small-group reading instruction offers a powerful opportunity for differentiation and equitable learning opportunities. Using interleaved practice and intentionally considering how and when to scaffold learning opportunities help teachers connect whole-group and small-group learning goals. Additionally, teachers can leverage their own deep knowledge of curriculum standards and prerequisite skills for grade-level benchmarks to include nuanced questions, prompts, and cues in their small-group lessons. Integrating these ideas with a lens toward readers' day-to-day experiences across the literacy block can help teachers ensure that readers themselves see the connections between their learning opportunities and their growth as skilled, proficient readers.

LAUNCH YOUR REFLECTION

Let's reconnect with Dr. Harris, the principal we met at the beginning of this chapter (page 50). Now that you've read this chapter, consider the following questions.

- As you reread how Dr. Harris describes her challenge to support teachers at her school, what recommendations would you suggest she use to help teachers make connections between small-group instruction and whole-group lesson goals?

- What guidance or support for aligning small-group and whole-group instruction would you like to receive from instructional leaders at your school?

RECHARGE YOUR SMALL-GROUP READING INSTRUCTION

The following are some questions you can use to apply the chapter concepts to your own classroom context.

- How might I consider both whole-group instruction (core instruction and the curriculum standards aligned with that instruction) and data-informed learning goals when planning for upcoming small-group reading instruction?
- How can I avoid reteaching whole-group instruction during small-group lessons?
- How can I connect to whole-group instruction with connected text, including text selection considerations, if my students are building foundational skills?
- What might interleaved practice look like for my readers in a small-group reading lesson?
- If asked, would my readers be able to explain how whole-group and small-group instruction connect to support them as readers? If not, what can I do to help them see that connection?

EXPAND YOUR TOOLBOX

To continue your learning, see the "Leading the Learning Action Guide" (page 201) to support you and your colleagues. In the action guide for this chapter, you'll find in-action videos that spotlight teaching strategies as well as differentiated professional learning activities you can try out with your team. Additional tools that support this chapter topic can be accessed online (visit **go.SolutionTree.com/literacy**).

CHAPTER 4
HOW DO I PLAN FOR SMALL-GROUP INSTRUCTION?

Planning for small-group reading instruction requires deep content knowledge, an understanding of students as readers, and knowledge of various evidence-based instructional practices. Teachers must also be familiar with available curriculum resources, whether they be optional materials or required for fidelity of implementation. Familiarity with curriculum resources includes knowing the text students will use during small-group lessons, which teachers need to preview in order to support meaningful text discussion. Teachers must also consider the logistics of materials management and organization, including deciding when and how they will reorganize and prepare materials from day to day for subsequent lessons. Considering these demands, it is understandable why planning for small-group instruction can be challenging for some teachers. However, they can demystify this planning by consistently using a set of planning considerations.

In this chapter, we explore those planning considerations, including reading content knowledge for teaching, and we offer examples of lesson structures and instructional routines that teachers can implement during their small-group instruction. We also revisit the ABC Reader Profile Framework (chapter 1, page 17) as a support tool to determine the data-informed instructional focus for each small group. We share ideas for organizing, managing, and preparing materials, and we conclude the chapter with examples of research outcomes that we think you'll find relevant to your instructional practices.

As you read this chapter, consider your own experiences planning small-group reading lessons with the curriculum resources that are accessible to you. Use the following questions to frame your thinking as you read.

- How might I use the ABC Reader Profile Framework (chapter 1, page 17) to determine instructional focus areas (such as decoding, fluency, and comprehension)?
- After I've identified my broad instructional focus data, how can I determine skill-specific learning targets for small-group reading instruction?
- How can I ensure that I utilize reading content knowledge and reading research in my small-group instruction?
- If using an adopted curriculum with lesson plans provided: How can I identify the research-proven instructional routines embedded in the lesson plan structures? How do these routines align with my students' data-informed needs?

Consider the following example of Mrs. Valdez.

MEET THE TEACHER: MRS. VALDEZ

> Mrs. Valdez is a third-grade teacher who has been teaching in her local school district for twenty years. During her time in the district, she has used a wide variety of curriculum materials to plan for small-group instruction. Despite having a wide array of curriculum options, Mrs. Valdez recently feels that she needs more clarity in deciding which curriculum materials to use when she plans lessons. She appreciates the autonomy in instructional decision making, but she wishes she knew more about the research base of each of the optional materials to inform her decision.

Does Mrs. Valdez's difficulty selecting curriculum materials for small-group reading lessons resonate with you? What should Mrs. Valdez look for when identifying curriculum materials as options for instructional planning? How can she ensure curriculum materials are grounded in evidence-based research?

We'll revisit these ideas and questions at the end of the chapter to identify ways to support instructional practices for small-group lesson planning in your classroom.

Intentional Planning

Reading experts Kristin Conradi Smith, Steven J. Amendum, and Tamara W. Williams (2022) describe small-group reading instruction as expensive. They elaborate to explain that small-group instruction requires time to manage and plan for effective differentiated instruction, which is costly. Given the time commitment and cost, teachers committed to small-group instruction should ensure their efforts are aligned with research evidence to achieve intended learning goals.

Research indicates that small-group instruction is an effective approach to impact student reading achievement within specific skill sets (Gersten et al., 2017; Neitzel et al., 2021; Wanzek et al., 2016). Conceptualizing small-group instruction as supplemental and differentiated to meet targeted literacy goals provides teachers with a framework for intentional planning. Teachers may have varying levels of autonomy in selecting curriculum materials and developing and implementing lesson plans for small-group instruction. Regardless of your school's approach to lesson plan implementation and the selection of curriculum materials, we believe the planning considerations we share in this chapter apply to you. Intentionally planning by identifying instructional foci and lesson goals and aligning them to reader data and observations is valuable for all small-group reading instruction, regardless of the lesson source. Additionally, teachers can deliver impactful lessons with clear intention when they understand the lesson structure and how and why instructional routines are embedded in lessons to support readers. Hopefully, this consideration helps frame your reading of this chapter so the planning considerations that we share can reinvigorate your planning practices, regardless of the curriculum materials you use.

The following video shows a principal sharing his thoughts on the importance of planning for small-group instruction.

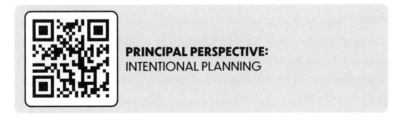

PRINCIPAL PERSPECTIVE:
INTENTIONAL PLANNING

DETERMINE DATA-INFORMED INSTRUCTIONAL FOCUS AREAS

To identify instructional foci for small-group instruction based on data, teachers need access to valid, up-to-date, and insightful information about readers' strengths, skills, and behaviors. Teachers can use data from a variety of sources, including observations, informal and formal assessments, summative assessments, and curriculum-based measures. Teachers can use these data to differentiate instruction, increase intervention support, and make grouping and other instructional decisions. To read more about data sources that support data-informed decision making, revisit chapter 2 (page 35).

Teachers can use the ABC Reader Profile Framework (chapter 1, page 17) to synthesize reading data to identify reading focus areas for instruction. This tool can also help determine which students to group together for small-group lessons based on the instructional focus area identified. Using high-level decision making aligns with Conradi Smith and colleagues' (2022) recommendation to consider three focus areas for lessons: (1) decoding, (2) fluency, and (3) comprehension.

Our suggestions in the ABC Reader Profile Framework are similar, as we identify decoding, bridging processes (which include fluency), and comprehension as potential focus areas while acknowledging the role self-regulation and reader motivation play in planning. For example, a teacher might use an informal assessment for phonics to determine that word recognition should be a key instructional focus area and to prioritize which specific phonics learning goal to target. Alternatively, teachers might notice an opportunity to provide instruction in both oral reading prosody (fluency) and making inferences (reading comprehension), and they can plan to coordinate instruction in these areas of reading during a series of small-group lessons with a dialogue-rich fiction text that offers opportunities for both goal areas.

Figure 4.1 includes an example of how teachers can use the ABC Reader Profile Framework to determine overarching focus areas for a first-grade reader named Jake. Notice in this example that the teacher not only indicated Jake's asset-based strengths but also considered his needs and the standard benchmark expectations for his grade level to determine his reading goals.

After identifying the instructional focus area, it is important to determine targeted learning goals for each small group and, ultimately, for each reader. The next sections offer recommendations to help narrow your instructional planning from a reading focus area to more specific learning goals anchored in reading skills or strategies.

Decoding

	Pre-Alphabetic	Partial Alphabetic	Full Alphabetic	Consolidated Alphabetic	Automatic
	☐ Readers use cues such as pictures, context cues, and guessing strategies. ☐ Readers notice semantic rather than phonological relationships. ☐ Readers' connections are more arbitrary than systematic.	☐ Readers use emerging grapheme–phoneme connections, such as the first letter sound. ☐ Readers' connections are incomplete, and they use known phonetic cues to guide their decoding attempts.	☐ Readers attend to every letter in every word as they convert graphemes into phonological representations. ☐ Readers have working knowledge of most letter-sound correspondences and decode sequentially, though slowly.	☑ Readers use chunks to decode. They recognize multiletter patterns instantly (such as consonant blends, vowel teams, affixes, and so on) and use syllables and morphemes as chunks to support decoding. ☑ Readers teach themselves new connections as orthographic mapping further develops.	☐ Readers quickly and effortlessly decode, and most words are sight words. ☐ Readers use decoding processes that are highly automatic when they encounter unknown words. ☐ Readers have a variety of strategies at their disposal, especially when reading technical words.

Reader Goals:
Met year-end goal: uses chunks to decode. Future goal is to use processes more automatically to support decoding.

Fluency and Bridging Processes

	Word by Word	Local Grouping	Phrase and Clause	Sentence Prosody	Passage Expression
	☐ Readers focus on individual words or sounds. ☐ Less than one-quarter of the words are read aloud with appropriate expression.	☑ Readers focus on local word groups and may be mostly arrhythmic or monotone. ☑ More than one-quarter and less than one-half of words are read aloud with appropriate expression.	☐ Readers express the structure or meaning of words, phrases, clauses, and a few sentences. Intonation may reinforce rhythmic grouping, or reading may be monotone. ☐ More than half of the words are read aloud with appropriate expression.	☐ Readers express text, sentence structure, and meaning. ☐ Reading may be inconsistent but not monotone. Reading rate is at least fifty-five words per minute. ☐ More than three-quarters of the words are read aloud with appropriate expression.	☐ Readers convey elements as if reading for a listener and are expressive throughout. ☐ Readers consistently express the structure and meaning of sentences, paragraphs, and passages. Their reading rate is at least eighty words per minute.

Additional bridging processes to consider along this continuum include concepts of print, vocabulary knowledge, morphological awareness, and graphophonological-semantic cognitive flexibility.

Reader Goals:
On target for grade-level expectations; uses local word groups. Future goal is to express the meaning of phrases and some sentences with expression.

Source: Ehri, 1995; Lastiri, 2022; Mokhtari & Reichard, 2002; White et al., 2021.

FIGURE 4.1: Sample ABC Reader Profile for Jake.

continued ▼

SMALL GROUPS FOR BIG READERS

Comprehension

	Literal Comprehension	Inferential Comprehension	Evaluative Comprehension	Reorganization Comprehension	Appreciative Comprehension
	☑ Readers understand a text, including facts, ideas, vocabulary, events, and stated information. ☑ Readers can provide direct and explicit answers to questions extracted from a text.	☑ Readers make valid inferences from the information found in text. ☑ Readers understand the facts, even if they aren't explicitly stated in the reading material. ☐ Inferences made include generalizations, comparisons, assumptions, predictions, and so on.	☐ Readers analyze an author's intent, opinion, language, and style of text presentation. ☐ Readers evaluate the appropriateness of an author's devices and then make inferences based on the fact or idea implied in text.	☐ Readers use information gained from various parts of the text and rearrange it into new patterns that integrate the information into an idea for further understanding. ☐ Readers apply creativity or curiosity as they analyze, digest, and evaluate text to identify a unique view of a situation or event.	☐ Readers recognize the purpose, perspective, and philosophy of the author by understanding the deeper meaning of the text. ☐ Readers reflect and respond emotionally to the text while making connections. This requires a literal and inferential understanding, which is then used to evaluate and reflect.

Reader Goals:
Understands ideas presented directly; makes inferences from the information found in illustrations. Future goal is to use the information in the text (more than just illustrations) and broaden the types of inferences made.

Self-Regulation and Metacognition

	Initial Awareness and Control	Emerging Awareness and Control	Developing Awareness and Control	Skilled Awareness and Control	Independent Awareness and Control
	☑ Readers begin reading a text at the first word, paragraph, or page. ☐ Readers read slowly and carefully for all texts and purposes. ☑ Readers think about their understanding of text during or after reading.	☐ Readers think about what they know before they read. ☑ Readers slow down and pay closer attention to text when it becomes difficult. ☐ Readers employ a strategy to think about texts as they read (such as summarizing, visualizing, or asking questions).	☐ Readers preview the text before reading to anticipate content and determine a purpose for reading. ☐ Readers stop to think about what they're reading from time to time, regardless of text difficulty. ☐ Readers employ multiple strategies to think about text as they read (such as summarizing, visualizing, or asking questions).	☐ Readers preview the text before reading to anticipate content while noting the text's organization and structure to support their purpose for reading. ☐ Readers adjust reading speed to try to get back on track if they lose concentration or to deepen understanding. ☐ Readers employ multiple strategies to think about their reading (such as summarizing, visualizing, or asking questions) and seek opportunities to discuss their reading with others to check for understanding.	☐ Readers preview the text before reading by noting organization and structure and making inferences about how to prioritize content in alignment with reading purpose. ☐ Readers adjust rate, reread, and refocus flexibly according to text, purpose, and difficulty. ☐ Readers flexibly employ multiple strategies to think about their reading (such as summarizing, visualizing, or asking questions), seek opportunities to discuss their understanding, and use additional resources to connect, repair, or extend their learning.

Reader Goals:
Thinks about what he is reading during and after reading. Future goals is to think about the content of the text prior to reading and to gain a variety of strategies to support his understanding during reading.

IDENTIFY READERS' LEARNING GOALS

Identifying targeted learning goals for small-group instruction is a critical step to understanding the purpose of instruction. Using clearly defined, data-informed, skill-specific learning goals when planning can help teachers make instructional decisions about text, lesson materials, and learning experiences—such as instructional routines—to support learning outcomes. Teachers can lift reading-specific learning goals from state literacy curriculum standards—in alignment with reading assessment data—as one source for planning support. For example, a teacher may determine that an instructional focus area for a single small group is decoding, but after reviewing the specific results of the CORE Phonics Survey (CORE, 2008) and curriculum grade-level expectations, they can narrow the focus area more specifically as "students will decode one-syllable words with diphthongs (oi, oy, ou, ow)" (CORE, 2008).

This focused goal supports text selection and instructional routines that outline the explicit instruction and application opportunities necessary to yield positive student outcomes. Similarly, when a teacher utilizes a curriculum that includes premade lesson plans for small-group reading instruction, they can enhance their comprehension of the instructional routines and embedded lesson components by understanding the specific learning objectives of the lesson. This understanding enables teachers to align the instructional opportunities within the lesson with data-informed, skill-based needs of the readers, thereby improving their ability to meet those needs. To read about connecting learning goals to whole-group instruction, including spiraled instruction from previous whole-group units, revisit chapter 3 (page 49).

SELECT CURRICULUM RESOURCES THAT SUPPORT LEARNING GOALS

After skill-specific learning goals have been identified for small-group reading instruction, selecting text in alignment with instructional goals is an important next step. Teachers must determine characteristics of the text that support students as readers at their current point of instruction to make this choice. For example, if the readers' instructional focus area is decoding and the skill-specific learning goal is the vowel-consonant-e (VCe) pattern o_e /ō/, the lesson text should offer the opportunity to practice this phonics knowledge and apply it through decoding. In this case, a decodable text—one that serves as an *accountable text* for which readers can be held accountable for the instruction they received—would support instruction (ILA, 2020).

With instruction and available text options that are aligned to a systematic scope and sequence, an ideal accountable text would also offer readers the opportunity for ongoing practice with decoding words with previously taught phonics patterns and high-frequency words from previous small-group lessons. An additional consideration is the context of text selected, meaning whether the text is presented at the word, sentence, paragraph, or passage level. As curriculum standards call for more sophisticated applications of comprehension skills and strategies in intermediate grades, they also typically outline expectations for more complex text passages. It is important to keep these considerations in mind, even if a lesson requires chunking or strategic scaffolding for readers to access grade-level standards aligned with learning goals.

Other important factors to consider when selecting texts include the interest, representation, diversity, and level of engagement they provide. These elements include various aspects such as content, format, illustrations, and language. These additional components contribute to the overall reading experience and cater to the diverse learning needs of readers. This is particularly significant when planning a series of lessons, as it ensures a wide range of text experiences for readers. For additional considerations for text selection and to read more about those we've presented here, including examples, see chapter 5 (page 93).

To select appropriate text and instructional materials, teachers must become acquainted with and deeply understand the curriculum resources available. Devoting time to reading curriculum materials is an important but often overlooked initial step. Curriculum programs and resources are firmly grounded in research, have demonstrated their ability to produce positive student outcomes through field testing, and have undergone revisions based on valuable input from experienced educators in the field. Curriculum writers expect teachers to adapt materials and lessons based on readers' needs. In many curriculum programs, teachers can find annotations from the curriculum's authors in the form of introductions to a teacher's manual, margin notes in lesson plans, or online supplemental resources designed to support teachers in making instructional decisions (Ball & Cohen, 1996). Learning about the intent, organization, components, supplements, and any other instructional support from curriculum materials can have a long-term impact on teacher understanding and use of materials to anchor students' lessons.

Lesson Structures and Instructional Routines to Support Readers

It is difficult to dispute the comfort that clear expectations provide when preparing for a new and possibly unfamiliar experience. Imagine traveling to a new destination, trying a new art or fitness class, or preparing to present to your school's advisory council about a recently adopted curriculum. Knowing what to expect from each of these scenarios in advance would provide a level of comfort and increased confidence during the experience. The same is true for our readers as they join a small-group reading lesson. Readers may feel uncertain in this situation. Helping students anticipate how they will engage with the teacher and with other readers in their group will increase their confidence and prepare them for the lesson. Building common structures with predictable routines in lessons—whether through lesson planning, lesson facilitation, or both—is a great strategy to boost reader engagement. Predictable routines do more than just impact readers' confidence and expectations—they also promote equitable learning experiences, where the predictability of the lesson structure and routines increases the likelihood that all learners will have access to the lesson (Lindsey, 2022). To learn how predictable routines offer clarity for teacher and student roles, see chapter 6 (page 109).

Teachers often describe the small-group literacy block as a challenging part of their day simply due to its planning demands. Many teachers create between two to four small-group lessons daily with varying learning objectives and plan for differentiated, extended learning opportunities during individual centers, when students aren't engaged in small groups. For additional considerations for planning extended learning opportunities for students who aren't part of the pulled small-group lesson, see chapter 10 (page 179).

With this planning demand in mind, we encourage teachers to think about how they can incorporate predictable lesson structures and routines into their lesson plans. In doing so, there will be variability in the planning process, which leads to efficient lesson planning and delivery.

Although you know that identifying lesson structures and routines supports both teachers and students, you may be uncertain about how to determine a lesson's structure or select an evidence-based routine. The sections that follow provide guidance on how to structure lessons and create instructional routines that are aligned with your instructional focus areas. Additionally, for instructional purposes, the following sections include content-specific considerations derived from the knowledge of the reading material. These content-specific considerations may influence your decision-making process during the planning phase.

LESSON STRUCTURES TO FRAME READING OPPORTUNITIES

Teachers should structure small-group lessons to provide readers with learning experiences and application opportunities aligned with the instructional focus areas and skill-specific learning goals. A lesson structure helps teachers outline how they will facilitate the lesson. This facilitation can include delivering explicit, systematic instruction and monitoring readers' application of their learning in context. Clearly defined teacher and student roles from the onset of the planning process enable teachers to make decisions about lesson facilitation, pacing, and strategic scaffolding. To read more about these lesson facilitation considerations, see chapter 6 (page 109).

Lesson structures grounded in research are credible options for teachers because they include components that have yielded positive student outcomes in educational settings. In this section, we offer examples of lesson structure frameworks that have demonstrated evidence of student learning for teachers to consider. We also share examples of lesson structure templates that have been developed to offer teachers systematic frameworks to use for their instructional planning. The lesson structures highlighted in this section aren't necessarily the only lesson structures that are effective or currently endorsed by reading researchers in the field—they are simply the lesson structures that we have used in our work with teachers. Future research in the field may offer additional considerations for lesson structures that support both teachers and students in small-group reading lessons.

If you are teaching from a curriculum program that includes predetermined lesson plans for small-group reading instruction, you may find that you don't need to make lesson structure decisions during the planning process. However, we encourage you to learn more about the research-proven basis for structure of the lessons you'll be teaching. When teachers understand the intentional, underlying structure of lessons, their increased awareness contributes to a teacher-curriculum partnership in which the strengths of both the curriculum and the teacher's expertise are leveraged for student learning (Remillard, 2016).

During our experiences collaborating with districts, schools, and teachers, we have encountered lesson plan templates for small-group reading that are designed to support teachers through the lesson-planning process. The templates serve as outlines that provide predictable lesson structures grounded in research. Although lesson plan templates can run the risk of being overly prescriptive or limiting, they also offer a framework for organizing components of instruction to align skill-specific learning goals with reading experiences.

The figures that follow highlight sample lesson structures from districts where we provided coaching support. We encourage teachers (and school leaders) to engage in collaborative discourse prior to adopting lesson plan templates for small-group instruction. This important process allows teachers to explore the underlying research basis for a given lesson structure, offers opportunities for teachers to make connections between lesson structures and readers' needs, and increases the likelihood that teachers gain ownership over a lesson structure and its use in the classroom.

Figure 4.2 offers an example of a district-created guidance tool to help teachers determine potential lesson structures based on their grade level and the instructional focus needs of a given group of readers. With this tool, teachers in this school district have access to sample lesson templates based on the specific instructional focus that they selected for their grade level. For the remainder of this section, we'll use resources from this district as a case example for how to provide

Small-Group Planning Template Choices

Purpose: This document includes optional resources to support planning for small-group instruction.

Grades K–2	
Foundational Skills — Decodable Passage	Provides guidance on how to structure a lesson utilizing a decodable passage
Foundational Skills — Based on Structured Literacy	Provides guidance on how to structure a lesson based on specific foundational skills
Comprehension	Provides guidance on how to structure a lesson based on specific comprehension skills

Grades 3–5	
Foundational Skills and Comprehension	Provides guidance on how to structure a lesson that transitions from foundational skills to comprehension
Comprehension	Provides guidance on how to structure a lesson based on specific comprehension skills

Source: © 2023 by Orange County Public Schools. Used with permission.

FIGURE 4.2: Lesson template menu for small-group instruction.

teacher planning support for various small-group instructional focus areas. As you review these district resources, consider how they align with the guidance provided by your school or district. If you don't have similar structures for planning support, how might you lead the effort to identify evidence-based supports in your context? We hope that the examples in the rest of this chapter inspire you and offer guidance that informs your next steps for instructional planning.

In figure 4.3 (page 76), we provide an example of an assisted learning lesson template. This template offers an outline for foundational skills instruction in which readers are learning letter names or sounds based on assessment data. In addition to offering a structure for a single day's lesson, the format of this template provides space for lesson planning across a week of instruction. This allows teachers to determine the specific skills and letters of focus for the week's instruction on a single page. We offer this figure for you as an example to demonstrate how teachers and leaders in a school district created or adapted existing evidence-based resources into a tool that they could widely use for consistency.

Assisted Learning Lesson Template						
Sample Data to Support (circle all that apply): PASI (phonemic awareness) PSI (decoding) DSA (encoding) Fundations DIBELS Writing Analysis Other: _____							
	Day ____	Day ____	Day ____	Day ____	Day ____
Phonemic Awareness **(5–7 minutes)** Identifying initials sound, blending and segment, and so on					
Letter ID Activity **(1–2 minutes)** If students are not able to recognize at least 20 letters, start with letter ID. Choose letter(s) according to data. Letter focus: _____ Review of known or previously taught letters: _____					
Vocabulary or Language Comprehension **(3–5 minutes)** Use language stimulation techniques. Discuss the word meanings of any images used to connect to letters taught in the previous step.					
Letter Formation **(3–4 minutes)** Use path of movement oral prompts and primary lined paper until all letters are formed correctly, after which less structured paper or blank dry-erase boards may be used.					

Source: © 2023 by Orange County Public Schools. Used with permission.

FIGURE 4.3: Sample five-day assisted learning template.

Figure 4.4 offers an example from the same school district previously described to depict a foundational skills lesson template in alignment with a structured literacy approach. This district-adopted template offers teachers a clear structure to plan for explicit instruction. It is important to note, however, that while this template offers an example of lesson-specific guidance for elements in a single lesson, it doesn't offer a systematic scope and sequence of instruction. Determining the scope and sequence for systematic instruction is important, and should be part of higher-level planning based on evidence-based curriculum resources.

Group: _____	Week of: _____
colspan="2" **Foundational Skills Lesson Template**
Data to Support	**Resources**
☐ STAR ☐ DIBELS ☐ Writing analysis ☐ SBLIA ☐ Learning check	• Decodable passages • Raz-Plus syllable types • Syllable division • Decoding prompts • Visual drill cards • Kinesthetic approach in phonics resource • Phoneme articulation cards • BEST standard questioning support dashboard • Accountable talk question STEMs
colspan="2" **Lesson Plan**
Phonemic Awareness Task (1–2 minutes, if applicable)	
High-Frequency Words (2 minutes) Provide explicit instruction on high-frequency words using the read, spell, and write routine.	
Review Taught Sounds (2 minutes) Review concepts from previous lessons.	
Explicit Phonics Instruction (2–3 minutes) Review or introduce a new concept. Provide opportunities for multisensory instructional strategies.	
Encoding (1–2 minutes) Provide 3–4 words for students to apply the new skill by writing.	
Application (3 minutes) Students practice reading sentences or short passages that contain the focus skill.	
After Reading (2–3 minutes) Follow up with basic comprehension questions.	
colspan="2" **Upcoming Action Steps or Notes**
colspan="2"

Source: © 2023 by Orange County Public Schools. Used with permission.

FIGURE 4.4: Sample lesson template for foundational skills based on structured literacy.

Figure 4.5 (page 78) offers an example of a comprehension-focused lesson structure. You'll notice that the lesson is intended to be informed by data to identify a specific lesson learning goal. Once a learning goal has been determined, the lesson elements can be confirmed, including those that say "if applicable" in the template.

Group: _____	Week of: _____
Comprehension Lesson Template	
Data to Support	**Resources**
☐ STAR reading data ☐ i-Ready reading data ☐ Writing analysis ☐ Curriculum-based measures ☐ Learning check	
Connect / Build Knowledge (1 minute) Engage students by building meaning and relating the text to the students' prior experiences, knowledge of the world, or literacy experience. Make Predictions (if applicable)	
Vocabulary Preview (2 minutes)	
Explicit Comprehension Strategy (3–4 minutes) Provide explicit instruction on focus benchmark(s).	
Set a Purpose for Reading	
Students Read Independently (5 minutes) Monitor reading to prompt for the use of reading strategies and provide feedback.	
Discussion (3–6 minutes) Discuss the meaning of the text. Revisit the purpose and use of the comprehension strategy.	
Extension Activity (if applicable) Provide an activity for students to work on based on the targeted benchmark.	
Upcoming Action Steps or Notes	

Source: © 2023 by Orange County Public Schools. Used with permission.

FIGURE 4.5: Sample lesson template for comprehension skills.

PREDICTABLE, RESEARCH-PROVEN INSTRUCTIONAL ROUTINES

Predictable, evidence-based instructional routines result in efficient and effective small-group reading lessons. Effective instructional routines for small-group instruction (Lindsey, 2022):

- Translate research-based protocols
- Directly align to targeted, skill-based learning goals
- Support student application and transfer
- Apply to contexts beyond the small-group lesson to foster both short-term student learning outcomes and long-term reading development
- Require approximately fifteen minutes per lesson

Routines are supportive and effective in small-group reading lessons and are grounded in a lesson structure that supports interconnected learning goals, especially when considering foundational skills. For example, a single small-group reading lesson for decoding may include integrated instructional routines for phonemic awareness, spelling sounds, decoding practice at the word level, decoding practice in connected text, and encoding practice. A lesson focused on fluency can include an instructional routine for model reading and echo reading prior to students' independent reading and discussion of the text. In this way, lesson structures serve as overarching frameworks in which instructional routines are organized.

Additionally, while instructional routines support student learning outcomes in a single lesson, teachers can organize the progression of skills they will teach through routines in a clear scope and sequence, especially for foundational reading skills. Sample instructional routines for small-group reading instruction are presented in the figures that follow. These routines are examples and are not intended to be comprehensive. The quoted text in these figures exemplifies what the teacher may say during that routine step.

Figure 4.6 (page 80) offers an evidence-based routine for phonemic awareness. This routine is appropriate for readers who do not yet know letters (or not enough letters to read or build words) and are working to recognize and manipulate sounds in words. You'll notice that this routine offers an example where auditory phonemic awareness alone is included.

Routine for Phonemic Awareness Instruction	
Introduce and Model	Determine a phonemic awareness skill based on curriculum scope and sequence (or reader data if scope and sequence are not available). This example demonstrates blending phonemes in CVC words. "We can blend sounds to make words. When we blend sounds, we slide through sounds to connect each one and make a word. I can use these sound boxes (Elkonin boxes) and this counter to help me slide through each sound that I hear. Watch me slide through the sounds: /s/ /ĭ/ /p/. The word is *sip*."
Rehearse as a Group	Distribute Elkonin box template and counter to each reader. Prompt readers to practice using their individual Elkonin box with the same model word and with an additional word.
Have Readers Practice	Prompt readers to practice blending with their sound box and counter using the same predictable oral prompts. For example: /m/ /ă/ /p/—readers whisper each sound to themselves as they slide the counter across the sound boxes. Readers may practice individually (though simultaneously to each other) or chorally. Be sure to refrain from using *r*-controlled vowels or irregular CVC words.
Conclude Routine	"You just listened to the sounds while you slid through each word, and that is going to help you so you can read and write words."

Source: Adapted from Keesey, Konrad, & Joseph, 2015, as cited in Lindsey, 2022.

FIGURE 4.6: Routine for phonemic awareness instruction.

You'll find examples in research that highlight auditory-only phonemic awareness instruction and those that link phonemic awareness instruction with phonics instruction to help readers connect the sounds in words to the graphemes that represent them. Knowing that phonemic knowledge and learning to read are reciprocal, we encourage you to carefully consider whether the routine for phonemic awareness instruction (figure 4.6) is the right match for your readers' needs rather than assume that it is the routine you should use. If readers have some letter knowledge, the routine for alphabet instruction (figure 4.7) or the routine for introducing sound-spelling relationships (figure 4.8, page 82) may be a better fit, and both still offer opportunities for phonemic awareness practice linked with phonics instruction.

Figure 4.7 offers an evidence-based routine for alphabet instruction. This routine is appropriate for readers who are learning letter names and sounds. You'll notice it includes opportunities to learn and practice the letter name, sound, and formation. This routine is effective for initial instruction and ongoing review.

	Routine for Alphabet Instruction
Review Previously Taught Letters (Visual Drill)	Identify a set of previously learned letters, displaying each letter on individual letter cards with an embedded picture. Then, follow these four steps. *Note:* This visual-review deck does not need to include all known letters, as that may grow to be too large and inefficient for pacing. Consider letters that have been previously taught that readers may need to review. 1. Show a single visual drill letter card with an embedded picture. 2. "What letter?" Pause for readers' choral response. 3. "What sound does it spell?" Pause for readers' choral response. 4. Use corrective feedback by modeling, as needed.
Introduce and Model	1. Show a single visual drill letter card for a new letter. 2. "This letter is [name], [sound]. Say [name]." Pause for readers' choral response of the letter name. 3. "Sound [name]." Pause for readers' choral response of the letter sound. 4. "[Name] spells [sound], like at the beginning of the word [target word with embedded picture]." 5. "This is the uppercase letter [name, sound]. Your turn [point to uppercase letter]." Pause for readers' choral response. 6. "This is the lowercase letter [name, sound]. Your turn [point to lowercase letter]." Pause for readers' choral response. 7. Have readers repeat the sound at least three times. You might have them use different voices (for example, whisper voice, talking voice), tell their partner the sound, or repeat the sound as they trace the letter on the table.
Find and Read	1. Show a mix of letters (such as magnet letters or letter tiles). Prompt readers to find the target letter while saying the letter name and sound. 2. Show a connected text (poem, paragraph, big book, and so on) that is print salient (enlarged, redundant text that catches the reader's eye). Prompt readers to find instances of the target letter as they say the letter name and letter sound.
Model and Practice Letter Formation	1. Model the formation of the target letter—both uppercase and lowercase. Prompt readers to form the letter using path of movement directions in which the voice is stretched to coordinate with letter formation construction. 2. Prompt readers to make the letter sound as they practice forming the letter: "Write the letter that spells the sound [sound] and say its sound." "Write the letter named [name] and say its sound." *Note:* This step can be adapted to include multisensory instruction in which readers write on tactile surfaces.
Conclude Routine	1. Show the visual letter drill card used in the Introduce and Model step of the routine. 2. "This letter is [name], [sound]. Say [name]." Pause for readers' choral response of the letter name. 3. "Sound [name]." Pause for readers' choral response of the letter sound. 4. "[Name] spells [sound], like at the beginning of the word [target word with embedded picture]. What word?" Pause for readers' to chorally say the target word that matches the embedded picture.

Source: Adapted from Jones et al., 2013, and Roberts et al., 2020, as cited in Lindsey, 2022.

FIGURE 4.7: Routine for alphabet instruction.

Figure 4.8 offers an evidence-based routine for introducing sound-spelling relationships. This routine is appropriate for readers who know letter names and are learning the sound associations, including patterns such as digraphs and diphthongs. You'll notice this routine includes opportunities for connected phonemic awareness practice, explicit instruction on new sounds, ongoing review, and applications of encoding and text reading.

	Routine for Introducing Sound-Spelling Relationships
Provide a Phonemic Awareness Warm-Up	Determine a phonemic awareness skill based on curriculum scope and sequence (or reader data if scope and sequence are not available). This example demonstrates blending phonemes in CVC words. Prompt students to listen to each sound and blend them together to make a word: "/s/ /ĭ/ /p/ . . . blend." Pause for readers' choral response. Repeat with six to eight words.
Review Sounds and Spellings	Review previously learned sound-spellings (this may include sound cards that show the recently learned spellings).
Introduce Sound-Spelling Relationships	1. Show the spelling. (Consider using a sound card.) 2. "This is one way to spell [sound]. Say [sound]." 3. "[Spelling] spells [sound]. Repeat after me." 4. Show the spelling sounds in several words. If there are any relevant spelling rules, share those with students. If there are other ways to spell this sound that students already know, discuss them together. Review examples (which may include sound cards on a sound wall).
Have Students Decode	Prompt students to decode eight words (at least half should have the target sound-spelling from the current lesson and the others may include review). Prompting should include students saying each sound and blending the sounds back together.
Have Students Encode	Prompt students to spell eight words (at least half should have the target sound-spelling from the current lesson and the others may include review). Prompting should include students saying each sound as they spell each part of the word.
Connect to Literacy Tasks	Remind readers they should use these skills during reading and writing tasks. If students are about to engage in an extended practice opportunity where they will need to read or write, make a direct connection to the activity.
Conclude Routine	Show the spelling. Prompt readers to tell a partner what sound the spelling represents.

Source: Adapted from Fien et al., 2015, as cited in Lindsey, 2022.

FIGURE 4.8: Routine for introducing sound-spelling relationships.

Figure 4.9 offers an evidence-based routine that facilitates readers' application of word recognition skills while reading decodable text. While the primary focus is the application and practice of taught phonics skills, there are opportunities to discuss the text, or even use this text for extended practice outside of the teacher-facilitated lesson. While this routine is outlined as a single day's lesson, it could be matched with previous routines within a week of instruction.

Routine for Reading a Decodable Text	
Introduce the Text	Introduce the text with a one-sentence connection to previous learning.
Prepare Readers for the Text	Explicitly teach or review phonics knowledge or a decoding strategy for students to apply in this text. Prompt students to read words in isolation using the phonics knowledge or decoding strategy (consider using a dry-erase board). Review high-frequency words by having students read the word, write the word, or engage in a read-spell-read routine.
Invite Students to Read the Text	Remind students to say each sound in the word and slide through the sound. Indicate if there is a stopping point (and, if reading the entire book, indicate what readers should do if they finish before others are done). Support readers and offer prompts and cues for different types of words. *Note:* To read about ways to monitor and support readers as they engage with text, see chapter 7 (page 137).
Discuss the Text	Ask a series of questions to check students' comprehension of the text. Relate questions to the purpose for reading.
Conclude Routine and Connect to Literacy Task	Prompt readers to share how they used their decoding knowledge while reading that day (they can share with a partner or the small group). Remind readers that they will have more opportunities to read and apply their decoding skills when they read other texts.

Source: Adapted from Lindsey, 2022.

FIGURE 4.9: Routine for reading a decodable text.

Figure 4.10 (page 84) offers an evidence-based routine for morphology instruction. This routine incorporates explicit instruction, practice, and application of morphology to support readers with authentic text reading. This routine may be used for a single day's small-group lesson, or it can be paired with a fluency or comprehension routine for subsequent days of instruction for readers to have more practice applying the morphology knowledge they gained from this routine.

Figure 4.11 (page 84) offers an evidence-based routine for fluency instruction. This routine incorporates phrasing and expression for readers to learn from models of fluency and to practice reading and rereading in various instructional contexts with immediate feedback. We find it important to note that, while readers' data may suggest a need for oral reading fluency, we caution teachers against focusing on fluency instruction alone for extended periods of time (such as repeated days and weeks of instruction). You may find it beneficial to pair a fluency routine with a routine for morphology or comprehension (or both) across a week of instruction. Some evidence-based curriculum resources include examples that combine fluency, morphology, and comprehension instruction in this way.

Routine for Morphology Instruction	
Name It	Introduce a new affix by reading it aloud, writing it on a dry-erase board, and prompting readers to chorally read the affix. If the affix corresponds to more than one sound (for example, -*ed* pronounced as /ed/, /d/, or /t/), provide additional explicit instruction and have students practice all pronunciations.
Provide a Sample Word	Provide a sample word using the affix. Write it on the dry-erase board. Offer a sentence with the word in context.
Define It	Provide a student-friendly definition of the affix. For example, the prefix *pre* means *before* and helps students understand the meanings of common words such as *pretest*, *preheat*, or *prepay*.
Have Students Generate Sample Words	Prompt students to think of other words using the target affix (in pairs or as a group).
Write It	Prompt students to write the prefix and two to three sample words.
Review It	Prompt students to review previously learned affixes through a visual drill (chorally responding).
Conclude Routine	Prompt students to read the target affix from that day's instruction and define it.

Source: Adapted from Toste, Capin, Williams, Kearns, & Vaughn, 2023.

FIGURE 4.10: Routine for morphology instruction.

Routine for Fluency: Phrasing and Expression	
Introduce the Reading Task	Explain that today, readers will be practicing reading text with appropriate phrasing and proper expression.
Model Reading	Explain to students how readers group words together in phrases and use emphasis to better understand a text's meaning. Explain how a reader also pauses after an action to show where an action took place and how readers pause and change voice to show when they see punctuation. Then, follow these four steps. 1. Display an enlarged text or distribute individual copies of text with phrase-cued markings. 2. "I will read this passage to you in short phrases to make it sound smooth, as if I were talking. When I see the slash marks, it will remind me to pause. When I see two slash marks, I will pause for a longer time at the end of each sentence." 3. "Follow along as I read." 4. Slide your finger under each word as you read, slightly exaggerating the emphasis.
Discuss Modeled Reading	Prompt readers to discuss reading by asking questions such as: - What did you notice about how I changed my voice to show feelings? What did you hear? Where in the text did you hear it? - What did you notice about how I grouped words together to make my reading sound smooth? - What did you notice about my voice when I got to the end of a sentence?
Practice Together: Choral Reading or Echo Reading	Prompt readers to practice by using choral reading or echo reading. **Choral reading:** The teacher and the students read together in unison, with the teacher's voice at a slightly higher volume to guide the reading in unison. **Echo reading:** The teacher reads a chunk of text with modeled expression, after which readers repeat the same chunked text in unison, emphasizing the modeled reading expression.

Have Students Practice	Prompt readers to practice reading the text on their own (as part of the lesson or outside of the lesson as an extended practice opportunity). Listen to each student as they read and note areas for feedback. Use echo reading to provide modeling or corrective feedback to emphasize phrasing or expression.
Conclude Routine and Connect to Literacy Task	Prompt readers to use their fluency practice from reading that day while they read other texts on their own, even if they don't have the phrasing marks.

Source: Adapted from Florida Center for Reading Research, n.d.

FIGURE 4.11: Routine for fluency—Phrasing and expression.

Figure 4.12 offers an evidence-based routine for comprehension instruction. You'll notice that this routine offers options for facilitation in each routine step, based on the lesson goals and readers' needs. We don't recommend that you try to do all the options in each step, but rather focus on those that support the readers to think deeply about the text and build their understanding and knowledge, both individually and collectively, with your support during the lesson.

Routine for Comprehension Instruction	
Warm Up With Word Study	Introduce and teach how to read and write multisyllabic words. Teach any prefixes or suffixes, if applicable, to promote morphological awareness.
Prepare Readers for Text Reading	Set a purpose for reading. Activate prior knowledge and introduce three to five key vocabulary words. Make a prediction. Demonstrate and explain any strategies or skills for this lesson (if applicable).
Monitor Readers During Text Reading	Monitor students and offer feedback (questions, prompts, or cues) to support readers to fix their mistakes. If students are orally reading, gradually shift to all silent reading. Identify stopping places to check for meaning. Use think-alouds or questioning to monitor progress and model thinking.
Discuss Text Reading	Discuss text and reconnect to the purpose for reading. Some of the following suggestions can be used for text discussion or extended to collaborative or independent practice. • Check predictions. • Discuss what students learned and understood. • Clarify any points of confusion. • Retell or summarize the text. • Ask or answer comprehension questions using evidence from the text to support responses. • Make inferences. • Practice and revisit vocabulary. • Finish any graphic organizers.
Conclude Routine and Connect to Literacy Task	Prompt readers to use their thinking as readers that day while they read other texts on their own.

FIGURE 4.12: Routine for comprehension instruction.

As we noted earlier, these routines serve as evidence-based samples, and we encourage you to use them to springboard your planning with your readers in mind. The order of elements in these routines is important because it supports the building of the skill or learning target. Notice that each routine contains an introduction toward the start of the routine and ends with a closure or summary. Within each routine, students have the opportunity to interact and engage with the content as well as apply their new learning. Using predictable routines such as these will help students know what to expect and will support you and your team as you plan for small-group instruction.

The following video shows the flow of a sample first-grade lesson. The lesson is intentionally sequenced to build foundational skills. There is one part of the flow missing—as you watch, consider how you would incorporate writing toward the end of the lesson.

The following video shows a sample morphology routine.

Logistics for Organizing, Managing, and Preparing Materials

Organizing, managing, and preparing materials may seem like obvious aspects of lesson planning that don't warrant discussion. Yet, we continue to learn from teachers who have personalized approaches to managing, organizing, and preparing materials for multiple lessons each day that offer efficiency and sustainability for their small-group practices. In table 4.1, we provide material logistics, considerations, and tips to help set you up for increased success in your small-group lessons.

TABLE 4.1: Organizing, Managing, and Preparing Materials

Material Logistics	Considerations	Tips and Examples
Text: How or where should I store texts for small-group lessons?	• How many copies of the text do I have for the lesson? • Can students keep their own copy in book bags or toolboxes? • Where should I store word cards or sentence strips (for lessons where students aren't yet reading connected text)? • Will students from more than one group need access to the same text? • Do students have digital access to this text on devices to read at centers or at home?	• 8.5 × 11–inch bins with lids provide stackable storage for texts and other materials for each group. Slanted file-folder boxes provide a side-by-side storage option for lesson texts. • If using student book bags or toolboxes, two-gallon bags are an affordable, flexible option for students to store their own texts. This option also gives them text access during extended practice opportunities outside of the small-group lesson.
Instructional Materials Selection: What additional materials should I have accessible at the small-group table?	• What materials are lesson-specific for each group (such as high-frequency word cards or sound-spelling visual support cards)? • What materials might be helpful to have accessible for all groups? • Are there materials that need to be posted for my readers to view from the small-group table?	• Lesson-specific materials (such as word cards, sound-spelling cards, or picture sorts) can be stored in a folder or plastic gallon bag in the same storage space as the text for the lesson or group. • General materials to use across all groups may include dry-erase boards, dry-erase markers (in an easy-to-access storage cup), dry-erase board erasers, Elkonin box templates (when building foundational skills), or scaffolding prompt cue cards or standards-based question prompts on a ring. • Consider having a clear space behind or near the small-group table for reference supports that students may need as they read (such as sound walls, anchor charts, and so on).
Use of Student Toolboxes: Are there materials that students could store in personal toolboxes for both small-group lessons and extended practice opportunities?	• What materials do students need to access while at the small-group table and during extended practice opportunities? Would it be more efficient for them to have a toolbox that "travels" with them (if they move around the room), or can they easily get what they need from their desks?	• Student toolboxes may be large enough to include texts (current and recent familiar texts to reread or various texts to read with different purposes) and personal materials they need for both the small-group table and extended practice opportunities.

continued ▶

Material Logistics	Considerations	Tips and Examples
Teacher Materials: Are there materials that would be helpful for me to have nearby for small-group instruction?	• What note-taking format will I use to capture my observations during small-group lessons? • What office supplies might be helpful to have accessible near my small-group table for efficiency?	• Access to multiple blank copies of observational tools such as the reader observation tool (page 141) can support teachers to quickly take notes about their observations. • Office supplies to consider include pencils, pens, highlighters, index cards, self-stick notes (to mark pages and text excerpts), tape (for unexpected book repair), and possibly even scissors (to chunk articles into excerpts or cut sentence strips into word cards, as needed).
Materials to Manage Time: What might help me to manage time?	• Do I have clear access to a clock at all times during small-group lessons? • Is my plan for which groups to meet with on a given day easy for me to access or within view?	• Ensure that a classroom clock (or computer with time posted) is visible from the small-group table. • Consider keeping a one- to two-week grouping planner posted near the small-group table to help you track and manage the frequency, day, and time you meet with each group.
Plan for Preparing for the Next Day: When will I prepare the materials needed for the next day of small-group lessons?	• What materials will students need for tomorrow's lesson? • What instructional materials will I need for tomorrow's lesson? • When is there an opportunity to preview and prepare for tomorrow's lesson (such as a quiet moment after school, a planning period after the literacy block, or before school tomorrow)?	• Identifying a predictable time of day to prepare materials for the next day's lesson makes planning efficient and increases the likelihood that you'll maintain practices and meeting times with each group on the following day. • Predictable lesson structures and routines should make organizing and managing materials predictable for teachers as well, since they know what they might need to add (or take) from the stored materials from one lesson day to the next.

Teacher Content Knowledge

One thing we admire most about elementary teachers is the broad range of content knowledge expertise that they possess, not only for the grade level they teach but for each grade level and content area in which they are certified or credentialed.

At the same time, considering the grade-level expectations of readers in any one grade requires significant depth of knowledge for teaching. This deep knowledge of reading content and reading instruction intersect, helping teachers interpret reading data and observations, make planning decisions, and deliver facilitation and scaffolding techniques. In this section, we offer highlights of what we refer to as *reading research translations to practice*. We hope these highlights refresh or affirm your reading content knowledge for teaching and will support you in implementing the ideas from this chapter to your small-group lesson plans.

The following are some word recognition highlights.

- *Explicit instruction* means readers are directly told what they need to know, and may include introducing a skill or concept (visual and oral), definition, example, and scaffolded practice.
- *Systematic instruction* suggests that components of skills are taught in a logical, connected way, most often presented by a scope and sequence.
- Studies continue to demonstrate that early phonemic awareness and spelling-sound knowledge predict decoding, which in turn can predict fluency and comprehension (Caravolas et al., 2019; Torppa et al., 2016).
- Blending and segmenting phonemes are the most critical subskills of phonemic awareness because of their direct support for decoding and encoding (Hatcher, Hulme, & Snowling, 2004).
- Teaching letter names and sounds together (rather than teaching letter names prior to letter sounds) leads to the best sound-spelling outcomes for readers (Piasta & Wagner, 2010).
- Offering continuous blending opportunities in phonemic instruction decreases the likelihood that readers will forget the beginning sound of a word as they read (Weisberg & Savard, 1993).
- Phonics instruction should include decoding, which provides readers with opportunities to use sound-spelling relationships to read (Lindsey, 2022).
- Creating an orthographic map by linking a word's spelling to its pronunciation and meaning can help a reader retrieve the word's meaning and pronunciation automatically from memory when they encounter the word in a text (Ehri, 2020). Giving students the opportunity to decode a word one to eight times can promote memory storage of the orthographic map (Nation, Angell, & Castles, 2007).

The following are some bridging process highlights in fluency, vocabulary, print concepts, morphology, and so on.

- Kindergarten vocabulary knowledge predicts second-grade reading comprehension (Roth & Lee, 2002).
- Readers need to learn digital text concepts through explicit systematic instruction, similar to how they learn print concepts (Shamir & Korat, 2015).
- Multisyllabic words contain complex sound-spelling patterns related to morphology (prefixes, suffixes) and etymology (study of word origins) rather than the alphabet (Lindsey, 2022).
- Combining syllable instruction and morphology instruction supports the widest range of multisyllabic reading (Austin & Boucher, 2022).
- Instructional practices such as reader's theater, echo reading, choral reading, and paired reading have been shown to positively impact reading prosody and reading comprehension (Kuhn, 2020).

The following are some language comprehension highlights.

- Second-grade listening comprehension predicts seventh-grade reading comprehension (Lervåg, Hulme, & Melby-Lervåg, 2018).
- Comprehension-focused interventions can promote reading comprehension gains in readers who have specific difficulty with comprehension (Lee & Tsai, 2017).
- Not all readers monitor their own reading comprehension, yet instruction in comprehension monitoring has been found to be effective (National Reading Panel, 2000).
- Instruction in text structure has yielded positive student outcomes for both narrative text (Fitzgerald & Spiegel, 1983) and nonfiction text (Pyle et al., 2017).
- *Compreaction* refers to a reader comprehending and reacting in response to a text, such as laughing at a funny character (Duke & Cartwright, 2021).
- Readers' knowledge (academic and cultural) affects reading comprehension (Hwang & Duke, 2020).

The following are some self-regulation and motivation highlights.

- Successful reading experiences lead to motivation in the same way that strong motivation to read leads to successful reading outcomes (Toste, Didion, Peng, Filderman, & McClelland, 2020).
- Many young readers benefit from learning how to engage in mental activities such as thinking before, during, and after reading; monitoring understanding; and determining how to help themselves when meaning breaks down (Shanahan et al., 2010).

We hope these highlights empower teachers to look for research-proven connections in the impactful learning experiences they are planning for their students. Effective reading instruction lays the foundation for academic success across all subject areas, making it a critical focus area for elementary educators. Continuing to support teachers in deepening their understanding of reading content and refining their instructional practices will undoubtedly contribute to enhanced student learning outcomes.

Summary

Crafting comprehensive lesson plans for small-group reading instruction requires a breadth of content knowledge, awareness of students' strengths and needs as readers, and a repertoire of evidence-based practices. Additionally, knowing and understanding the structure of your curriculum resources, including available text, will support you in implementing lessons. With all that is required to plan for small-group instruction, including materials organization and management, it is evident why creating lesson plans for this important time can be overwhelming. With lesson structures and routines and the knowledge of your students as readers, you can apply your understanding of reading instruction to streamline the lesson-planning process and build lessons that feel familiar to readers while giving them the tools they need to grow.

LAUNCH YOUR REFLECTION

Let's reconnect with Mrs. Valdez, the teacher we met at the beginning of this chapter (page 66). Now that you've read this chapter, consider the following questions.

- As you reread Mrs. Valdez's challenge to identify the underlying research basis of curriculum material options in her district, what recommendations might you suggest for her?
- How do you ensure that the instructional recommendations in the curriculum materials are grounded in research?

RECHARGE YOUR SMALL-GROUP READING INSTRUCTION

The following are some questions you can use to apply the chapter concepts to your own classroom context.

- How can I employ predictable routines to promote equity, efficiency, and engagement in my instruction?
- If using an adopted curriculum with lesson plans provided: How can I identify the research-proven instructional routines embedded in the lesson plan structures?

- What are the data-informed instructional focus areas for each of my groups of readers? How do their instructional focus areas align with the instructional routines I plan to teach?

EXPAND YOUR TOOLBOX

To continue your learning, see the "Leading the Learning Action Guide" (page 201) to support you and your colleagues. In the action guide for this chapter, you'll find in-action videos that spotlight teaching strategies as well as differentiated professional learning activities you can try out with your team. Additional tools that support this chapter topic can be accessed online (visit **go.SolutionTree.com/literacy**).

CHAPTER 5

HOW DO I SELECT AND EVALUATE TEXT?

A deep understanding of instructional text is critical when planning for small-group instruction. Teachers' multifaceted understanding of a text impacts their instruction and decision making, whether they are using an adopted curriculum or selecting text on their own. This chapter offers a protocol for teachers to evaluate instructional text, including how to consider quantitative and qualitative aspects such as text structure, language features, syntax, and more. Additionally, the protocol prompts teachers to characterize students by their background knowledge of the topic and level of interest.

As you read this chapter, consider your own experiences. The following questions may also help frame your thinking as you read.

- How do I typically select texts?
- What factors impact my decision making?

Consider the following example of Mrs. Potter.

MEET THE TEACHER: MRS. POTTER

Mrs. Potter is a second-grade teacher. The school district where she works purchased many resources to support teaching and learning. Mrs. Potter

> is grateful for the variety of texts at her fingertips. However, with an abundance of resources, making decisions about which text to use and when to use it has become overwhelming. She typically chooses leveled text—as she hopes this will provide access for all her students—but she feels that this does not fully support all the areas of reading she strives to include in her classroom learning. She wonders how to best select text for a variety of instructional purposes.

Does Mrs. Potter's challenge resonate with you? Have you identified strategies to help her overcome it?

We'll revisit these ideas and questions at the end of the chapter to identify and plan for text selection strategies that you want to try with your own students.

Text Definition

When we think about the definition of *text*, we may each view what constitutes a text differently. Therefore, for the sake of common language, we want to make sure to begin our text discussion by defining what we mean by text. Although we share print text in this chapter, we want to expand how we define text. Text can be print or nonprint. Text can be digital. Each type of text requires its own analysis and identification of potential challenges and supports for readers. Figure 5.1 shows the range of text types as defined by the Common Core State Standards (CCSS). The texts are categorized by grades K–5 and 6–12.

	Narrative Text			Informational Text
	Stories	**Plays**	**Poetry**	**Discipline-Specific Text**
K–5	Adventure, fantasy, mystery, realistic fiction, folktales, fables, tall tales	Brief, one-act plays	Nursery rhymes, narrative poems, free verse, limericks	History texts, science texts, art texts, technical texts, biographies, autobiographies
6–12	Mystery, thriller, horror, detective fiction, historical fiction, science fiction, mythology, graphic novels	Multi-act plays, films	Epics, ballads, haikus, sonnets, narrative poems, free verse	History texts, science texts, art texts, technical texts, biographies, autobiographies, essays, memoirs

Source: Adapted from the National Governors Association for Best Practices (NGA) and Council of Chief State School Officers (CCSSO), 2010.

FIGURE 5.1: Range of text types.

As we begin to explore the critical role text plays in our small-group lessons, we want to encourage you to choose a variety of texts that will help your readers access more complex language, build knowledge, and engage in the literacy tasks you have planned for them.

Text Selection

Before we dig into why text selection is critical for instruction—specifically small-group instruction—we would like you to complete a little exercise. As you read the excerpts of the following texts, think about the following questions.

- What do you notice you are doing?
- What does your reading "sound" like?
- What do you do when something doesn't make sense?
- What do you do when you come across a word you don't know?
- How do you try to comprehend?

Figure 5.2 is a nonfiction text about Alzheimer's disease.

The Basics of Alzheimer's Disease

Alzheimer's disease is a progressive neurological disorder that primarily affects memory, cognitive function, and the ability to perform everyday activities. Named after the German physician Alois Alzheimer, who first identified the disease in 1906, it has become a growing concern in an aging global population.

Unraveling the Mechanisms

Alzheimer's disease is characterized by the accumulation of abnormal protein deposits in the brain. Beta-amyloid plaques and tau tangles disrupt the normal functioning of nerve cells, leading to their degeneration and eventual death. The exact cause of these protein build-ups remains unclear, but genetic and environmental factors are believed to play a role.

Risk Factors and Prevalence

Several risk factors increase the likelihood of developing Alzheimer's disease. Age is the most significant, with the risk doubling every five years after the age of sixty-five. Genetics also play a role, as those with a family history of the disease face a higher risk. Other factors, such as cardiovascular health, head injuries, and lifestyle choices, can contribute to the development of Alzheimer's.

Signs and Symptoms

Alzheimer's disease progresses in stages, and symptoms can vary from person to person. Early signs often include mild forgetfulness and difficulty in concentrating, while later stages may involve significant memory loss, confusion, and challenges in communication. Behavioral changes, mood swings, and difficulty in performing routine tasks are also common indicators.

Diagnosis and Challenges

Diagnosing Alzheimer's disease can be challenging, as there is no single test for it. Medical professionals rely on a combination of cognitive assessments, medical history, and neurological exams to make an accurate diagnosis. Advanced imaging techniques, such as brain scans, may also be used to detect changes in the brain associated with Alzheimer's.

Source: OpenAI, 2024a.

FIGURE 5.2: Understanding Alzheimer's disease text example.

Figure 5.3 is from a memoir about Alzheimer's disease.

> **ALZHEIMER'S DISEASE: GRIEF ARRIVES EARLY**
>
> We tend to think of grief as something we have to deal with after a loved one dies. Before that, as disease ravages the person we love, we refer to our sorrow, our despair, the waves of tears that come at odd times. But we don't usually mention grief. We consider the weightiness of grief as something that awaits us at the end, after death. Alzheimer's, though, is a death before dying. So grief needs to be embraced early on. You will watch as the person you know so well fades from view. Alzheimer's piracy is unpredictable and unrelenting. The disease is in control; it will steal what it chooses when it chooses and there is nothing you can do to stop it.
>
> When I sat with my father, I anchored myself in the faith that his soul was unencumbered by dementia. I imagined a clear, calm lake far beneath the choppy waters of Alzheimer's. I felt I had entered a different reality, a sort of suspended state where I could look at the disease from enough of a distance that, no matter what was going on physically, his spirit still whispered to me. Those visits had a serenity to them, despite my sorrow. I would often drive away from my parents' house and have to pull over to the side of the road to sit in my car and cry. This is my reality now, I told myself. I'm straddling two worlds—the spiritual realm of faith in the soul's endurance, its imperviousness to disease, and the physical realm of loss, helplessness, and sorrow beyond measure.

Source: Davis, 2021, p. 37.

FIGURE 5.3: *Floating in the Deep End* book excerpt.

Figure 5.4 is an excerpt from a scientific journal article abstract about Alzheimer's disease.

"Limbic-Predominant Age-Related TDP-43 Encephalopathy (LATE): Consensus Working Group Report"

We describe a recently recognized disease entity, limbic-predominant age-related TDP-43 encephalopathy (LATE). LATE neuropathological change (LATE-NC) is defined by a stereotypical TDP-43 proteinopathy in older adults, with or without coexisting hippocampal sclerosis pathology.

LATE-NC is a common TDP-43 proteinopathy, associated with an amnestic dementia syndrome that mimicked Alzheimer's-type dementia in retrospective autopsy studies. LATE is distinguished from frontotemporal lobar degeneration with TDP-43 pathology based on its epidemiology (LATE generally affects older subjects), and relatively restricted neuroanatomical distribution of TDP-43 proteinopathy. In community-based autopsy cohorts, ~25% of brains had sufficient burden of LATE-NC to be associated with discernible cognitive impairment.

Many subjects with LATE-NC have comorbid brain pathologies, often including amyloid-ß plaques and tauopathy. Given that the "oldest-old" are at greatest risk for LATE- NC, and subjects of advanced age constitute a rapidly growing demographic group in many countries, LATE has an expanding but under-recognized impact on public health. For these reasons, a working group was convened to develop diagnostic criteria for LATE, aiming both to stimulate research and to promote awareness of this pathway to dementia.

We report consensus-based recommendations including guidelines for diagnosis and staging of LATE-NC. For routine autopsy workup of LATE-NC, an anatomically-based preliminary staging scheme is proposed with TDP-43 immunohistochemistry on tissue from three brain areas, reflecting a hierarchical pattern of brain involvement: amygdala, hippocampus, and middle frontal gyrus. LATE-NC appears to affect the medial temporal lobe structures preferentially, but other areas also are impacted. Neuroimaging studies demonstrated that subjects with LATE-NC also had atrophy in the medial temporal lobes, frontal cortex, and other brain regions. Genetic studies have thus far indicated five genes with risk alleles for LATE-NC: GRN, TMEM106B, ABCC9, KCNMB2, and APOE.

The discovery of these genetic risk variants indicate [sic] that LATE shares pathogenetic mechanisms with both frontotemporal lobar degeneration and Alzheimer's disease, but also suggests disease-specific underlying mechanisms. Large gaps remain in our understanding of LATE.

Source: Nelson et al., 2019.

FIGURE 5.4: "Limbic-Predominant Age-Related TDP-43 Encephalopathy (LATE)" abstract excerpt.

Reflect on the following questions about the texts you just read.
- What impeded your understanding?
- What made comprehension possible?

Although you are the same reader, your reading experience and your depth of comprehension may differ based on the text. This is a great time to revisit the Active View of Reading (chapter 1, page 17).

As you read the memoir excerpt (figure 5.3, page 96), you may have had an emotional response to how the author describes caring for someone with Alzheimer's. This is a great example of a text that offers an opportunity to explore theory of mind or practice analyzing figurative language (verbal reasoning) in a narrative text. This text would not lend itself to lessons on nonfiction text structure. On the other hand, figure 5.2 (page 95) is a great text to practice identifying nonfiction text structure and analyzing how the more traditional informational text structure helps facilitate the author's message. The journal abstract (figure 5.4, page 97) requires specialized background knowledge to make sense of its contents. You may have found yourself using your morphological knowledge to unpack words like *neuroimaging* or *pathogenetic*.

As you read through the three texts, you may have noticed that each text helped build your knowledge of Alzheimer's disease by exposing you to its vocabulary and related concepts, which then helped you make connections in the last excerpt, the journal abstract. The order of the texts was intentional to demonstrate how using coherent sets of text can scaffold a more difficult text. Table 5.1 highlights possible instructional areas based on the Active View of Reading that align with the three text excerpts we shared.

TABLE 5.1: Instructional Opportunities by Text

Text	Possible Instructional Areas Based on the Active View of Reading
Understanding Alzheimer's disease	• Genre (reading-specific background knowledge) • Text structure (reading-specific background knowledge) • Text features (reading-specific background knowledge) • Content knowledge (language comprehension) • Vocabulary strategies (active self-regulation)
Floating in the Deep End	• Cultural knowledge (language comprehension) • Genre (reading-specific background knowledge) • Inference (verbal reasoning) • Metaphors (verbal reasoning) • Theory of mind (language comprehension)
"Limbic-Predominant Age-Related TDP-43 Encephalopathy (LATE)"	• Word recognition strategies (active self-regulation) • Vocabulary strategies (active self-regulation) • Decoding skills (word recognition) • Morphological awareness (bridging processes) • Genre (reading-specific background knowledge) • Language structure (language comprehension)

Although we designed this activity to simulate what a reader in your classroom may experience, it also helps us understand why text selection is important and the variety of instructional opportunities each text type offers. This activity is a reminder that not all texts work for the skill or strategy that may be your instructional focus. If you are focusing on informational standards, you must be intentional about the text you choose to highlight that specific standard (more on this to come). Evaluating text prior to instruction is critical to the success of the lesson.

Text Alignment to Lesson Purpose

Selecting text that aligns with the instructional focus of your small-group lesson is crucial for ensuring that students can effectively practice and apply the targeted skills in a meaningful and supportive context.

Consider the following video of a fifth-grade teacher briefly sharing how she selects texts for her classroom.

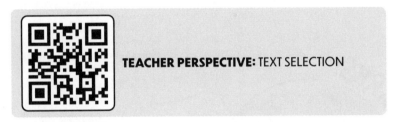

We briefly alluded to the importance of finding text that aligns with the instructional focus for your small-group lesson, and we believe this conversation needs to be emphasized.

When thinking about text selection, consider the following questions.

- What is the instructional focus of the lesson?
- What type of text will best serve this instructional focus?
- What specific text showcases the specific skill or strategy that is the instructional focus?

Figure 5.5 offers a visual representation of this decision-making process.

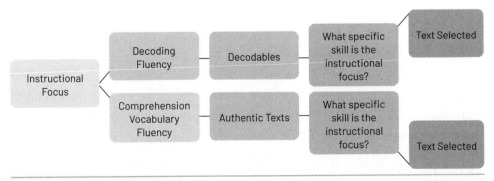

FIGURE 5.5: Text selection decision-making tool.

What is the difference between the text types? This is a question that comes up often when we work with teachers. Just like Mrs. Potter, who we met at the start of the chapter, teachers have access to many different texts, which sometimes may cause analysis paralysis. Therefore, to simplify the process, it is important to think about the purpose of our small-group lesson.

A *decodable text* has a clear purpose. If the focus of a lesson centers on a phonics pattern and the emphasis is on applying the patterns to a text, then a decodable is the most appropriate text. Decodable texts are written to reflect the phonics scope and sequence. Many decodable texts have natural-sounding language, tell a story, or focus on a topic. However, the main objective of a decodable text is to practice and apply foundational reading skills. Therefore, although we may ask comprehension questions, the depth of the comprehension work is limited by the controlled language used to help readers practice decoding. Figure 5.6 shows a decodable text. You may notice that it is presented as an informational text on sharks and the main objective is to practice the *r*-controlled vowel pattern.

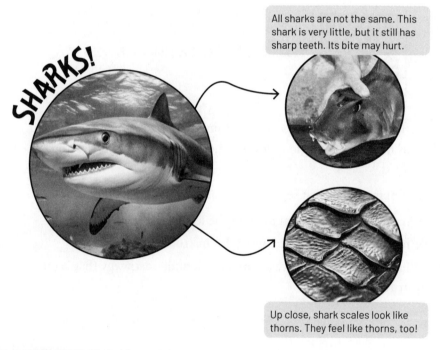

Source: Helfer, 2016. Used with permission.

FIGURE 5.6: Sample decodable text.

Authentic text is a term that describes the types of texts that can be used to build knowledge, reading comprehension skills, fluency, and vocabulary or as an anchor text for writing. Authentic texts require significant analysis since not all authentic texts (fiction and nonfiction) allow readers to practice the skill or strategy of the instructional focus. Additionally, because authentic texts may be beyond a reader's word recognition ability, scaffolds must be planned to ensure access for all readers. Figure 5.7 is an authentic informational text about tide pools (OpenAI, 2024b, 2024c, 2024d). This lesson focuses on text structure to help the author convey meaning. Although the readability is not complex, readers can engage in conversations about text structure while analyzing the text features and describing how the content is organized in the text itself.

Exploring Tide Pools

Tide pools are fascinating mini-ecosystems found along the shoreline. Let's dive in and learn more about these watery wonderlands!

Tide pools are rocky depressions filled with seawater. They form when the tide goes out, leaving behind little pools. Imagine them as tiny aquariums where sea creatures live!

High and Low Tides

Tide pools change with the tides. During high tide, they fill up with water. At low tide, they're exposed, revealing their secrets.

Source: OpenAI, 2024b, 2024c, 2024d.

FIGURE 5.7: Sample informational text.

Text Considerations

Prior the Common Core State Standards in 2010, text levels and text complexity were indirectly referenced. Standard 10 explicitly discusses text complexity by stating the expectation that readers will "read and comprehend complex literary and informational texts independently and proficiently" (NGA & CCSSO, 2010). Components that impact text complexity include quantitative and qualitative factors, reader variables (motivation, knowledge, and experiences), and the complexity of the task assigned.

The variables identified by the CCSS are important considerations in analyzing texts. We propose that we think more deeply about the potential obstacles and supports that may impact or aid how successful our readers will be with the text. Teachers should not generally apply these considerations to all readers but instead use them as a lens to provide scaffolds and differentiate instruction. The Active View of Reading (Duke & Cartwright, 2021) provides the lens that will help us identify instructional opportunities, supports, and challenges within a text.

Let's take a look at a text we used for instruction during a small-group lesson for fourth graders. Linda Bennett's (2014) informational text *The Battle Against Pests* explains what pesticides are, including the arguments for and against the use of pesticides. During whole-group instruction, readers learned to identify and explain an author's perspective of a topic in an informational text. Our first step in selecting an informational text was to find one that provided opportunities to explore this specific standard. We needed a text that demonstrated how an author communicates different perspectives on the same topic. Table 5.2 highlights our analysis and considerations for *The Battle Against Pests*.

TABLE 5.2: *The Battle Against Pests*—Text Considerations

What might engage my learners in the text? How interesting is the text?	The topic of pesticides is not the most exciting topic for most, let alone fourth graders. Therefore, we knew this would be one of the challenges of this particular text. One of the first decisions we made was to focus just on the pages that highlighted this standard. This allowed us to meet the goal of the lesson.
	We decided to engage readers in the activity of identifying the author's perspective by covering the subtitles on two pages. This was an attempt to pique curiosity and gamify the task. This proved to be a successful decision because readers were immediately intrigued by what was beyond the cover.

What kind of prior content knowledge is needed?	We predicted that the topic of pesticides may be unfamiliar with the readers we were meeting with. Therefore, we chose to explain to readers what pesticides are, and why and when they are used. This was a very brief conversation. The goal for this lesson was to identify ways that the author presents her perspective on pesticides. We were not focused on teaching about pesticides, so we were confident in our decision to stay concise during this phase of instruction.
What kind of vocabulary knowledge is needed to understand the text?	We determined that the meanings of the following vocabulary words would be important to aid comprehension. • famine • organic • tragedies • beneficial Again, we only briefly introduced the words. Our routine for introducing the words was: 1. Say the word while pointing to it in the text. 2. Have readers repeat the word. 3. Provide a reader-friendly definition of the word. 4. Give synonyms or examples of the word. This was not meant to have a vocabulary focus; therefore, the purpose of introducing the words was to provide access to the content that may have been unfamiliar.

*Visit **go.SolutionTree.com/literacy** for a free reproducible version of this table.*

Beyond identifying potential challenges and supports in the text, we must also consider the opportunities for instruction that are naturally reflected in the text. Therefore, aligning the text to the purpose of the lesson is a critical step in the planning process.

Text Accessibility

Aligned with your reading experience at the start of the chapter, we want to address how texts are used as a scaffold for accessibility. Our intentional arrangement of the texts about Alzheimer's disease enabled you to make connections in the memoir and even in the medical journal abstract (even if you did not fully understand what you were reading due to the technical language used). We share two ways to scaffold for two different purposes: (1) knowledge building and (2) word recognition.

KNOWLEDGE BUILDING

When we select a text where readers have limited to no background knowledge on the topic, we often plan to activate prior knowledge and build knowledge to help readers with the content or topics they will read about. However, if we provide too much support prior to reading, we may actually decrease students' motivation to read or limit opportunities for them to authentically engage with text. It is almost like readers realize we did all the work for them!

The following video shows students reading a biography of Helen Keller. As you watch the video, notice how the readers are building knowledge of Helen Keller and her family.

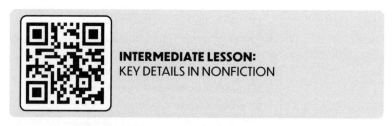

INTERMEDIATE LESSON:
KEY DETAILS IN NONFICTION

WORD RECOGNITION

Let's revisit the text *The Battle Against Pests* (Bennett, 2014). This text is printed in a curriculum series in four different variations: (1) approaching, (2) on-level, (3) beyond, and (4) English language learner (ELL). If analyzed through the quantitative lens, each variation increases in complexity as it relates to word recognition. For students who may still be developing their word recognition skills, starting with a book that is more accessible will allow them to learn the concepts, understand new vocabulary, and build a *schema*—a set of related knowledge or concepts—for a topic. This intentional sequencing of texts will help scaffold students to access more complex texts.

Teachers can also accomplish this with a variety of texts about the same topic. Using readability measures only, the text *Turtle Rescue* by Pamela Hickman (2005) is complex. *Turtle Rescue* is a nonfiction text that discusses the conservation efforts by scientists, governments, and conservationists to protect sea turtles. If you analyze the book, you will notice that there are many vocabulary words and ideas that you can introduce with more accessible text to facilitate grade-level text comprehension.

Figure 5.8 shows an example text set to provide scaffolding. The other texts range from realistic fiction to less complex informational text that introduces readers to topic-related vocabulary to facilitate word recognition and understanding. Using text sets that progressively increase in complexity provides a scaffold for readers for more difficult text.

Text	Text Components
Turtle, Turtle, Watch Out! by April Pulley Sayre (2010)	• **Introduction of Vocabulary:** turtle, nests, leathery, hatchlings, flippers, yolk sac, horizon, crawl, journey, islands, sargassum, coral reef • **Familiar Story Structure:** narrative structure (realistic fiction) • **Repetitive Key Words or Phrases:** turtle, crawls, waves, watch out, escape
Sea Turtles by Gail Gibbons (2020)	• **Introduction of Vocabulary:** turtle, reptiles, paleontologists, flippers, loggerhead, migrate, nesting, leathery, clutch, hatch • **Expository Story Structure:** descriptive text structure with text features (diagrams, labels, pictures, pronunciation support) to support informational text provided • This text expands on concepts presented in the first text with specific vocabulary and text features.
On-Grade-Level Text *Turtle Rescue* by Pamela Hickman (2005)	• **Introduction of Vocabulary:** turtle, reptiles, loggerhead, migration, nesting, leathery, clutch, hatch, conservation, eggs, hatchlings, endangered • **Expository Story Structure:** variety of expository text structures, limited support by text features • This text contains more sophisticated labels of concepts that have been previously introduced in prior, more accessible, texts.

FIGURE 5.8: Cohesive text set to scaffold word recognition and vocabulary.

As we discussed, text can be scaffolded for various purposes, and in this section, we explored scaffolding text to build knowledge and word recognition. The following video shows a teacher using text to support word recognition. Beyond this video snapshot, the readers also engage in interleaved practice through decoding, building knowledge about the winter, and finding text evidence to support reasons why winter activities require skill. To learn more about interleaved practice, revisit chapter 3 (page 49).

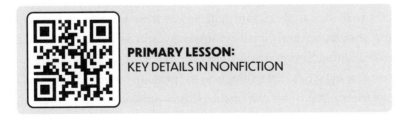

PRIMARY LESSON:
KEY DETAILS IN NONFICTION

Artificial Intelligence for Text Creation

You can use artificial intelligence (AI) to create text tailored to your readers' interests and levels. Given specific quantitative features, such as readability information and content areas, AI tools can generate text to support your learning goals.

There are various AI tools that allow you to tailor text to a student's or students' interest and reading level. A prompt such as "Create a short text at a second-grade level about dinosaurs" can be used to scaffold knowledge building through text.

Earlier in this chapter, you read a nonfiction text on Alzheimer's disease (figure 5.2, page 95). This text was generated by AI, and the prompt was, "Create a nonfiction text on understanding Alzheimer's disease." You can also use AI to create texts that highlight specific text features. For example, you might say, "Create an informational text on ocean life that contains a glossary." You can extend this text into more of an activity or task by following up with the prompt, "Generate two questions in which the reader needs to use the glossary to respond."

Creating text using AI allows teachers to focus on other areas of the lesson, such as grouping, routines, instructional strategies, and much more. Remember to perform basic fact-checking before using AI-generated texts. In addition to generating text on any content area, AI enables the creation of diverse and inclusive content, representing the cultural and diverse backgrounds of your students.

Representation in Texts

We want to conclude this chapter with a consideration that we feel is just as important as the academic goals you have for your students. We encourage you to have a critical eye for the types of books you use in your classroom. As Jerie Blintt (2020) shared in ILA's blog, "Students seeing themselves in the stories they read to foster a sense of belonging, recognition, and most of all, validation, is crucial—representation matters." Texts in classroom libraries and texts selected for instruction should reflect your students' diverse physical, cultural, and linguistic backgrounds.

Student agency and voice are critical to situating them at the heart of the reading process, allowing for more engagement. Providing opportunities for students to choose texts that they find relevant and reflect their interests will go a long way in fostering student agency. Small groups are also the perfect context to elevate student voice. Emma Samman and Maria Emma Santos (2009) define *voice* as our ability to express ourselves and willingness to speak up on behalf of others. Through access to a variety of texts, we can foster a classroom community grounded in deep connections, acceptance, mutual respect, student agency, and voice.

Summary

A deep understanding of instructional text is critical when planning for small-group instruction. Teachers should analyze texts for accessibility, instructional opportunities, and their ability to engage the reader. Texts serve a very specific purpose, whether that be to apply foundational skills with decodable texts or to engage in knowledge building or comprehension work in authentic texts.

LAUNCH YOUR REFLECTION

Let's reconnect with Mrs. Potter, who we met at the start of the chapter (page 93). Now that you've read this chapter, consider the following questions.

- Does Mrs. Potter's challenge resonate with you?
- Have you identified strategies to overcome the challenge shared?

RECHARGE YOUR SMALL-GROUP READING INSTRUCTION

With the perspectives you've gained from this chapter, what text would you select to support students to do each of the following?

- Build knowledge
- Apply standards
- Practice word recognition patterns
- Develop morphological awareness
- Build fluency

EXPAND YOUR TOOLBOX

To continue your learning, see the "Leading the Learning Action Guide" (page 201) to support you and your colleagues. In the action guide for this chapter, you'll find in-action videos that spotlight teaching strategies as well as differentiated professional learning activities you can try out with your team. Additional tools that support this chapter topic can be accessed online (visit **go.SolutionTree.com/literacy**).

CHAPTER 6
HOW DO I ENGAGE MY READERS DURING SMALL-GROUP INSTRUCTION?

To maximize time devoted to small-group instruction, we must be intentional about how we engage our readers throughout each lesson. An effective lesson with high student engagement begins with an intentionally crafted plan, and the facilitation of a well-planned lesson is critical for the lesson's effectiveness. Teachers make many decisions when designing lesson plans, regardless of whether the lesson was written by the teacher or if it came from a curriculum resource. Understanding the purpose of each instructional step and considering how the lesson experiences support students toward meeting the learning goals enables teachers to plan and make facilitation decisions, including pacing, student roles and response opportunities, the use and timing of strategic scaffolds, and more.

In this chapter, we share instructional strategies to support effective small-group instruction while also increasing the likelihood that students are engaged and are doing the heavy lifting in each lesson. We provide small-group lesson snapshots and lesson videos with various instructional focus areas. Each of these examples of small-group instruction in action includes annotations and engagement notes organized by teacher facilitation moves and student engagement opportunities.

As you read this chapter, consider your own perceptions of your facilitation and student engagement during your small-group lessons. The following questions can help frame your thinking as you read.

- During the planning process, what facilitation strategies can I anticipate using to enhance student engagement and success?
- Do my students have ample opportunities for applied practice and ownership during small-group instruction? Do the opportunities and time allotted for student practice and application match the actual time spent on practice and application during the lesson?
- How do my engagement strategies align with the instructional focus of my lesson (comprehension and metacognition, building foundational skills, and so on)?
- How does clarity about teacher and student roles impact student engagement opportunities and my planning process?

Consider the following example of Mrs. Atkins.

MEET THE TEACHER: MRS. ATKINS

> Mrs. Atkins has been teaching for ten years and considers small-group instruction to be a critical opportunity to differentiate instruction in her classroom. Each week, she invests one to two hours of planning for small-group lessons. But despite her best efforts, she finds that her lessons do not always go as intended. Specifically, she notices that lessons frequently take longer than planned, and she worries that "teacher talk" often outweighs opportunities for student application and practice. Mrs. Atkins is looking for ways to maximize instructional time and increase opportunities for her students to have more ownership during instruction.

Do Mrs. Atkins's reflections resonate with you? Have you identified strategies to overcome any of the challenges that she's shared?

We revisit these ideas and questions at the end of the chapter to identify and plan for engagement strategies you can try with your own students.

Teacher Facilitation and Student Engagement

Mrs. Atkins's experience describes a challenge we have heard from many teachers—their small-group reading lessons don't seem to unfold as planned. Teachers aren't alone in recognizing a disconnect between lesson plans and lessons in action. Researchers have long asserted that lesson plans, the actual facilitation of plans, and learning experiences or outcomes don't always align as intended (Remillard, 2018; Remillard & Heck, 2014; Ziebell & Clarke, 2018). In fact, this phenomenon is prevalent enough in the field of education for it to be depicted in various theoretical models.

In their framework, the Visual Model of the Curriculum Policy, Design, and Enactment System, educational researchers Janine T. Remillard and Daniel J. Heck (2014) describe and situate research on the *enacted curriculum*—how curriculum unfolds in the classroom during instruction. For our purposes in this book, we find what Remillard and Heck (2014) describe as the operational curriculum to be of particular interest. The *operational curriculum* describes what happens after the curriculum is put into teachers' hands, and then moves from descriptions of instructional objectives and the means for achieving them to actual classroom learning experiences and outcomes.

There are various reasons why a disconnect between the teacher-intended curriculum and student outcomes might occur through the enacted curriculum. These reasons include teachers being unfamiliar with the instructional strategies listed, the content or the authors' intent, or the learning outcomes of the particular lesson. In addition, students may not respond to the lesson in the way the teacher or the curriculum anticipated. Fortunately, there are ways that teachers can work toward closely aligning the intended curriculum and intended student outcomes. Consider the following musical performance analogy to further understand this phenomenon.

Just like teachers, musicians perform based on a plan that has already been written. This performance exists whether they wrote the music themselves or were provided a piece of sheet music. Due to this similarity, James Dean Brown (2009) used a music analogy to compare the written curriculum to a piece of composed sheet music, where the enacted curriculum represents how the music is performed. As teachers may expect, if the same piece of music was played by different musicians, there would likely be differences in each musician's performance, interpretation, and the nuances conveyed.

Sheet music has embedded instructions for the performer to support delivery. For example, sheet music might list a *crescendo*, a note to increase the volume of the music at specific points. It is then up to the performer to determine how loudly they will play the notes and at what speed to increase the volume. Stylistic interpretations, differences in tone and tempo, and even deciding when and where to breathe impact the overall musicality of a performance. So if two performers play from the same sheet music on the same instrument, there will be noticeable differences in their performances.

Brown (2009) uses this analogy to describe the potential for variance in the enacted curriculum despite teachers using the same adopted curriculum. Like Brown, we believe the same analogy applies to small-group reading lessons. There are a multitude of ways teachers could implement the lesson given the variation in facilitation and engagement strategies they employ. We find it helpful to align the teacher-intended curriculum, enacted curriculum, and student learning outcomes to strategically plan for student engagement opportunities with the learning goals. Although this may be an extra step in planning for some teachers, we consider it to be a critical one to optimize student engagement. Just as composers leave performance guidance for musicians through annotations such as dynamics, suggested tempo, and style, teachers can explicitly map out dynamic practices to maximize student ownership and engagement.

Taking teacher facilitation and student engagement into consideration may sound like a lesson-specific task. Although this is true to an extent, the facilitation considerations we provide in this chapter can apply to all grade levels and topics. In the sections that follow, we present five facilitation considerations and examples of lesson snapshots and videos that highlight teacher facilitation and student engagement in action.

REFOCUS THE ROLES OF STUDENTS AND TEACHER

Explicitly planning for student and teacher roles during a small-group reading lesson ensures the lesson plan, the teaching and learning experience, and learner outcomes strongly align. We suggest that you clearly define the roles of students and the teacher for each small-group reading lesson. We aren't suggesting that lessons be written out as scripts, as the word *role* might suggest. Instead, we promote the idea of running a high-speed "dress rehearsal" of the lesson, considering when and how to facilitate student engagement throughout the lesson. This enables teachers to visualize when and how students will respond and initiate with action, both individually and collectively.

When we plan small-group lessons—either teacher-written or from a curriculum resource—we often rely on a bank of teacher and student actions that align with our instructional goals. For example, using instructional routines in lesson plans (or identifying routines in curriculum resources) can offer predictable teacher and student actions, planned in alignment with lesson goals. Whether we are teaching a lesson to build foundational skills and read decodable text, support oral reading fluency through work on phrasing, or show students how to make inferences about characters based on text evidence, there are predictable facilitation strategies and student engagement look-fors.

The lesson observation and reflection tool (Center for the Collaborative Classroom, n.d.a), found in figures 6.1 and 6.2 (page 114), provides examples of teacher and student roles. This tool is organized by observable teacher and student actions to plan and look for within lessons. This tool was adapted and developed using a framework for teacher and student actions, and it is designed to help teachers review and reflect on engagement during small-group instruction. In figure 6.1, the version we developed for lessons with an emphasis on building foundational skills, teacher and student actions are highlighted with considerations of predictable routines for teaching phonemic awareness, phonics, and text decoding applications. To learn more about how to plan predictable routines in your instruction, visit chapter 4 (page 65).

Small-Group Instruction Lesson Reflection and Observation Tool: Foundational Skills		
During small-group reading instruction, the teacher:	**Observed**	**Notes**
Prepares materials as needed for the lessons (such as high-frequency word cards, spelling-sound cards, spelling-sound wall cards, and so on)		
Uses continuous blending for phonological awareness tasks ("ssuunn" rather than /s/ /u/ /n/)		
Engages in phonological awareness, phonics, and high-frequency word instruction based on students' data		
Allows students to do the work and provides corrective feedback during instruction, only as needed (for instance, students practice sounds without the teacher making the sounds)		
Monitors students' accuracy, decoding, and comprehension during instruction		
Documents observations of students reading to inform future instruction		
During small-group reading instruction, the students:	**Observed**	**Notes**
Do the work to practice and demonstrate their mastery of foundational skills, such as phonological awareness, phonics, and high-frequency word activities		
Engage in reading (and possibly rereading) of text		
Discuss the text (with partners, the whole group, or the teacher)		
Take responsibility for their learning and behavior		

Source: Adapted from Center for the Collaborative Classroom, n.d.a.

FIGURE 6.1: Reflection and observation tool for small-group instruction with an emphasis on building foundational skills.

*Visit **go.SolutionTree.com/literacy** for a free reproducible version of this table.*

The version in figure 6.2 was developed for lessons with an emphasis on building fluency, comprehension, and metacognition. Teacher and student actions are highlighted with consideration of students taking ownership over generating independent thinking, contributing to text discussions, and reflecting about their own reading processes and reading identities.

Small-Group Instruction Lesson Reflection and Observation Tool: Fluency, Comprehension, and Metacognition

Note: This may also include polysyllabic decoding or morphology instruction.

During small-group reading instruction, the teacher:	Observed	Notes
Prepares materials as needed for the lesson (intentional text selection, materials for word study, if included, and so on)		
Encourages students to talk to each other, not to the teacher		
Asks carefully-crafted questions based on lesson goals and guided by data, curriculum standards, and reading comprehension (including self-monitoring and metacognition)		
Monitors students' comprehension and fluency		
Asks students how they think the teacher could help them as a reader (general or specific to the lesson text)		
Documents observations of students reading to inform future instruction		

During small-group reading instruction, the students:	Observed	Notes
Apply, practice, and discuss reading strategies or procedures introduced during text discussions		
Engage in reading and rereading the texts (reading independently and in pairs, echo reading, reading for listeners) and sharing their thinking; opportunities to record thinking through writing may be included, such as reading journals		
Take responsibility for their learning and behavior		

Source: Adapted from Center for the Collaborative Classroom, n.d.a.

FIGURE 6.2: Reflection and observation tool for small-group instruction with an emphasis on fluency, comprehension, and metacognition.

*Visit **go.SolutionTree.com/literacy** for a free reproducible version of this figure.*

Later in this chapter, we provide concrete examples of teacher and student actions to assist teachers in delineating teacher and student roles during reading lessons, including how and where the roles intersect.

OFFER STRATEGIC SCAFFOLDING

It can be challenging to know when and how to scaffold during guided practice, collaborative learning, and independent practice within small-group lessons. To differentiate instruction and simultaneously meet individual students' needs, teachers make critical decisions about when and how to intervene while maintaining high levels of student engagement and success in authentic reading tasks. Asking questions, offering prompts, providing cues, and offering direct explanations are examples of scaffolds teachers can execute to engage students (Frey & Fisher, 2011). Table 6.1 provides definitions and examples of strategic scaffolds. Understanding the nuanced differences in scaffolding approaches and strategies supports teachers with their decision making.

TABLE 6.1: Strategic Scaffolds and Reading Examples in Action

Strategic Scaffold	Reading Examples in Action
Asking Questions Teacher poses a question to check for understanding. While student responses offer a formative assessment opportunity, the intent is not to assess—it is to uncover misconceptions or errors to gauge whether additional scaffolding is needed or if students are ready for less supported applications of learning or more rigorous tasks.	After independent student reading of the text *Sunny Days, Starry Nights* (Kintz, 2016): **Teacher:** *Why is it dark at night even when the sun is still shining?*
Prompting Used as a follow-up to questioning when misconceptions or errors are present: Teacher poses a follow-up question to prompt students to do their own cognitive or metacognitive work. Prompting questions may reference, for example, previous learning; background knowledge; or known concepts, rules, or procedures.	After independent student reading of the text *Sunny Days, Starry Nights* (Kintz, 2016): **Teacher:** *Why is it dark at night even though the sun is still shining?* **Student:** The Earth is going around the sun. **Teacher:** *You are right. Did you already know that before reading this text, or did you learn that from the author?* **Student:** I already knew it. **Teacher:** *What did you learn from the author in this text about why it is dark at night even when the sun is still shining?* [Prompt to use text evidence.]

continued ▶

Cueing Used as a more directive approach as a follow-up to questioning or prompting: Teacher shifts students' attention to something they may have missed or overlooked. Cues may be gestural, verbal, physical, environmental, or positional. Cues may be taught in initial instruction so they can be effectively used as a scaffold without additional explanation for their use in the moment.	After independent student reading of the text *Sunny Days, Starry Nights* (Kintz, 2016): **Teacher:** *Why is it dark at night even though the sun is still shining?* [Students offer text evidence that does not directly answer the question.] **Teacher:** *Turn to page 6. Use the text and the diagram on this page to find out why it is dark at night even when the sun is shining.* [Narrow focus on text excerpt and cue for attention to text and diagram.]
Directly Explaining Used as the most direct approach if prompting or cueing are unsuccessful—or, in the case of reading instruction, when explicit reteaching is needed to support a reading application task: Teacher offers a direct explanation, which may include giving students the answer. Afterward, the teacher monitors student understanding by prompting them to explain in their own words and checking for their understanding.	After providing the cue to look at the diagram on page 6, the student is still unable to explain why it is dark at night even when the sun is shining. **Teacher:** *I am looking to answer the question about why it is dark at night even when the sun is shining. In this diagram, I notice that the sun is shining on parts of the Earth. I also see that other parts of the Earth are not getting direct sunlight. I'm now looking at the text to see if it can help me answer that question further. Oh, yes, I see something that can help me here* [reads sentence aloud and makes connection].

Source: Frey & Fisher, 2011.

Later in this chapter, we offer examples of each scaffold using lesson excerpts, and we highlight video examples of strategies in action. To learn more about responding to students on the spot, visit chapter 7 (page 137).

CONSIDER ECONOMY OF LANGUAGE

In the book *Teach Like a Champion 2.0*, Doug Lemov (2015) uses the economy of language theory in relation to lesson facilitation to highlight how teachers can practice lessons using fewer words, which provides a clearer message for students. Lemov (2015) suggests that teachers need to be direct, clear, and concise when sharing content or eliciting responses to maximize the opportunity for students to respond. The economy of language theory is used in multiple disciplines outside of education, including translating, informational writing, and branding. When applied to a lesson facilitation context, the words teachers select for small-group reading lessons matter.

Table 6.2 provides applied examples of the economy of language principle. Although there is nothing wrong, per se, with the teacher language in the word-heavy questions and prompts on the left side of the table, the examples on the right that apply the economy of language principle clearly and succinctly state the task or question, which uses less instructional time. This clarity of language allows the teacher to dedicate more lesson time to student practice and application.

TABLE 6.2: Strategic Scaffolds and Reading Examples in Action

Word-Heavy Question or Prompt	Modified Question or Prompt Using the Economy of Language
Repeatedly during a blending routing (after directions have already been provided): *Look at the word* [points to the initial letter in the word]. *Think about how you would blend the word. Get ready. Your turn* [swipes finger under word].	Repeatedly during a blending routine (after directions have already been provided): • [Points to the initial letter in the word] • [Points to temple as a cue to think] • [Points to the initial letter in the word] • Blend [swipes finger under word].
When you were reading this text, you were probably wondering about why Helen was acting so angry and throwing tantrums around her family. I know I was wondering that when I was reading, too, and it even made me think about when my kids used to have tantrums when they were babies. Why do you think she was so angry and throwing tantrums around her family?	*Now that you've had a chance to read, why do you think Helen was acting so angry and throwing tantrums around her family?* [After intentional use of wait time, initiate students to turn to a partner to discuss or call on a student to share their thinking and text evidence.]

Our small-group instructional time is precious and fleeting, and using the economy of language principle preserves time for student ownership and engagement.

ESTABLISH NORMS FOR STUDENT-TO-STUDENT ENGAGEMENT

When compared to whole-group instruction, small-group instruction provides a unique coaching opportunity between teacher and students due to the reduced teacher-student ratio and more personalized setting. Small-group instruction also provides students with opportunities to engage in discussions and collaborative work with their classmates. To maximize student-to-student engagement and discourse, establishing norms for when and how students work together during small-group instruction is helpful. Norms should be planned, taught, and practiced, and teacher lesson planning and facilitation should highlight and support the norms that are in place (Dixon, Brooks, & Carli, 2019). Examples of norms for small-group reading instruction include the following.

- Respond with classmates using one voice together during choral responses (such as oral blending, oral segmenting, and oral decoding).
- Before telling your partner a word or correcting something you heard in their reading, ask if they would like reading help.

- When sharing your thinking about a text, help classmates understand your thinking by saying where you found the text evidence to support your thinking.
- When classmates share where they found text evidence during a discussion, look for and find the evidence in your own text.
- When a classmate shares their thinking, ways to respond might include:
  + Agreeing ("I agree with you because . . .")
  + Building on one another's thinking ("In addition to what you said, I think . . .")
  + Disagreeing respectfully ("I disagree with you because . . .")

Teachers can support students with the language to engage in rich discourse by introducing, modeling, and practicing question stems.

CONSIDER INSTRUCTIONAL PACING

Maximizing instructional time during small-group reading lessons carries implications for student engagement and learning outcomes and impacts the teacher's ability to meet with a targeted number of small groups each day. It is important for teachers to monitor lesson pacing so students remain focused and engaged. Pacing also ensures that teachers complete lessons in a reasonable amount of time. Additionally, it is important that lessons not feel rushed; teachers should provide students with ample time to generate and share their thinking and reading applications. Finding this pacing balance can be challenging, but with practice and intentional use of facilitation strategies, it is attainable. According to the Center for the Collaborative Classroom (2023), examples of facilitation considerations to support instructional pacing goals include the following.

- Facilitate the lesson according to the lesson plan (with planned scaffolding, if needed) to the greatest extent possible. Although it may be tempting to capitalize on "teachable moments" within the lesson, in most cases, making a mental note of additional possible learning opportunities is more advantageous than adding to the lesson in the moment. This affords the teacher the time to intentionally plan a lesson and align resources. At the same time, if it is challenging to complete a lesson during a single small-group session, consider how you can teach the lesson over two days with intentional chunking.
- Listen carefully to partner discussions, which allows teachers to gauge when students are ready to come back together. In addition, in some instances, it may not be necessary for students to share partner discussions with the entire small group. If a teacher monitors students'

responses and identifies consistency across student thinking, it may be more advantageous to advance their learning to the next part of the lesson. Alternatively, if the teacher prompts students to share their thinking after partner discussions, they should intentionally determine the order in which they share their ideas to help develop students' collective understanding in a meaningful way.

- Aim to prepare lesson materials in advance to the greatest extent possible. Finding a predictable part of a teacher's day to prepare materials for the next day's small-group lessons provides time to consider the planned lessons and what will be needed.

- Consider a materials management system that is responsive to the teacher's needs. For example, how can teacher and student materials be separated and stored for each individual small group? What materials are needed for every small group? Having a clear plan in place for material storage and management enables teachers to quickly transition between groups and increases the likelihood for efficiency and consistency from day to day and week to week.

Engagement Strategies in Action

Now that we have introduced five approaches to support lesson facilitation and student engagement, we offer concrete examples of each in sample lesson vignettes and videos. Feel free to read this section in order or prioritize one or two of these strategies based on your own personal goals for improving student engagement in your small-group reading lessons.

PHONEMIC AWARENESS LESSON SNAPSHOT

Consider the following lesson snapshot that highlights facilitation and engagement strategies in action during one routine of a foundational skill–building lesson. In this snapshot, the teacher provides a brief review of phoneme blending of CVC words using previous, explicitly-taught consonant and vowel sounds (consonants: *m, s, f, l, r, n, v, z*; vowels: *a, i, u*) followed by an instructional routine that provides student practice with blending three phonemes in CVC words. Dialogue is included in this lesson snapshot in addition to teacher-planned facilitation strategies designed to support student engagement and accuracy.

> **Teacher:** We can blend sounds together to make words. When we blend sounds, we slide through each sound. Listen to me slide through three sounds: */ssŭŭnn/*. When I slide through all of the sounds quickly to blend, I hear that the word is sun.

Now it's your turn. Listen to me slide through three sounds: /ffŭŭnn/. When I say "blend," use one voice together at our table to blend the sounds into a word. /ffŭŭnn/, blend.

Students: [Responding chorally, in unison] fun

Teacher: /mmĭĭss/

Students: [Responding chorally, in unison] miss

Teacher: /ffĭĭzz/

Students: [Responding chorally, in unison] fizz

Note: This routine continues with four additional CVC word blending tasks: fill, zip, run, nap. As readers respond chorally, the teacher ensures that their voice is off and they are not inadvertently mouthing the blended word to avoid unintentional scaffolding.

Teacher-prepared facilitation moves, if needed:

If readers "lose" an individual sound as they attempt to blend the phonemes, teachers might use the following strategy.

Introduce (or reintroduce) hand gestures to model producing individual sounds and blending. These may be used by the teacher during student choral responses or by the students, as needed.

- **Shoulder, Elbow, Wrist:** Teacher stretches their left arm out straight while holding up the pointer and middle fingers on their right hand. Teacher taps their shoulder while producing the first sound, elbow while producing the second sound, and wrist while producing the third sound. While blending, the teacher starts at the shoulder again and slides their fingers down their entire arm.
- **Hand Tap and Slide:** Teacher holds their left hand out flat, palm facing up. While producing individual sounds, the teacher taps their palm with the pointer, middle, and ring fingers of their right hand. While blending, the teacher slides their right hand across their left hand from wrist to fingertips (making a "swish" sound during the motion).

If readers produce an incorrect consonant or vowel sound while chorally blending (in this example, fizz), teachers might use the following strategy.

On a dry-erase board, draw three boxes attached side by side or three lines.

Teacher: /ff/ [Points to first box or line], /ĭĭ/ [points to second box or line], /zz/ [points to third box or line]. Now, you say each sound as I point.

Students: [Responding chorally, in unison] /ff/ [as teacher points to first box or line], /ĭĭ/ [as teacher points to second box or line], /zz/ [as teacher points to third box or line].

CHAPTER 6: How Do I Engage My Readers During Small-Group Instruction?

> **Teacher:** Blend.
>
> **Students:** fizz
>
> If readers continue to produce incorrect consonant or vowel sounds while chorally blending, teachers might use the following strategy.
>
> Distribute Elkonin box laminated templates and colored counters to add manipulatives to this routine to make it more concrete and to ensure that each reader is engaged in producing and blending sounds. Teacher provides an explicit review of how readers will listen, produce, and slide the counter for each sound, followed by blending the sounds to produce the CVC word. This review includes at least one modeled example. ← *Strategic Scaffolding: Providing a Direct Explanation*
>
> If one or more readers seem reluctant to share during the choral group response, teachers might use the following strategy.
>
> **Reading Cups:** Teacher directs readers to create "reading cups" by cupping their hands together and placing their "cup" over their mouths to offer a more personal opportunity for whispered individual or choral rehearsal prior to choral response. ← *Clear Teacher Facilitation and Student Engagement Roles*
>
> As readers practice, the teacher carefully observes readers' body language for increased confidence and willingness to attempt blending while also listening for the sounds coming from individual readers. After readers have practiced, the teacher might say the following.
>
> **Teacher:** Reading cups down. Ready, blend.
>
> [Students respond in unison.]

In addition to the annotations embedded in the preceding lesson snapshot, examples of teacher facilitation are outlined in the following.

- The teacher provides an initial explicit description and example of phoneme blending at the start of the routine. Then, the teacher relies on a previously taught, predictable routine to prompt students when it is their turn to blend. Instead of a question like "What word do you get when you blend these three sounds together?," the teacher can use the prompt "blend." To learn more about using and introducing predictable routines, revisit chapter 4 (page 65).
- The teacher intentionally uses continuous blending when presenting individual phonemes in the CVC words in this lesson practice. This strategy is based in research findings that having students blend words with continuous sounds (even during phonemic awareness practice) leads to stronger word-reading outcomes (Gonzalez-Frey & Ehri, 2021).

To learn more about planning for continuous blending, revisit chapter 4 (page 65).

- The teacher checks that their own participation in the instructional routine doesn't offer unintended scaffolding (such as mouthed or voiced responses in unison with students' choral responses).
- The teacher prepares evidence-based instructional scaffolds in advance to use only if needed. These instructional scaffolds are informed by their careful observations of students' responses. Examples of scaffolds include Elkonin boxes (Elkonin, 1963), concrete manipulatives for added multisensory instruction, and corrective feedback specific to the targeted skill.

Examples of student facilitation are outlined in the following.

- Students are expected to engage in choral response following the teacher's prompts and cues.
- Students use reading cups to prepare for choral response, a support strategy the teacher uses to increase their risk-taking and participation in a safe, supportive context, if needed.
- Students have differentiated opportunities for process and product to convey their knowledge of phoneme blending, if needed. To learn more about differentiating content, process, or product, revisit chapter 2 (page 35).

Here's a video snapshot of a lesson that highlights predictable routines for phoneme segmenting and the use of reading cups for decoding.

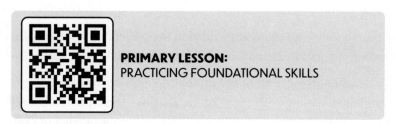

PRIMARY LESSON:
PRACTICING FOUNDATIONAL SKILLS

DECODING LESSON SNAPSHOT

The following lesson snapshot features teacher facilitation and student engagement strategies in action during one routine of another foundational skill–building lesson. In this snapshot, the teacher reintroduces the short vowel *e* by name, sound, and articulation, after which students have an opportunity to practice decoding CVC words with medial short *e*. Dialogue is included in this lesson snapshot in addition to teacher-planned facilitation moves designed to support student engagement and accuracy, if needed (Center for the Collaborative Classroom, 2021a).

CHAPTER 6: How Do I Engage My Readers During Small-Group Instruction?

Reintroduction of Short e, /ĕ/

Teacher: Today, we are going to revisit the spelling sound /ĕ/. [Points (or shows) the sound wall card for /ĕ/ that displays a book on the edge of a table.] The picture of the book on the edge of the table will help us remember that short e spells /ĕ/ because the word *edge* starts with /ĕ/. [Writes the letter e on a dry-erase board, or both the uppercase and lowercase e, depending on systematic scope and sequence of the letter name and sound instruction.] The letter e spells /ĕ/. What sound does it spell?

Students: [Responding chorally, in unison] /ĕ/

Teacher: [Prompts readers to continuously hold the /ĕ/ sound if they produce a single, distinct sound when responding.] Use your finger to trace the lowercase letter e on the table while you spell the /ĕ/ sound. [Models once, if readers don't start tracing immediately, and says, "Your turn."]

Students use their fingers to trace an imaginary e on the table in front of them while voicing /ĕ/, held continuously as they trace.

Teacher monitors readers individually to determine whether corrective feedback is needed.

Teacher: Now let's use what we know about letters and their spelling sounds to read words. [Displays CVC words for readers to decode on a dry-erase board.] Look at the first word. [Points under the first letter of the first word (set).] Sound?

Students: [Responding chorally, in unison] /ss/ ← *Economy of Language*

Teacher: [Points under the middle letter of the first word (set).] Sound?

Students: [Responding chorally, in unison] /ĕĕ/

Teacher: [Points under the final letter of the first word (set).] Sound?

Students: [Responding chorally, in unison] /t/

Teacher: [Points back under the first letter of the first word (set).] Blend. [Sweeps under the word from left to right as readers respond chorally.]

Students: [Responding chorally, in unison] set

Note: This routine continues with four to seven additional CVC word blending tasks. CVC words may all include the medial short e or may be a mix of words with medial short e and any other previously taught short vowels and consonants. Take care not to use r-controlled or irregular CVC words as decodable words for this routine. As readers respond chorally, the teacher ensures that their voice is off and they are not inadvertently mouthing the blended word to avoid unintentional scaffolding.

Teacher-prepared facilitation moves, if needed:

If readers produce an incorrect vowel sound as they attempt to produce the spelling sound /ĕĕ/, teachers might do the following.

- Add articulation instruction to the alphabet instruction: "When you make the sound /ĕĕ/, you are going to open your mouth just a little [model], drop your chin down [model], and stretch the corners of your mouth [physically model]."
- Introduce a mnemonic gesture to help readers remember the /ĕ/ sound, with a link to the articulation: Using the thumb and pointer finger (with other fingers on the hand folded down), place each finger on either side of your mouth (at the corners of your lips) as you say, "/ĕĕ/, e spells /ĕĕ/."

If readers use incorrect letter formation while tracing the letter e on the table, teachers might do the following.

- Offer corrective path-of-movement prompts—like across, over, around, and open—or other predictable path-of-movement cues provided by an adopted curriculum resource. *Strategic Scaffolding: Cueing*
- Distribute tactile boards for readers to trace the letter, offering a multisensory, tactile support.

If readers produce incorrect consonant or vowel sounds while chorally blending, or produce accurate individual sounds but incorrectly blend the CVC word, teachers might do the following.

- Distribute Elkonin box laminated templates and a sample of magnet letters (based on those used in the lesson) to add manipulatives to this routine to make it more concrete. This will ensure that each reader is engaged in identifying spelling sounds, producing spelling sounds, and blending CVC words correctly. Provide an explicit review of how readers will slide the magnet letter into the designated Elkonin box while producing each spelling sound, followed by blending the sounds to produce the CVC word. This review should include at least one modeled example.

Strategic Scaffolding: Providing a Direct Explanation

If one or more readers seem reluctant to share during the choral group response, teachers might do the following.

Reading Cups: As in the phonemic awareness lesson snapshot, direct readers to create reading cups by cupping their hands together and placing their "cup" over their mouths to offer a more personal opportunity for whispered individual or choral rehearsal prior to choral response.

As readers practice, the teacher carefully observes readers' body language for increased confidence and willingness to attempt blending while also listening for the sounds coming from individual readers. After readers have practiced, teachers might say the following.

> **Teacher:** Reading cups down. Ready, blend.
>
> [Students chorally respond, in unison.]

Clear Teacher Engagement and Student Facilitation Roles

In addition to the annotations embedded in the preceding lesson snapshot, examples of teacher facilitation included in this snapshot follow.

- The teacher provides an initial explicit description of the connection between a grapheme (*e*) and phoneme (/ĕ/) at the start of the routine.
- The teacher provides opportunities for the students to apply sound-spelling knowledge to analyze words. This strategy is grounded in research that promotes opportunities for students to create an orthographic map as they decode (Chambrè, Ehri, & Ness, 2020). In this part of the lesson snapshot, the teacher relied on a previously-taught, predictable routine to prompt students when it was their turn to blend. To learn more about orthographic mapping and using and introducing predictable routines, revisit chapter 4 (page 65).
- The teacher gives instruction on letter names and letter sounds concurrently. This strategy stems from research that links the teaching of alphabet names and sounds together with improved student outcomes and effective learning of both letter names and sounds (Miciak et al., 2018; Piasta & Wagner, 2010).
- The teacher prompts students to orally produce the sound for each letter in the CVC word prior to blending based on their knowledge of students' current decoding skills. As students become more proficient with decoding CVC words, wait time, followed by the prompt "blend," may be a more efficient routine.
- The teacher prepares evidence-based instructional scaffolds to use only if needed and based on their careful observations of students' responses. Examples of scaffolds include Elkonin boxes (Elkonin, 1963), tactile boards for added multisensory instruction to increase attention and engagement (Shanahan, 2020), and articulation instruction to promote word reading (Boyer & Ehri, 2011).

Examples of student facilitation are outlined in the following.

- Students are expected to engage in choral response following the teacher's prompts and cues.

- Students build toward whole-word decoding by producing individual spelling sounds for initial, medial, and final graphemes prior to blending. Based on students' current proficiency and automaticity when decoding, this approach supports their success, which in turn promotes their engagement.
- Students have differentiated opportunities for process and product to practice and convey their decoding knowledge, as needed. The introduction of magnet letters provides a decoding and encoding connection and is based on research that spelling supports reading by improving phonics knowledge and word reading (Møller, Obi Mortensen, & Elbro, 2022). To learn more about differentiating content, process, or product, revisit chapter 2 (page 35).

The following is a video snapshot of a lesson that highlights clear teacher-student roles to support spelling-sound learning and decoding practice.

PRIMARY LESSON:
BUILDING LETTER KNOWLEDGE

PROSODY LESSON SNAPSHOT

The following lesson snapshot features teacher facilitation and student engagement strategies in action during a fluency lesson–based prosody, a method to support students as they group words together in phrases to make their reading sound smooth. In this snapshot, students hear and discuss a model of oral reading fluency and read a phrase-cued version of the text *Sunny Days, Starry Nights* (Kintz, 2016). The teacher facilitates students' oral reading fluency through modeling, providing text with supports, and using echo reading as an instructional strategy. Dialogue is included in this lesson snapshot in addition to teacher-planned facilitation strategies designed to support students' oral reading fluency (adapted from Center for the Collaborative Classroom, 2021b).

> This lesson includes a text that is being revisited to support fluency instruction. In this curriculum resource, the text used in this lesson—*Sunny Days, Starry Nights* (Kintz, 2016)—was previously used in a lesson to build foundational skills by practicing embedded high-frequency words and phonics patterns.

Preparing to Read the Text

Teacher: Remember, we read this text, *Sunny Days, Starry Nights*, during a different small-group lesson. This text was written by Corinn Kintz, and Gail Guth selected the photographs and designed the illustrations. This book is nonfiction, and it gives us information about day and night. Today, we are going to use this book to build our oral fluency, or what it sounds like when we read out loud.

Listen as I read page 1 of the book, and you and your partner will talk about what you notice about my reading. [Teacher reads page 1 of the text aloud with an intentional combination of rushed and halted phrasing.] What did you notice about the way I read this? Turn to your partner.

[Partners discuss their observations of the teacher's reading (as the teacher monitors), offering ideas.]

Student 1: It sounded like you didn't know what you were reading about.

Norms for Student-to-Student Engagement

Student 2: It sounded like you knew some of the words, but you were pretending that some of the other words were hard for you.

Student 3: It sounded like you were a kid reading who doesn't know all the words—not like a teacher.

Teacher: Yes, when I was reading, I wasn't grouping the words together to read fluently or smoothly. My reading didn't sound smooth like talking, and the sentences were hard for you to understand because of the way I read. Today, you are going to practice grouping words together as you read so your reading sounds like talking.

Reading Phrase-Cued Text to Build Prosody

Teacher passes out a copy of a phrase-cued, reprinted version of the text on paper to each reader.

> Excerpt of Phrase-Cued Text from *Sunny Days, Starry Nights* (Kintz, 2016)
>
> Look outside. // How can you tell / it is daytime? // Can you see the sun / high in the sky? // You can see it / on a sunny day. // But even on a rainy day, / it is light outside. // It is light on foggy / and snowy days, / too. // The sun is there. //
>
> Once it is night, / the sky is not as bright. // Though there may be starlight / or moonlight, / it is dark. //
>
> So why do we have day / and night? // Once nighttime comes, / does the sun stop shining? //

Teacher: Take a few moments to look over your text. [Teacher observes as readers preview their text.] What do you notice about this text?

[Students share their observations of the text, offering ideas.]

Student 1: This has the same words from the book, but it's not put together like a book—it's just words on a page.

Student 2: The words from the book are here, but the pictures are not.

Student 3: This page has words from the book with lines on it.

Teacher: Find and point to the first section on your paper. Notice that each section on the sheet has words from one page of the book. Follow along in the first section while I read the page 1 text aloud. [Teacher reads aloud, using the marks in the sentences to naturally phrase their reading.] What did you notice about the way I read the text this time?

[Students share their observations of text reading, offering ideas.]

> Strategic Scaffolding: Questioning

Student 1: When you got to the lines on the page, you stopped.

Student 2: It sounded like usual teacher reading—the way you usually read to us.

Student 3: I could understand what you were saying this time.

Teacher: Yes, and when I was reading, the marks between words helped me know which words to group together to make the reading sound like talking.

Echo Reading Practice With Phrase-Cued Text

Teacher: Now you're going to practice grouping the words together by echo-reading with me. As I read, notice what I do with my voice to make the reading sound like talking so you can do the same thing with your voice when it's your turn. I'm going to use the marks between the words to help me know which words to group together. You should pay attention to the marks when you echo-read.

[Students echo-read from the phrase-cued text.]

After this lesson snapshot, the teacher offers students feedback and explains how fluency supports readers and listeners to better understand and enjoy text. Students will have additional opportunities to practice reading the phrase-cued text in pairs and independently outside of this small-group lesson. Students can also use the original book version of the text to practice their oral reading fluency without the scaffolds of the phrase-cued markings.

> Norms for Student-to-Student Engagement

If readers have difficulty describing the teacher's oral reading (either the nonexample or the model reading), the teacher might ask questions such as the following.

CHAPTER 6: How Do I Engage My Readers During Small-Group Instruction?

- What did my reading sound like?
- Did my reading sound like it usually sounds when I read to you? Why not?

Strategic Scaffolding: Prompting

If readers seem to have difficulty decoding the text during echo reading, the teacher might provide on-the-spot, explicit instruction like the following.

- For high-frequency words: Teacher names the word and describes the word's meaning, followed by information to support orthographic mapping of the word.
- For decodable words: Teacher provides an explicit explanation of the phonics pattern applied in the word to support accurate decoding.

Strategic Scaffolding: Providing a Direct Explanation

If readers continue to have difficulty with accuracy, the teacher may choose to use the text for a decoding instructional purpose prior to resuming instruction focused on fluency.

If readers have quick success improving their prosody during echo reading, consider differentiating the task by directing readers to pause longer for the double lines (at the end of a sentence) compared to the single lines (within sentences).

In addition to the annotations embedded in the preceding lesson snapshot, examples of teacher facilitation included in this snapshot are outlined in the following.

- The teacher models oral reading fluency using both examples and nonexamples of reading with smooth prosody, or phrasing. The teacher asks questions to invite students' observations, but also explicitly shares the reading characteristics in each example related to oral reading fluency.
- The teacher uses intentionally-developed text with phrase-cued scaffolding to support the instructional goals of this lesson. Beyond this lesson, students have additional opportunities to practice phrasing during their oral reading using both a printed version of the text without phrase-cued scaffolds and the book version of the nonfiction text, which includes photographs and illustrations.
- The teacher provides opportunities for students to turn and talk to their partner during the lesson. This maximizes opportunities for students to share their thinking and maintains their engagement during instruction.
- The teacher uses an instructional hook aligned with the learning goal of the lesson (through the disfluent example of teacher reading) to engage students and offer a counterexample to the model fluent reading they provide in the next step of the lesson.

Examples of student facilitation are outlined in the following.

- Students engage in both partner conversation and small-group discussion about oral text reading after direct prompting and questioning from the teacher.
- Students have clearly defined roles in the echo-reading process, during which they use both the teacher's model oral reading and the phrase-cued text scaffolds to improve their phrasing as they read.
- Students gain increased responsibility to practice and apply grouping words to improve phrasing during oral reading by engaging in a collaborative learning practice task (paired reading) and independent practice (independent reading of the phrase-cued text, non-phrase-cued text, and original nonfiction book). To learn more about guided practice and collaborative learning, visit chapter 10 (page 179).

MAKING INFERENCES LESSON SNAPSHOT

The following lesson snapshot features teacher facilitation and student engagement strategies in action during a comprehension lesson based on making inferences about characters' feelings using text evidence. In this snapshot, students read an excerpt from a chapter-book biography that recounts the life of Helen Keller. The author uses features of narrative nonfiction to depict experiences in Keller's life. While this is a nonfiction text, true stories like biographies can be similar to fiction in many ways, and both biographies and fictional stories include characters or real people and their experiences.

In this lesson snapshot, the teacher facilitates students' inferences and identification of textual evidence as they work toward explaining differences in individuals' perspectives and how one or more of the people in the biography develop throughout the text. This lesson is also designed to support students to deepen their thinking about text and monitor their own understanding. Dialogue is included in this lesson snapshot in addition to teacher-planned facilitation moves that are designed to support student engagement, deepen text comprehension, and address readers' misconceptions, if needed (adapted from Center for the Collaborative Classroom, 2021a).

> **This lesson is a day 2 follow-up lesson anchored in a biography of Helen Keller.**
>
> On day 1, four students are introduced to the text and build knowledge around what it means to be deaf and blind, including learning about historical discrimination against individuals with disabilities. Students also use features of the chapter book and elements of the biography genre

(cover, back cover [including the braille alphabet], and table of contents) prior to reading twelve pages of chapter 1 independently. As students read, the teacher monitors their individual oral reading fluency and accuracy, jotting down observations. After reading, students engage in a discussion about the chapter, including their own reflections about what they read. They consider how sharing their own thinking and discussing text with others help them think about the text in ways they would not have thought of on their own. Students are assigned to read the second chapter independently during their independent reading extended practice opportunity station prior to their small-group meeting the following day (which may include additional reading on day 1 or independent reading on day 2 prior to small-group instruction).

Preparing to Read the Text

Teacher: Since yesterday, you read the second chapter of this biography. What happened in the chapter that you read?

Student 1: Helen was getting very angry and making bad choices.

Student 2: Yes, and her dad said that they might have to send Helen away out of their house.

Teacher: Okay, so you noticed some character actions and feelings as you were reading. Remember, yesterday we talked about how readers discuss their own thinking about what happens in stories and what the characters say and do. What are you thinking about what you've read so far? Turn to your partner to share. ◀ Strategic Scaffolding: Questioning

[Student 1 and student 2 adjust their seating to face one another as they discuss their thinking about what they've read so far. Student 3 and student 4 do the same. As partners discuss, the teacher leans toward them to listen in on the partner discussions.] ◀ Norms for Student-to-Student Engagement

Teacher: Let's come back together. What did you and your partner discuss about what you're thinking as you're reading?

Student 2: I think Helen is having tantrums because it's the only way that she can let people know that she's angry, since she can't talk.

Student 3: I agree with Emily [student 2] because she can't say anything that she is thinking, and so her only choice is to show how mad she is.

Teacher: Skylar [student 4], what have you been thinking about as you read this chapter?

Student 4: I wonder if her parents are mad at her for hurting her sister.

Student 3: I wonder that too, and I wonder if they are secretly afraid of Helen and think that she might hurt them too.

Teacher: I'm noticing that you are using events from the text and your own ideas to wonder about what characters are thinking and why they might be doing the things they are doing. When you use evidence the author has provided from the text with your own ideas in this way, you are actually making inferences, which can help you better understand the text and enjoy the text even more. Today, you're going to have a chance to reread page 16, and as you're reading, I want you to think about this question: "Why are Helen's parents worried?"

[Shows a graphic organizer on a dry-erase board.] You see this question at the top of the graphic organizer that we are going to use to capture our thinking today. As you read, look for evidence from the author that helps you answer this question. Also, think about your own ideas and how they help you to understand why Helen's parents are worried.

[Teacher gives readers time to read page 16 silently and monitors their reading.]

Discussing the Text, Sharing Independent Thinking, and Making Inferences

Teacher: Now, let's try this out together. What are some clues that the author is describing in this part of the book about why Helen's parents are worried?

Student 1: Helen's apron catches on fire.

Teacher: OK, but before that, something important happened. Turn to your partner and talk about what happened before Helen's apron catches on fire. *— Strategic Scaffolding: Cueing*

[Partners discuss what happened as teacher monitors.]

Teacher: So, what happened first?

Student 1: She spilled water on her apron.

Teacher: [Records event on graphic organizer] Okay, then what happened after that?

Student 4: She tried to get it dry. *— Strategic Scaffolding: Prompting*

Teacher: [Records event on graphic organizer] Okay, so she moved it closer to the fire to get it dry, and then what happened?

Student 3: Her apron caught on fire.

Teacher: [Records event on graphic organizer] Okay, so now I want you to think about what the parents said. Grayson, do you remember?

Student 1: Her parents said that she could have been hurt.

Teacher: Yes, so what do we know about how Helens' parents are feeling based on what they said and what happened in this part of the chapter?

> Clear Teacher Engagement and Student Facilitation Roles

Student 4: I think they're feeling worried because Helen could have died, and she was putting herself and their whole family in a lot of danger when the apron was on fire in their house.

Teacher: So, we can infer that they're becoming more and more worried about Helen because some of the things that she is doing when she can't communicate or ask for help are putting her in danger—so our inference is that her parents are becoming more and more worried about Helen and her safety.

Setting Up Collaborative Learning Practice

Teacher: Now, I want you to reread page 17 of the text and think about this question: "How is Helen feeling about her baby sister and why might she be feeling that way?" After you read, at your desk, I want you and your partner to use this organizer to make an inference about why Helen may be feeling the way she's feeling about her baby sister.

[In pairs at their desks, students read and revisit the text to use the graphic organizer to make an inference about Helen's feelings toward her baby sister.]

Teacher-prepared facilitation moves, if needed:

If readers have difficulty recalling events from the chapter they previously read, the teacher might ask questions such as the following.

- What problems did Helen cause?
- How does Helen find out about the world?
- Why did Helen's father say they might have to send Helen away?

If readers continue to have difficulty, the teacher may share a specific event from the text. In this case, the teacher would try to let the readers drive the conversation as much as possible after sharing the event to get the discussion started.

> Strategic Scaffolding: Providing a Direct Explanation

When asked to share their own thinking, if readers recall events from the text only, the teacher might ask questions such as the following.

- What do you think about that?
- What does that make you wonder?

> If readers have difficulty completing the graphic organizer with their partner during the collaborative practice opportunity, the teacher might revisit the question and engage in guided practice to help readers infer.

In addition to the annotations embedded in the preceding lesson snapshot, examples of teacher facilitation included in this example are outlined in the following.

- The teacher prompts students to think about the story events they recall in addition to their own independent thinking related to those events. By asking for each and clearly delineating between the two, the teacher illustrates how readers make inferences by synthesizing evidence from the text with their own thinking.
- The teacher uses frequent opportunities for students to turn and talk to their partner during the lesson. This maximizes opportunities for students to share their thinking and offers teachers more time to monitor students' understanding and gauge their engagement. In instances where the teacher hears each partnership discuss accurate evidence from the text, the teacher can move to the next part of the lesson without sharing ideas with the whole group. This allows the teacher to maintain lesson pacing and affords more time for students to work toward the main learning goals.
- The teacher uses strategic scaffolds by deciding when to ask questions, offer prompts, or cue students for specific information. Each of these examples was evident in the lesson snapshot based on how the students responded and the teacher's careful observation and analysis of how to scaffold students' learning (Frey & Fisher, 2011).

Here's a video snapshot of a lesson that highlights part of this lesson with the teacher's questions, prompts, and cues in action.

INTERMEDIATE LESSON:
MAKING INFERENCES

Examples of student facilitation are outlined in the following.

- Students engage in partner conversation and small-group discussion about the text following the teacher's questions, prompts, and cues.

- Students' engagement in partnered discussions is evident based on their response when asked to talk to their partner. Students physically turn their bodies, share their ideas, and build on the ideas of one another.
- Student behavior indicates that a small-group norm for text discussion is to provide specific text evidence to support their thinking when contributing to discussions.
- Students gain increased responsibility to practice and apply making inferences. To facilitate this, students use strategies like engaging in a collaborative learning practice task using a graphic organizer after they complete a guided practice task led by the teacher during a small-group lesson. To learn more about guided practice and collaborative learning, see chapter 10 (page 179).

Summary

Facilitating high student engagement within an effective lesson begins with a well-thought-out plan. Whether the lesson comes from a curriculum resource or is written by the teacher, there are still many decisions to be made when planning for the lesson. To plan for and make decisions regarding lesson pacing, teacher and student roles, response opportunities, scaffolds, and more, it is helpful to first understand the purpose of each instructional step and how the experiences within the lesson support readers in reaching the intended learning goals. In this chapter, we explored instructional strategies that support effective small-group instruction, including strategies for student engagement and ensuring readers are doing the heavy lifting in each lesson. The chapter included small-group lesson snapshots and lesson videos with various instructional focus areas to create a shared vision of the practices shared.

LAUNCH YOUR REFLECTION

Let's reconnect with Mrs. Atkins, the teacher we met at the beginning of this chapter (page 110). Now that you have read this chapter, consider the following questions.

- As you reread how Mrs. Atkins describes her small-group reading instruction, what facilitation techniques to maximize student engagement come to mind?
- If you were going to observe her instruction to offer peer-to-peer feedback, what look-fors might you anticipate?

RECHARGE YOUR SMALL-GROUP READING INSTRUCTION

The following are some questions you can use to apply the chapter concepts to your own classroom context.

- What facilitation moves for student success and engagement might I anticipate prior to the next lesson I will teach to maximize student learning and engagement?
- Do my students have ample opportunities for applied practice and ownership during small-group instruction? How do the opportunities for student practice and application in the lesson plan compare to the actual time spent on practice and application during lesson facilitation?
- How do my engagement strategies align with the instructional focus of the lesson (such as comprehension and metacognition, building foundational skills)?
- How might my understanding of teacher-student roles impact student engagement opportunities in my lessons?

EXPAND YOUR TOOLBOX

To continue your learning, see the "Leading the Learning Action Guide" (page 201) to support you and your colleagues. In the action guide for this chapter, you'll find in-action videos that spotlight teaching strategies as well as differentiated professional learning activities you can try out with your team. Additional tools that support this chapter topic can be accessed online (visit **go.SolutionTree.com/literacy**).

CHAPTER 7

HOW DO I MONITOR AND RESPOND TO MY STUDENTS AS READERS?

Monitoring and responding to readers during text reading in small-group instruction requires nuanced decision making. Nell K. Duke (2020) states that "there's an art—and science—to providing prompts" (p. 26) that support readers when they encounter difficulties in a text. In this chapter, we focus on the ways teachers can monitor students' understanding and their progress toward skilled, proficient reading. We share research-informed strategies and practices for observing students' reading behaviors and deciding when and how to intervene. We also discuss ways teachers respond to students' text reading both through immediate, on-the-spot responses and by planning for responses in subsequent small-group lessons.

As you read this chapter, consider ways you might respond when listening to students read. How will your observations inform the way you choose to offer prompts and cues to support your readers? How might you coach them through the reading challenges they encounter without doing the work for them?

The following questions may also help frame your thinking as you read.

- What should I do when a student encounters a word they struggle to read?
- How can I monitor students' text reading progress to guide my instruction?

- What can I listen for to respond to my readers with in-the-moment scaffolds?
- What are ways I can adjust my instruction to respond to students within and beyond a single small-group lesson?

Consider the following example of Ms. Locke.

MEET THE TEACHER: MS. LOCKE

> Ms. Locke recognizes that listening to her students read is critical to developing their reading skills and behaviors. During a small-group lesson, she asks each reader to read to her orally as the other readers in the group read silently to themselves. As she listens, she notices that two of her students struggle when they encounter multisyllabic words. To address this challenge, she helps the students decode the unfamiliar words on the spot by offering prompts and cues linking to previous instruction. However, the more Ms. Locke listens to her students, the more she notices that they may be experiencing different challenges when they come across unfamiliar words. How should she respond?

Does Ms. Locke's challenge in deciding how to respond to her students as readers resonate with you? How can Ms. Locke respond to each student's individual needs within and beyond this lesson?

We'll revisit these ideas and questions at the end of the chapter to identify ways to support instructional practices for small-group lesson planning in your classroom.

Monitoring and Responding to Readers

The vignette about Ms. Locke shares common challenges for all teachers: How do we support readers as they engage with text? How should we respond when readers encounter a challenging word as they read? How do we support students to learn and apply *fix-up strategies*—or techniques that skilled readers use to be aware of their own mistakes and to know how to correct their decoding or improve their understanding of a text? For example, how might we help a reader know what to do when their comprehension of the text breaks down due to a challenging narrative text structure or lack of content knowledge on a nonfiction topic? The decisions teachers make during instructional moments like these can shape how and to what extent readers build their independent reading skills for future text reading.

Teachers may wonder how much support to provide, or when to intentionally refrain from intervening to allow for productive struggle. They may wonder what to say or not to say. For example, if a reader encounters an unfamiliar word, how should the teacher respond in that moment? Should they say the word? Should they prompt the reader to connect to previously taught concepts? Should the teacher offer the reader a cue to support a subsequent attempt of the unknown word—whether for decoding or vocabulary knowledge? These are all possible teacher responses to this student's challenge.

We know that decisions like these must be made repeatedly in each small-group lesson every day. Knowing how to monitor students' text reading and deciding when and how to respond to readers during text reading are important elements of lesson facilitation. These complex decisions impact teachers' on-the-spot responses to coach students' reading behaviors, but they may also result in subsequent instruction to address students' needs through carefully-crafted future lessons. During small-group lessons, readers need opportunities to practice reading connected text to apply the skills and strategies they learned. Depending on the reader's decoding proficiency and the learning goal, teachers may present connected text for readers at the word, sentence, paragraph, passage, or chapter level. In each of these instances, readers should have the time and space for independent reading opportunities, whether oral or silent.

It's important to avoid instructional practices such as *round-robin reading*—where each reader orally reads a text segment as the other readers follow along before their turn—during this reading practice time (Kuhn, 2014). To maximize each reader's time with text and to provide opportunities for them to receive teacher feedback in risk-free settings, readers should be able to read at their own pace where they aren't being watched (and waited on) by their reading peers. Instead, we recommend establishing reading norms in which readers independently practice their text reading by silently reading or whispering to themselves at their own pace without giving attention to the reading progress of their reading peers participating in the small-group lesson (Shanahan, 2009). During this time, teachers can individually monitor one reader at a time as the reader reads aloud from a chunked excerpt of the independent text. This allows teachers to astutely listen for opportunities to provide individualized coaching that supports each reader's practice. To learn more about instructional routines that support independent text reading during small-group lessons, revisit chapter 4 (page 65).

Teachers can use the following ideas as they plan for how they will monitor and respond to readers in their classroom.

- **Provide scaffolding:** Offer questions, prompts, cues, and—when required—direct explanations. Scaffolded support helps readers navigate challenging texts while gradually building their independence.
- **Encourage self-monitoring:** Prompt students to reflect on their text comprehension by asking questions like "Does that make sense?" or "How can I help you in the part you just read?" Encouraging self-monitoring helps students recognize when and how to get unstuck on their own.

- **Teach fix-up strategies:** Explicitly teach students strategies to overcome word recognition, morphemic, or comprehension obstacles.
- **Foster independence:** Encourage independent problem-solving and critical-thinking skills by allowing for productive struggle and resisting the urge to intervene immediately.
- **Reflect and adjust:** Reflect on how effectively you monitor and respond to students as readers. Adjust teaching practices based on ongoing assessment data and your observations of students' progress. Try out the tools in this chapter to refine your on-the-spot support for readers.

The following is a video snapshot of a lesson that highlights the teacher individually monitoring readers as they independently read the text *Winter Fun* (Arego, 2016).

PRIMARY LESSON:
SUPPORTING INDEPENDENT
READING–GRADE 2

When teachers listen to readers during independent reading opportunities, they can determine whether readers are applying taught skills and strategies as they read. This includes discerning if and how readers are using decoding skills to aid in word recognition, demonstrating bridging processes (such as fluency, vocabulary knowledge, or morphological awareness) with increasing automaticity, using taught comprehension strategies to extract meaning from text, and monitoring their own reading processes for the progressive use of strategic decision making to stay engaged and connected with text.

To support their organization of observations in this area in real time, we recommend that teachers consider using a framework to capture their observations of reading and any notes that come to mind as they monitor students. For example, if a teacher wants to use an analytic protocol to record their observations of readers' behaviors across instructional components of reading, one tool we recommend is the Listening to Reading–Watching While Writing Protocol (Duke et al., 2020). This open-access tool was designed as an informal assessment to use during daily instruction to help teachers focus their attention on particular aspects of readers' behaviors. It concentrates teachers' attention on multiple applications of the reading process, including decoding, fluency, vocabulary, comprehension, and metacognition.

As another example, a teacher can use the Individualized Daily Reading Conference Record (Center for the Collaborative Classroom, 2023) to frame individual reading conferences. This tool guides them while they frame their observations and questions during one-on-one, informal conference settings. This informal assessment tool also provides a space for teachers to summarize their conference observations, which includes making notes of readers' progress on the continuum of reading development, goal setting, and identifying next steps for instruction. Although this is an example of a program-specific tool, teachers may still want to use it and adapt it for their own use. Both tools serve as supports for us during our collaboration with teachers and readers. Teachers can use powerful tools like these, as well as less structured observation tools, to record their notes and wonderings as they monitor their readers.

Figure 7.1 provides a structured observation tool based on the categories of the ABC Reader Profile Framework (chapter 1, page 17). This tool offers a space for teachers to record their own anecdotal notes based on their observations of readers. Figure 7.1 is an example of how the same framework can be repeated on a single page to capture multiple observations of readers during a lesson. Each box of reader notes can be cut and filed individually using a teacher-created informal assessment tracking system and can be readily available to share with parents and caregivers, other teachers, and specialized instructional support personnel.

Reader:	Date:	Reader:	Date:
Text Title:		Text Title:	
Text Characteristics:		Text Characteristics:	
Decoding		Decoding	
Fluency and Bridging Processes		Fluency and Bridging Processes	
Comprehension		Comprehension	
Self-Regulation and Metacognition		Self-Regulation and Metacognition	

Reader:	Date:	Reader:	Date:
Text Title:		Text Title:	
Text Characteristics:		Text Characteristics:	
Decoding		Decoding	
Fluency and Bridging Processes		Fluency and Bridging Processes	
Comprehension		Comprehension	
Self-Regulation and Metacognition		Self-Regulation and Metacognition	

FIGURE 7.1: ABC Reader Profile Framework reader observation tool.

*Visit **go.SolutionTree.com/literacy** for a free reproducible version of this figure.*

When teachers are unsure about which tool to use, we often encourage them to take some time to try out different tools during their own instruction to see which offers the best fit for their instructional and informal assessment needs.

Responding to Readers on the Spot

In the previous section, we shared how the ABC Reader Profile Framework can be used to frame observations of readers as they engage with text during small-group lessons. This framework can also be useful for teachers to monitor and respond to readers. Identifying and practicing on-the-spot scaffolds during interactions with readers promotes their reading success. At the same time, we can frame scaffolds to allow readers to internalize the support they receive, thereby increasing the likelihood that their learning transfers to reading opportunities with other texts.

When responding to readers as they engage in independent reading, it can be helpful to start by classifying the response by area of reading. In the following tables, we provide examples of possible prompts and cues based on the area of support needed. Table 7.1 includes prompts for decoding and word recognition.

TABLE 7.1: Prompts Based on the ABC Reader Profile Framework for Decoding and Word Recognition

When Attempting to Decode an Unknown Word, the Reader . . .	Teacher Prompt or Cue and Explanation
. . . uses the wrong sound for a letter once	Point. Say, "Sound" or "Try a different sound." These cue and prompt options direct readers to the part of the word that is incorrect by giving specific feedback of where to focus and refocus in spelling-sound recognition followed by word blending.
. . . continually uses the wrong sound	Point to a visual cue (sound wall, sound wall card, visual drill card for the sound-spelling relationship). Ask, "What sound?" (You might also prompt for the picture on the visual cue if it will help the reader with the sound-spelling relationship. This is not to suggest that the teacher would point to a picture in the reader's text, but rather a picture on a tool such as a sound card to support the spelling-sound relationship.) Point to the letter in the text. Ask, "What sound?," then say, "Blend" (swipe under the word as the student reads).

. . . pronounces short individual phonemes	"Slide through the word" or "Slide through each sound."
	These prompt options are helpful when readers are focused on reading by individual graphemes within a word. Continuous blending, also referred to as *connected phonation*, has been found to be a more effective approach for readers at this stage. By using this practice of stretching out individual sounds—/sssääättt/—readers are less likely to forget the beginning sounds of a word by the time they get to the end of the word (Weisberg & Savard, 1993). This practice also reduces the likelihood of students adding an unintended vowel sound when pronouncing a phoneme (for example, "tuh" for /t/; Gonzalez-Frey & Ehri, 2021). This is a helpful swap for the traditional "sound it out" prompt used by many teachers.
. . . tracks illustrations on the page more than individual words	"Put your eyes on the word."
	This prompts readers to focus on the word during decoding practice, which will reinforce the expectation that the reader should apply word recognition skills.
. . . incorrectly pronounces or has difficulty decoding an unknown word part (inflected ending, prefix, and so on)	"Break the word apart." or
	(Cover the affix / inflected ending) "Read."
	(Uncover the affix / inflected ending) "Read the whole word."
	These options prompt readers to see how they can break words into parts, which is useful as they encounter more complex words. These prompts also support accurate decoding. For follow-up prompts related to meaning, see table 7.2 (page 144).
. . . incorrectly attempts to read a word with an unknown sound-spelling relationship or a phonetically irregular word	"This part of the word spells the /_____/ sound." or
	"This word is _____."
	If readers are attempting to decode a word with a sound-spelling relationship that they have not learned and cannot identify, it is more helpful to explicitly provide the unknown spelling-sound or to provide the entire word than to use the other prompts included in this table that might result in the student guessing.

Visit **go.SolutionTree.com/literacy** *for a free reproducible version of this table.*

Table 7.2 includes prompts for fluency and bridging processes.

TABLE 7.2: Prompts Based on the ABC Reader Profile Framework for Fluency and Bridging Processes

When Reading With Fluency Challenges (or Other Bridging Processes Such as Vocabulary, Morphology, or Print Concepts), the Reader . . .	Teacher Prompt or Cue and Explanation
. . . reads a word but conveys word-meaning confusion (facial expression, verbalization ["huh?"])	"What does that word mean?" This provides students with the first opportunity to share word learning strategies and word knowledge, which helps them to identify themselves and the text as the primary source of information when encountering a vocabulary challenge.
. . . reads a word with an unknown word part (inflected ending, prefix) conveyed by word-meaning confusion (such as pausing, facial expression)	"What do you know about the word parts?" Teachers may consider using physical cues while asking the following questions for individual word parts: • (Cover the affix / inflected ending) "What do you know about this word part?" • (Uncover the affix / inflected ending) "What do you know about this part?" • "What clues can you use from the word parts in this word?" These prompt options are helpful to draw students' attention to morphemes in the unknown word (or word parts that convey meaning).
. . . reads without expression or attending to punctuation	Point. "What does this mean?" "Try it again with the _____." These questions prompt readers to focus on their expression in response to punctuation, which can support their fluency and also aid in comprehension. *Note:* If students are reading word by word, this prompt may not be appropriate for frequent use unless the focus of the small-group lesson is fluency.

*Visit **go.SolutionTree.com/literacy** for a free reproducible version of this table.*

Table 7.3 includes prompts for comprehension, self-monitoring, and metacognition.

TABLE 7.3: Prompts Based on the ABC Reader Profile Framework for Comprehension, Self-Monitoring, and Metacognition

When Reading, the Reader . . .	Teacher Prompt or Cue and Explanation
. . . substitutes a word (or words) and doesn't appear to notice the error	(Extended pause) Rather than providing a correction that interrupts the reader's text reading, wait to see if the reader recognizes that they made an error and self-corrects. If not, you might ask, "Is there anything I can help you with?"
	"Did that make sense?" These questions prompt the reader to consider whether their text reading makes sense, which is helpful to convey that readers should derive meaning from text while reading.
	"Try reading that again." This prompts the reader to reread, which conveys that this strategy can be helpful, and the reader may benefit from learning more about the word and sentence from a subsequent reading.
	(Ignore) If the words students substitute (or possibly even omit) are articles or words that are insignificant to the overall meaning of the text, ignoring the error may provide teachers with opportunities to use other cues to support the reading (rather than prioritizing minor errors in text reading).
. . . reads correctly without any decoding errors with perceived comprehension	"Is there anything I can help you with?" or "How can I support (help) you as a reader with this text?" Asking these questions when students read accurately conveys that sometimes readers have challenges deeply comprehending text, even if they read the words correctly. Additionally, asking this question when students make an error but also when they don't will keep readers from automatically assuming that these teacher prompts mean they made a mistake.
. . . reads correctly without any decoding errors, but comprehension seems to be limited	"Tell me about what you just read." This question offers a risk-free entry point to discuss the readers' comprehension of the text. If an opportunity for increased self-monitoring or comprehension is uncovered, the follow-up question of "How can I support (help) you as a reader with this text?" offers an opportunity to discuss the challenges presented in the text.

Visit **go.SolutionTree.com/literacy** *for a free reproducible version of this table.*

As outlined in the explanations for these recommended responses to readers, the rationale for the various questions, prompts, and cues are as important as the language of the responses themselves. In each case, the intent of the teacher's response is to provide support in the text at hand and to aid students' in internalizing reading strategies for future text reading when words, phrases, or text passages no longer make sense to them. In addition to using these prompts with readers, teachers can create an anchor chart of fix-up strategies that readers can use while reading independently to further support students' internalization of reading strategies.

We don't intend these tables to be exhaustive in terms of how a teacher might respond but rather starting points for teachers to consider as they listen to their students during independent reading opportunities. We encourage teachers to think about which of these reading scenarios best represents their readers' needs and how their typical responses align with the recommended prompts and cues. Are there places where a teacher notices more or less alignment to their usual responses? If so, teachers may want to focus on a few responses that feel new to them and try them out during their instruction with students.

The following is a video snapshot of a lesson that highlights the teacher individually monitoring and responding to readers as they independently read the text *Family Reminders* (Danneberg, 2009). During the reading, the teacher listens to fourth-grade reader Amalie to monitor her reading and determine how to offer support. What do you notice about how the teacher's responses assist Amalie in decoding words with prefixes and making inferences in the text passage?

INTERMEDIATE LESSON: SUPPORTING INDEPENDENT READING

Figure 7.2 is a sample reader observation tool for one of the readers in the video.

Reader: Amalie	**Date:** 5/13
Text Title: Family Reminders	
Text Characteristics: historical fiction novel, limited context offered in chapter 1 for setting, multisyllabic words (common prefixes, suffixes, and inflected endings)	
Decoding	"Unlit"
Fluency and Bridging Processes	Inconsistent phrasing and expression
Comprehension	Unsure if she understands the clues the author provides that something terrible has happened (expression does not yet convey meaning)
Self-Regulation and Metacognition	Not able to articulate where or how she might need help in the text reading (despite decoding errors). Eager to read and interested in fiction topics

FIGURE 7.2: Sample reader observation tool based on the ABC Reader Profile Framework.

Leveraging Observations as Opportunities for Future Instruction

When teachers offer on-the-spot feedback through intentional monitoring and responding, readers have increased awareness of the reading skills that assist them in decoding and making sense of text. This proficiency in responding to students can also have positive impacts on their reading confidence, contributing to a cyclical pattern in which both competence and confidence are strengthened by the other (Lindsey, 2022).

At times, teachers may notice reader challenges and trends that are better addressed outside of the current lesson. For example, if multiple readers fail to attend to nonfiction text features during independent text reading, teachers may choose to plan a subsequent small-group lesson on the mapping and planning of text features. This sets a purpose for reading and can be followed by a discussion about what they learned from the text and how the text features contributed to their learning. In this example, choosing not to address the reader challenge in the lesson where it was observed provides an opportunity to intentionally plan a follow-up lesson with a learning goal aligned directly with student need as evidenced by data.

Alternatively, with the same example, the teacher may already have a future unit planned on the spiraled curriculum standard of nonfiction text features. Knowing this in advance allows the teacher to choose to intentionally wait and address this group's instructional needs during whole-group instruction. At that time, the teacher can carefully monitor individual students during the whole-group lesson to gauge their proficiency and determine if additional small-group lessons would be helpful. In each of these examples, the teacher intentionally refrains from inserting a "teachable moment" into the lesson with the knowledge that other instructional opportunities would allow for more intentional planning and connections to other parts of the literacy block.

Summary

Supporting readers as they engage with text involves a delicate balance of monitoring to provide support and fostering their independence and identities. When readers encounter difficulties such as challenging words, sophisticated text structures, or unfamiliar content, teachers must make strategic decisions to guide students and empower them to employ fix-up strategies. When teachers make targeted observations and intentionally decide how to respond to readers, they empower students to become independent and confident readers who are equipped to navigate a variety of texts effectively.

LAUNCH YOUR REFLECTION

Let's reconnect with Ms. Locke, the teacher we met at the beginning of this chapter (page 138). Now that you've read this chapter, consider the following questions.

- As you reread the challenge Ms. Locke was experiencing, what advice would you offer her on how to respond?
- How can Ms. Locke respond to each student's individual needs within and beyond this lesson?

RECHARGE YOUR SMALL-GROUP READING INSTRUCTION

The following are some questions you can use to apply the chapter concepts to your own classroom context.

- What should I do when a student encounters a word they struggle to read?
- How can I monitor students' text reading progress to guide my instruction?
- What can I listen for to respond to my readers with on-the-spot scaffolds?
- How can I adjust my instruction to respond to students within and beyond a single small-group lesson?

EXPAND YOUR TOOLBOX

To continue your learning, see the "Leading the Learning Action Guide" (page 201) to support you and your colleagues. In the action guide for this chapter, you'll find in-action videos that spotlight teaching strategies as well as differentiated professional learning activities you can try out with your team. Additional tools that support this chapter topic can be accessed online (visit **go.SolutionTree.com/literacy**).

CHAPTER 8
HOW DOES WRITING CONNECT TO MY SMALL-GROUP INSTRUCTION?

Literacy instruction includes opportunities for writing development through explicit instruction and purposeful tasks. Teachers can plan explicit, consistent writing opportunities into their small-group instruction. This instruction includes supporting early readers to develop encoding skills that equip them to build word knowledge and communicate their thinking. Extending writing tasks beyond small-group instruction for collaborative and independent practice also strengthens students' literacy skills. This chapter provides concrete ways teachers can integrate writing opportunities both within small-group instruction and as extensions beyond lessons.

As you read this chapter, consider your own perceptions of integrating writing during and after your small-group lessons. The following questions can frame your thinking as you read.

- What are some ways I make time for daily writing?
- How does the content of my small group serve as a springboard to writing for a variety of purposes?

Consider the following example of Mr. James.

MEET THE TEACHER: MR. JAMES

> Mr. James teaches fourth-grade English language arts. He has found a lot of success in ensuring that his planning time reflects both reading and writing. What he has found is that his students would benefit from daily writing practice to support their writing fluency and application of writing strategies on a more consistent basis. He wonders how he can extend the work done in small groups to include writing when finding time can be a challenge. He also wonders how to ensure that the writing tasks are authentic and provide opportunities to apply what they have learned.

Do Mr. James's reflections resonate with you? Have you identified strategies to overcome any of the challenges that he's shared? What strategies would help Mr. James integrate reading and writing instruction? How can small-group instruction serve as a scaffold for daily writing practice opportunities?

We revisit these ideas and questions at the end of the chapter to identify and plan for knowledge-building strategies you may want to try with your own students.

The Reading and Writing Connection

You may be wondering why a book on small-group reading instruction includes a chapter on writing. We understand that many schools teach reading and writing as separate subjects. However, we believe reading and writing draw on shared knowledge funds, as shown in figure 8.1. When integrated, the reciprocity between both literacy processes allows for deeper understanding of each. Writing contributes to students' growth as readers in both reading comprehension and foundational skills.

Reading	Writing
Phonological awareness	Rhyming, alliteration
Alphabetic principle	Letter formation
Phonics knowledge	Understanding of spelling and relationship of graphemes and phonemes
Decoding	Spelling, encoding, orthographic mapping
High-frequency words	Orthographic mapping
Print concepts	Directionality, spacing, punctuation
Reading fluency	Attention to punctuation and fluency in writing to communicate ideas
Vocabulary	Word choice

Morphological knowledge	Word choice
Graphophonological-semantic cognitive flexibility	Orthographic mapping, word choice
Cultural and other knowledge	Discipline-specific writing, narrative writing, memoirs
Reading-specific background knowledge	Text structure, transition words, text type (narrative, expository, argumentative), genre, point of view, purpose, cohesiveness, elaboration, summarizing
Verbal reasoning	Creating mood, tone, theme, characterization, tensions, literary devices
Language structure	Syntax, grammar, punctuation, sentence and paragraph structure, sentence elaboration
Theory of mind	Point of view
Motivation and engagement	Motivation and engagement
Executive function skills	Goal setting, planning, organizing, drafting, revising
Strategy use	Awareness of task, audience, and purpose

Source: Duke & Cartwright, 2021.

FIGURE 8.1: Relationship between reading and writing.

In this chapter, we frame the discussion for writing instruction to align with four recommendations from the What Works Clearinghouse (WWC) Educator's Practice Guide *Teaching Elementary School Students to Be Effective Writers* (Graham et al., 2012), shown in figure 8.2. These recommendations emphasize that instructional decisions in writing are made as a result of the instruction students receive while in a small-group reading lesson. Note that we make connections to these recommendations throughout this chapter by specifying the associated WWC recommendation number.

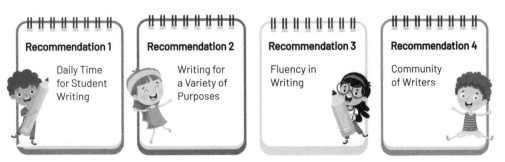

Source: Graham et al., 2012.

FIGURE 8.2: Recommendations for teaching elementary students to be effective writers.

Writing Instruction in Small-Group Lessons

In an article for *Education Week*, author and practitioner Wiley Blevins states his belief that writing should be integrated into every reading lesson, even in the earliest grades (Sawchuk, 2023). A research advisory by the International Literacy Association (2020) confirms the importance of connecting reading and writing instruction: "Writing and the teaching of writing enhance not only students' comprehension and fluency when reading but also their recognition and decoding of words in text" (p. 2).

Small-group reading provides an opportunity to integrate and connect authentic writing tasks, even when reading-based learning goals serve as the primary instructional focus. For example, when readers practice encoding words based on learned spelling-sound relationships, they are developing skills to support writing fluency (WWC recommendation 3) while building confidence they can apply to daily extended writing opportunities in the literacy block (WWC recommendation 1). Readers can write responses to reading tasks to enhance comprehension and build knowledge as well as use text as a springboard for writing for varied purposes and audiences through both independent and collaborative writing tasks (WWC recommendation 2). Authentic connections between reading and writing support community-building for readers and writers through shared experiences that promote a literacy-rich environment (WWC recommendation 4). With intentional opportunities for reading and writing integration, readers become adept at decoding, understanding individual words, and comprehending text (Graham et al., 2018).

Writing to Support Word Recognition

Recommendation 2 of the WWC report emphasizes that students need to be writing for a variety of purposes. Encoding is included as part of an effective structured literacy routine and is used in tandem with decoding practice to support word recognition skills. Encoding assists students in acquiring and applying letter-sound correspondence and decoding. Let's revisit the instructional routines shared in chapter 4 (page 65) to review the ways teachers can include writing to extend student learning as it relates to the reading learning goal (see figure 8.3).

The encoding piece of the lesson in figure 8.3 is directly related to the target sound-spelling focus within the lesson. Through the opportunity to immediately apply learning within the context of writing, readers gain a strong sense of the sound-spelling relationship and build toward their automaticity with letter patterns.

Routine for Introducing Sound-Spelling Relationships	
Provide a Phonemic Awareness Warm-Up	Determine a phonemic awareness skill based on curriculum scope and sequence (or reader data if scope and sequence are not available). This example demonstrates blending phonemes in CVC words. Prompt students to listen to each sound and blend them together to make a word: "/s/ /ĭ/ /p/ . . . blend." Pause for readers' choral response. Repeat with six to eight words.
Review Sounds and Spellings	Review previously learned sound-spellings (this may include sound cards that show the recently learned spellings).
Introduce Sound-Spelling Relationships	1. Show the spelling. (Consider using a sound card.) 2. "This is one way to spell [sound]. Say [sound]." 3. "[Spelling] spells [sound]. Repeat after me." 4. Show the spelling sounds in several words. If there are any relevant spelling rules, share those with students. If there are other ways to spell this sound that students already know, discuss them together. Review examples (which may include sound cards on a sound wall).
Have Students Decode	Prompt students to decode eight words (at least half should have the target sound-spelling from the current lesson and the others may include review). Prompting should include students saying each sound and blending the sounds back together.
Have Students Encode	Prompt students to spell eight words (at least half should have the target sound-spelling from the current lesson and the others may include review). Prompting should include students saying each sound as they spell each part of the word.
Connect to Literacy Tasks	Remind readers they should use these skills during reading and writing tasks. If students are about to engage in an extended practice opportunity where they will need to read or write, make a direct connection to the activity.
Conclude Routine	Show the spelling. Prompt readers to tell a partner what sound the spelling represents.

Source: Adapted from Fien et al., 2015, as cited in Lindsey, 2022.

FIGURE 8.3: Routine for sound-spelling relationships.

Encoding also supports readers in identifying irregular and regular high-frequency words. Orthographic mapping, which links spelling, phonology, and meaning, is a powerful process for helping students retrieve words from their working memory (Ehri, 2014). A simple routine that incorporates orthographic mapping is the *read, spell, read routine*: The teacher displays a high-frequency word for students, and they then read the word, spell the word, and read the word again. To learn more about orthographic mapping, see chapter 4 (page 65).

The following video shows encoding within a small-group lesson. As you view the lesson, consider how the teacher might have selected the focus for the guided spelling.

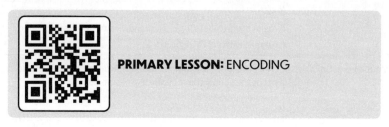

PRIMARY LESSON: ENCODING

Writing Samples for Understanding Word Recognition Skills

In addition to helping readers develop foundational skills, writing provides another data point for teachers to learn about their readers. The way students write provides insight into their understanding of sound-spelling relationships. Teachers can evaluate which sound-spelling relationships students have and have not mastered. The following samples illustrate a primary student's writing for a variety of audiences and purposes. In the following section, we share how informal writing samples can be used to understand Luke, who is in kindergarten, as a reader.

The first writing sample (figure 8.4) is from a spelling inventory. A spelling inventory is a window into a reader's control of phonics patterns. In this example, the phonics patterns Luke mastered are visible. The student word list is mud, nap, set, fog, rib, life, shack, and stone. The errors Luke made when writing some of the words demonstrate what skills he attempted and which he confused. Luke wrote four of the five words with short vowel sounds correctly. However, he wrote the two words with long vowel sounds the same way as the short vowel pattern.

Source: © 2024 by Luke. Used with permission.

FIGURE 8.4: Writing sample of a student word list.

The second writing sample (figure 8.5) shares a story Luke wrote using a laptop computer. While he was writing, the computer autocorrected the word *raccoon*. He spelled the remaining words by sound. During the writing process, the teacher

CHAPTER 8: How Does Writing Connect to My Small-Group Instruction?   155

helped Luke find the *caps lock* button for capitalization (when he asked) and where to locate the *period* button. At the word level, similar to the spelling inventory, the patterns Luke mastered are confirmed. This writing example provides insight into Luke's application of the high-frequency words *and* and *with*. However, Luke still hasn't mastered long vowel patterns, as evidenced in the example. The text is intended to read, "Luke and a dog and a raccoon eating a quesadilla. And a cat with a bison." Luke attempted to spell *eating* as *eden*.

> Luke And a dog and a raccoon Eden a casuda.
> And a cat with a bisin.

Source: © 2024 by Luke. Used with permission.

FIGURE 8.5: Writing sample of a writer-generated narrative story.

The final writing sample (figure 8.6) is a piece that Luke wrote out of frustration about a babysitter. The teacher didn't provide any assistance during writing. When reviewing these writing samples, it becomes evident how important it is to consider more than one data source to identify strengths and opportunities for growth. The text is intended to read, "You are the worst babysitter." The third writing sample offers another window into Luke's word recognition skills.

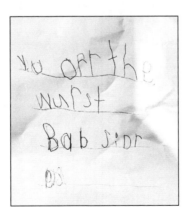

Source: © 2024 by Luke. Used with permission.

FIGURE 8.6: Writing sample of a writer-generated note.

Let's reflect using the ABC Reader Profile Framework. What are some of Luke's strengths and growth opportunities regarding his word recognition? Our interpretation of Luke's ABC Reader Profile is provided in figure 8.7 (page 156). In the same way we have used the framework previously, the teacher not only indicated Luke's asset-based strengths but considered grade-level expectations in alignment with state curriculum standards to determine his personal reading goals.

156 SMALL GROUPS FOR BIG READERS

Decoding

	Pre-Alphabetic	Partial Alphabetic	Full Alphabetic	Consolidated Alphabetic	Automatic
	☐ Readers use cues such as pictures, context cues, and guessing strategies. ☐ Readers notice semantic rather than phonological relationships. ☐ Readers' connections are more arbitrary than systematic.	☐ Readers use emerging grapheme-phoneme connections, such as the first letter sound. ☐ Readers' connections are incomplete, and they use known phonetic cues to guide their decoding attempts.	☑ Readers attend to every letter in every word as they convert graphemes into phonological representations. ☑ Readers have working knowledge of most letter-sound correspondences and decode sequentially, though slowly.	☐ Readers use chunks to decode. They recognize multiletter patterns instantly (such as consonant blends, vowel teams, affixes, and so on) and use syllables and morphemes as chunks to support decoding. ☐ Readers teach themselves new connections as orthographic mapping further develops.	☐ Readers quickly and effortlessly decode, and most words are sight words. ☐ Readers use decoding processes that are highly automatic when they encounter unknown words. ☐ Readers have a variety of strategies at their disposal, especially when reading technical words.

Reader Goals:
Short vowel patterns mastered; long vowel patterns not yet mastered. High-frequency words: like, and, with. Met year-end goal: emerging grapheme-phoneme connections and phonetic cues. Future goal is to use chunks, such as multiletter patterns, to support decoding.

Fluency and Bridging Processes

	Word by Word	Local Grouping	Phrase and Clause	Sentence Prosody	Passage Expression
	☑ Readers focus on individual words or sounds. ☑ Less than one-quarter of the words are read aloud with appropriate expression.	☐ Readers focus on local word groups and may be mostly arrhythmic or monotone. ☐ More than one-quarter and less than one-half of words are read aloud with appropriate expression.	☐ Readers express the structure or meaning of words, phrases, clauses, and a few sentences. Intonation may reinforce rhythmic grouping, or reading may be monotone. ☐ More than half of the words are read aloud with appropriate expression.	☐ Readers express text, sentence structure, and meaning. ☐ Readers may be inconsistent but not monotone. Reading rate is at least fifty-five words per minute. ☐ More than three-quarters of the words are read aloud with appropriate expression.	☐ Readers convey elements as if reading for a listener and are expressive throughout. ☐ Readers consistently express the structure and meaning of sentences, paragraphs, and passages. Their reading rate is at least eighty words per minute.

Additional bridging processes to consider along this continuum include concepts of print, vocabulary knowledge, morphological awareness, and graphophonological-semantic cognitive flexibility.

Reader Goals:
On target for grade-level expectations. Future goals are local word groups and reading some words with expression.

CHAPTER 8: How Does Writing Connect to My Small-Group Instruction? | 157

Comprehension

Literal Comprehension	Inferential Comprehension	Evaluative Comprehension	Reorganization Comprehension	Appreciative Comprehension
☑ Readers understand a text, including facts, ideas, vocabulary, events, and stated information. ☑ Readers can provide direct and explicit answers to questions extracted from a text.	☑ Readers make valid inferences from the information found in text. ☑ Readers understand the facts, even if they aren't explicitly stated in the reading material. ☐ Inferences made include generalizations, comparisons, assumptions, predictions, and so on.	☐ Readers analyze an author's intent, opinion, language, and style of text presentation. ☐ Readers evaluate the appropriateness of an author's devices and then make inferences based on the fact or idea implied in text.	☐ Readers use information gained from various parts of the text and rearrange it into new patterns that integrate the information into an idea for further understanding. ☐ Readers apply creativity or curiosity as they analyze, digest, and evaluate the text to identify a unique view of a situation or event.	☐ Readers recognize the purpose, perspective, and philosophy of the author by understanding the deeper meaning of the text. ☐ Readers reflect and respond emotionally to the text while making connections. This requires a literal and inferential understanding, which is then used to evaluate and reflect.

Reader Goals:
Understands ideas presented directly; makes limited inferences. Future goal is to broaden inferences made to include comparisons, assumptions, and predictions.

Self-Regulation and Metacognition

Initial Awareness and Control	Emerging Awareness and Control	Developing Awareness and Control	Skilled Awareness and Control	Independent Awareness and Control
☑ Readers begin reading a text at the first word, paragraph, or page. ☑ Readers read slowly and carefully for all texts and purposes. ☑ Readers think about their understanding of text during or after reading.	☐ Readers think about what they know before they read. ☐ Readers slow down and pay closer attention to text when it becomes difficult. ☐ Readers employ a strategy to think about texts as they read (such as summarizing, visualizing, or asking questions).	☐ Readers preview the text before reading to anticipate content and determine a purpose for reading. ☐ Readers stop to think about what they're reading from time to time, regardless of text difficulty. ☐ Readers employ multiple strategies to think about text as they read (such as summarizing, visualizing, or asking questions).	☐ Readers preview the text before reading to anticipate content while noting the text's organization and structure to support their purpose for reading. ☐ Readers adjust reading speed to try to get back on track if they lose concentration or to deepen understanding. ☐ Readers employ multiple strategies to think about their reading (such as summarizing, visualizing, or asking questions) and seek opportunities to discuss their reading with others to check for understanding.	☐ Readers preview the text before reading by noting its organization and structure and making inferences about how to prioritize content in alignment with reading purpose. ☐ Readers adjust rate, reread, and refocus flexibly according to text, purpose, and difficulty. ☐ Readers flexibly employ multiple strategies to think about their reading (such as summarizing, visualizing, or asking questions), seek opportunities to discuss their understanding, and use additional resources to connect, repair, or extend their learning.

Reader Goals:
Thinks about reading during and after reading. Future goals are to think about the content of the text prior to reading, and gain a variety of strategies (visualization, summarization, and asking questions) to support understanding.

Source: Ebri, 1995; Lastiri, 2022; Mokhtari & Reichard, 2002; White et al., 2021.

FIGURE 8.7: Sample ABC Reader Profile for Luke.

Writing to Enhance Reading Comprehension

Researchers Steve Graham and Michael Hebert (2010) conducted a meta-analysis that included student writing samples. Students in this study wrote about text they read. Graham and Hebert (2010) analyzed more than one hundred studies, and they found that writing for many different purposes and in a variety of formats improved reading comprehension and learning. The ILA (2020) highlighted the benefits that writing provides for reading comprehension and retention. Writing can deepen students' comprehension of text through the following.

- Fostering explicitness and literal comprehension
- Promoting synthesis and integration of information
- Creating a personal response and reaction to the text
- Encouraging unique thoughts about text
- Facilitating new understandings and connections

Writing Opportunities in and Beyond the Small-Group Lesson

During small-group lessons designed to address comprehension-based learning goals, teachers should allocate instructional time for rich discussion of text that supports readers' deep thinking about text content. As readers summarize or synthesize their reading, gaining a stronger understanding of devices authors use is critical. Readers grow when they are able to apply their literal and inferential knowledge to reflect and respond to text. Readers' perspective of the text can be used to develop their own writing ability. Readers' use of strategies to make sense of their reading—such as goal setting, questioning, visualizing, predicting, and analyzing—also strengthens their writing skills. Offering opportunities within and beyond the small-group lessons provides continued time to write for a variety of purposes and more occasions for daily writing time (WWC recommendations 1 and 2).

Readers can engage in the following writing activities to support their comprehension of text (ILA, 2020).

- Provide written responses to text-dependent questions
- Make personal connections to the text excerpts provided
- Take notes to capture the main ideas and relevant details
- Summarize the text in their own words
- Create a story based on the text they read
- Apply their learning from a text through written expression
- Make a claim regarding the ideas presented in the text
- Respond to the text to build content-specific knowledge
- Write with the focus on building vocabulary

Time may be limited during small-group lessons, so incorporating writing tasks may not always seem possible. However, we encourage teachers to think about how activities like these can be connected to and introduced within text discussions in a small-group lesson and then completed during extended practice opportunities outside of the lesson. Students can complete extended practice opportunities independently or collaboratively. These extended writing opportunities provide a natural supplement to small-group instruction. To learn more about developing extended practice opportunities, see chapter 10 (page 179).

Let's revisit another instructional routine shared in chapter 4 (page 65), shown again here in figure 8.8. Writing opportunities can be linked to comprehension and text-based discussions. Consider how writing could be included in the instructional routine to extend student learning as it relates to the reading learning goal.

	Routine for Comprehension Instruction
Warm Up With Word Study	Introduce and teach how to read and write multisyllabic words. Teach any prefixes or suffixes, if applicable, to promote morphological awareness.
Prepare Readers for Text Reading	Set a purpose for reading. Activate prior knowledge and introduce three to five key vocabulary words. Make a prediction. Demonstrate and explain any strategies or skills for this lesson (if applicable).
Monitor Readers During Text Reading	Monitor students and offer feedback (questions, prompts, or cues) to support readers to fix their mistakes. If students are orally reading, gradually shift to all silent reading. Identify stopping places to check for meaning. Use think-alouds or questioning to monitor progress and model thinking.
Discuss Text Reading	Discuss text and reconnect to the purpose for reading. Some of the following suggestions can be used for text discussion or extended to collaborative or independent practice. • Check predictions. • Discuss what students learned and understood. • Clarify any points of confusion. • Retell or summarize the text. • Ask or answer comprehension questions using evidence from the text to support responses. • Make inferences. • Practice and revisit vocabulary. • Finish any graphic organizers.
Conclude Routine and Connect to Literacy Task	Prompt readers to use their thinking as readers that day when they read other texts on their own.

FIGURE 8.8: Routine for comprehension instruction.

The *discuss text reading* part of the lesson in figure 8.8 (page 159) provides opportunities for readers to share their comprehension of the text and reconnect to their purpose for reading. Teachers can pair each of these suggestions with a writing-in-response-to-text task to extend students' learning beyond the small-group lesson. For example, readers can make inferences and record evidence from the text to support their inferences using a graphic organizer. In this way, readers use their writing to extend their reading comprehension.

In figure 8.9, we provide an additional example to highlight a writing activity to simultaneously support students' comprehension and writing development. The following example exemplifies the continuum of the reading and writing integration process that begins in whole-group instruction, moves to standards-aligned small-group instruction, and ends with extended practice. To learn more about connecting whole-group and small-group content, revisit chapter 3 (page 49). Figure 8.9 highlights the alignment between instructional contexts and provides an example of a connected reading and writing task.

Whole-Group Instructional Focus: Explore how the text features in an informational text help to contribute to the meaning of the text.

Small-Group Reading Text: "Jellyfish Take Over!" (ReadWorks, n.d.)

Small-Group Reading Task: Explore how the text features in the jellyfish text help to contribute to the meaning of the text.

Writing (Extended Practice Opportunity): Reader self-selection of topic for RAFT (Role, Audience, Format, Topic)

Role: Zoologist

Audience: Zoo visitors

Format: Poster using text features

Topic: Zoo animal

Students will use the RAFT strategy to create a poster providing information about a zoo animal of their choice. The poster must include text features that organize the facts on their chosen zoo animal. Students are required to include at least three text features from the ones they have explored during whole-group texts and small-group texts.

Curriculum Benchmark: Explain how text features—including titles, headings, captions, graphs, maps, glossaries, and illustrations—contribute to the meaning of texts.

FIGURE 8.9: Example of a connected reading and writing task.

The example in figure 8.9 showcases a number of important benefits of integrating reading and writing tasks, including the following.

- The instructional focus aligned in whole group instruction and the extended practice opportunity.
- The mentor text illustrated how an author uses text features to organize and communicate their message.
- The reading task, conducted in small group, met the expectations and rigor of the standards through the support and guidance of the teacher.

- The writing task was an extended practice opportunity for students to apply connecting reading and writing to create their own piece by utilizing the same writing tools (text features) to communicate their learning about their chosen animal.
- Students worked collaboratively to create the poster, which facilitated a community of writers.
- Students built knowledge by extending the topic to other texts and literacy tasks.
- Students used discipline-specific language and vocabulary in their writing.
- Students were motivated and engaged because they selected the topic, collaborated with peers, worked with cohesive text sets, and interacted with mentor texts.

Writing Samples for Understanding Your Readers' Comprehension

In addition to extending opportunities for text comprehension, writing tasks also offer formative assessment data that teachers can use to determine future learning goals for students. The following samples illustrate how two students used writing to communicate their understanding of nonfiction text. In the following section, we explore how teachers can use these writing tasks to determine instructional opportunities for their small-group lessons.

In the first example, second grader Kamara was prompted to identify the central idea and two relevant details of a nonfiction text about volcanoes (figure 8.10, page 162). This was an open-ended writing task that was directly related to a skill reflected in grade-level standards: identifying the central idea and supporting details. Analyzing both the text and Kamara's response (included as a series of images in figure 8.11, page 162), it is evident that Kamara determined the central idea is that volcanoes cause many changes to the earth. When analyzing Kamara's two relevant details, you can see that only one directly supports the central idea: "Volcanoes can build new islands and mountains." The second relevant detail—"Volcanoes erupt and ash fills the air"—describes a detail she found on the previous page of text. Although there may be a logical leap to support the response that volcanic eruptions can cause changes to the earth, this detail is not directly relevant to the requested task.

This observation and analysis of student writing may warrant a follow-up lesson to teach the difference between relevant details and general facts presented in the text. Additionally, it is common for readers to identify details that they find interesting, which may not necessarily be relevant to the central idea. Kamara's written response provides an opportunity for her teacher to probe deeply and discuss the nuances of how authors present details in nonfiction text.

Volcanic ash is more than just a fine dust—it's a potent mixture of rock, minerals, and glass particles that erupts from volcanoes during volcanic events. Let's explore this fascinating phenomenon!

What Is Volcanic Ash?

Volcanic ash is tiny pieces of rock and glass that come out of a volcano when it erupts. It's not like the ash from a fire, but more like very fine sand. When a volcano erupts, it shoots this ash high into the sky, and it can travel far away from the volcano. Volcanic ash can cover the ground, buildings, and even cars!

Pompeii: An Example From the Past

Pompeii was a city in ancient Rome. A long time ago, a volcano called Mount Vesuvius erupted near Pompeii. The volcanic ash from the eruption covered the whole city. The people and buildings were buried under the ash for many years. Today, scientists and archaeologists have dug up Pompeii to learn more about how people lived a long time ago. The ash helped preserve the city, so we can see what it looked like back then.

Source: OpenAI, 2024e, 2024f, 2024g.

FIGURE 8.10: Identifying the central idea—Text excerpt.

Central Idea
The central idea of the text is volcanoes cause many changes to earth.

Volcanoes can build new islands and mountains.

Volcanoes erupt and ash fills the air.

Source: © 2024 by Kamara. Used with permission.

FIGURE 8.11: Student writing sample for identifying the central idea.

In the second example, another second grader, Ramiro, was prompted to read a nonfiction text about games from around the world. This example provides another lens in which to analyze student comprehension. Unlike the Kamara example, this task helps to capture a student's understanding of the target skill. After reading the text, he was given opportunities to write about his comprehension. (The text excerpt is shown in figure 8.12, page 164, and Ramiro's written response is shown in figure 8.13, page 164.) The prompt was anchored in the following curriculum benchmarks: (1) Explain how text features—including titles, headings, captions, graphs, maps, glossaries, or illustrations—contribute to the meaning of texts and (2) explain an author's purpose in an informational text. Ramiro was prompted to explain why the author added photographs to the text and why the author used the same colors for the headings and captions as they did for the countries on the map.

These prompts personify the author in a helpful way to position readers to think about the author's purpose for using text features, which links both curriculum benchmarks. In Ramiro's responses, he offered descriptions of the text that explained the author's use of text features. He was asked to not only identify the text feature but explain how it helped him learn more about the content he read. This process tapped into Ramiro's ability to transfer his understanding of text features to other texts.

In each response, you may wonder if Ramiro can articulate how and why the description of the author's use of text features is helpful to the reader. Ramiro stated that the colors for the headings, captions, and countries on the map are the same "so you could match them up." But he does not explain why matching them up is helpful, how it contributes to the meaning of the text, or how it supports the author's purpose of informing the reader in informational text. At the same time, you may notice that Ramiro filled every line with his response but did not save space to explain how the author used text features and why they were helpful. In this case, additional space for written response could offer more information about Ramiro's ability to elaborate on the author's use of text features. This scenario highlights both an example of identifying next steps for instruction and how teachers should consider implicit ways to convey expectations for student writing, such as through the amount of writing space they provide.

When it comes to analyzing reading comprehension, writing provides an opportunity to capture authentic student thinking. Students' ability to articulate their understanding and support their thinking through writing is a unique window into their comprehension.

Chile

While watching the game *Corre, Corre la Guaraca*, one sees children sitting in a circle, singing a song, while one child runs around the outside with a handkerchief. The goal is to drop the handkerchief behind someone without them noticing.

Nigeria

Ayoayo is a strategy board game where players strategically distribute seeds in carved holes, aiming to capture more seeds than their opponent. It's a game of skill and calculation, often reflecting the rich cultural heritage of the region.

Japan

Ayatori is the Japanese version of the string game known as *cat's cradle*. Children use a loop of string to form intricate patterns, passing the evolving shape back and forth between their fingers.

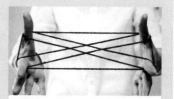

How to hold the string when playing *Ayatori*.

Source: OpenAI, 2024h.

FIGURE 8.12: Informational text about games from around the world.

1. What can you learn from the title?
   I can learn that there are lots of different games for kids around the world.
2. How do the headings help you understand the text?
   They can help me find infmation about the different games.
3. Find a map in the text. What does it show you?
   It shows the world. I see a compass rose directions NSEW Ghana Australia
4. Find a caption. What can you learn from it?
   The boys [indecipherable] are playing [indecipherable] the children in Australia are playing stuck in
5. Why did the author add photographs to the text?
   The photographs help you see how they play and what they look like
6. Why do you think the author used the same colors for the headings and captions as he did for the countries on the map?
   He used the same colors so you could match them up.

Source: © 2024 by Ramiro. Used with permission.

FIGURE 8.13: Student writing sample of how text features contribute to meaning and the author's purpose.

Summary

The integration of reading and writing instruction is strongly rooted in research. According to the ILA, "When reading and writing receive equal emphasis in literacy instruction, students become better readers and writers" (International Literacy Association, 2020). Teachers often face the challenge of limited time. The integration of reading and writing alleviates the demands of limited time and, more importantly, strengthens students' development in both areas. Reading and writing share many common processes, support students' acquisition of foundational skills, and deepen their comprehension. Extended practice opportunities that incorporate writing are a natural supplement to the small-group reading lesson and strengthen readers' engagement with text.

LAUNCH YOUR REFLECTION

Let's reconnect with Mr. James, who we met at the start of the chapter (page 150). Now that you've read this chapter, consider the following questions.

- Have you identified strategies to overcome any of the challenges that he shared?
- What strategies would help Mr. James integrate writing instruction?

RECHARGE YOUR SMALL-GROUP READING INSTRUCTION

The following are some questions you can use to apply the chapter concepts to your own classroom context.

- What are some ways I make time for daily writing?
- How does the content of my small group serve as a springboard for writing for a variety of purposes?
- How can small-group instruction serve as a scaffold for daily writing practice opportunities?

EXPAND YOUR TOOLBOX

To continue your learning, see the "Leading the Learning Action Guide" (page 201) to support you and your colleagues. In the action guide for this chapter, you'll find in-action videos that spotlight teaching strategies as well as differentiated professional learning activities you can try out with your team. Additional tools that support this chapter topic can be accessed online (visit **go.SolutionTree.com/literacy**).

CHAPTER 9
HOW DO I BUILD MY READERS' KNOWLEDGE?

Building knowledge is an essential condition for reading comprehension. Knowledge of a variety of topics facilitates understanding of text and promotes the retention of information. Interdisciplinary connections are aided by instruction that is grounded in knowledge building. According to Fisher and Frey (2022), "Elevating knowledge as an essential component of literacy instruction requires acknowledgment about the centrality of using an asset-based approach to learning" (p. 29). Small-group instruction affords the opportunity to build on a student's background knowledge using rich, high-quality texts and resources to plan instruction that focuses on both literacy and knowledge building.

As you read this chapter, consider your own perceptions of building knowledge during small-group lessons. The following questions can help frame your thinking as you read.

- What is the role of knowledge building in a small-group lesson, and how do I ensure access to the text for all students, including those who are building foundational skills?
- What are some examples of knowledge-building practices that I could incorporate into my small-group lessons?

Consider the following example of Mr. Duncan.

MEET THE TEACHER: MR. DUNCAN

> Mr. Duncan has been teaching for three years and understands that small groups offer an opportunity for students to deepen their content knowledge on a variety of topics. Each week, as he plans for small-group instruction, he tries to make knowledge building a focus. Specifically, he wants to ensure that all students have an opportunity to explore and learn about unfamiliar topics, expand on what they already know, and clarify misconceptions. But as Mr. Duncan begins to plan, he wonders how he can meet this goal for all readers, including those who are building foundational skills, using a common text.

Do Mr. Duncan's reflections resonate with you? Have you identified strategies to overcome any of the challenges that he shared?

We will revisit these ideas and questions at the end of the chapter to identify and plan for knowledge-building strategies that you want to try with your own students.

The Role of Knowledge Building in Literacy Instruction

Ana, one of the authors of this book, remembers a conversation she had with a colleague when she was a new teacher. During this conversation, she expressed her frustration with some of her students. Her frustration stemmed from her perception that students' lack of background knowledge contributed to why they struggled with reading comprehension. This conversation took place years ago, yet the response remains a vivid memory. Her colleague responded, "They have background knowledge. It may not be your background knowledge, but they have background knowledge." This conversation significantly shifted her thinking about the role of background knowledge. As educators, it is our responsibility to think about knowledge more broadly and shift our focus to building knowledge from an asset-based approach.

We are aware of the important role the word *recognition* (phonemic awareness, decoding, sight words, and so on) plays in developing skilled readers. Alongside word recognition, we also understand how language comprehension, working in tandem with word recognition, contributes to skilled, proficient reading. But what is the role of knowledge in reading comprehension? According to Gina N. Cervetti, Tanya S. Wright, and HyeJin Hwang (2016), knowledge and reading comprehension are intertwined. Knowledge allows students to have deeper comprehension and supports them as they learn while they read.

But how exactly do we define knowledge? The types of knowledge represented in table 9.1 include background knowledge, domain knowledge, cultural knowledge, and affective knowledge. Background knowledge can be further categorized into three subcategories: (1) episodic, (2) declarative, and (3) procedural.

TABLE 9.1: Types of Knowledge

Type of Knowledge	What It Is	What It Looks Like
Background knowledge	Episodic: related to events	Impact of weather on communities
	Declarative: facts associated with a topic	Timeline of key events in history
	Procedural: how to perform a specific task	Use of a budget for saving, spending, and managing income
Domain knowledge	Knowledge specific to a content area	Use of map elements (title, compass rose, cardinal directions, intermediate directions, symbols, legend, scale, longitude, latitude)
Cultural knowledge	Knowledge of the characteristics, history, values, beliefs, and behaviors of another ethnic or cultural group	Ability to explain the motivations, beliefs, and history of Cuban immigrants in Florida in the 1960s, and how they are similar to or different from Cuban immigrants in the 1980s
Affective knowledge	Knowledge of the mental states of others	Connections to the challenges experienced by immigrants in a new country

Knowledge provides a frame to help us organize incoming information and guides us through the process of reading text. Natalie Wexler described knowledge as Velcro: As we learn new information, existing knowledge serves as Velcro, adhering the new knowledge to what we already know (Loftus & Sappington, 2023). A schema allows the reader to move to more inferential thinking, have deeper connections with content and characters, and make connections across texts (Loftus & Sappington, 2023). As the reader's depth of knowledge grows, it provides access to other text, which in turn allows for more equitable learning and instruction.

In the following pages, we provide examples of each knowledge type with authentic texts.

BACKGROUND KNOWLEDGE

Episodic knowledge, a type of background knowledge, is related to events that the reader has experienced. If a reader with episodic knowledge reads the book *Hurricane* by David Wiesner (1990), they are more likely to infer how the characters, David and George, feel while they are sheltering from the storm. They would also be familiar with words or concepts such as spaghetti models, wind gusts, and storm surges, or the nuances between a tropical depression, tropical storm, and the various categories of hurricanes. *Declarative knowledge* refers to the facts associated with a topic. With the hurricane example, readers who have background knowledge on hurricanes would know facts such as hurricanes have an eye, hurricanes form in the ocean, hurricanes can be tracked, and hurricanes are given names. *Procedural knowledge* allows the reader to understand steps in hurricane preparedness, such as boarding up the house, setting up sandbags, or ensuring nonperishable items are available during and after the storm. This type of knowledge also helps readers make inferences about why those procedures must take place, and it works in tandem with episodic knowledge. A reader's prior experience with the events of a hurricane and the process to prepare for it help them connect why having nonperishable food is critical for surviving a hurricane.

DOMAIN KNOWLEDGE

Domain knowledge is specific to a content area and may consist of elements of background knowledge. This type of knowledge is critical to success in school. What differentiates domain knowledge from background knowledge is that background knowledge is grounded in personal experiences that are influenced by episodic, declarative, and procedural knowledge. Domain knowledge is associated with topics, concepts, and vocabulary in a subject and is agnostic of personal experience. Examples of domain knowledge may include the Great Depression, Leonardo da Vinci's impact during the Renaissance period, or photosynthesis. In these examples, the reader's domain knowledge is not tied to personal experiences but is derived from their prior learning through various types of texts, previous lessons, or visits to museums. Domain knowledge includes highly specialized concepts and vocabulary categorized as *Tier 3 words* (Beck, McKeown, & Kucan, 2002). For example, a student reading a text about space exploration will understand the text better if they know the words *astronaut* and *orbit*. The benefits of domain knowledge are uniquely tied to the subjects associated with that particular content area or discipline.

CULTURAL KNOWLEDGE

Cultural knowledge means that the reader knows about certain cultural characteristics, contexts, values, symbols, beliefs, and behaviors of their own cultural group or that of another. Having cultural knowledge also includes understanding a culture's norms or system of rules that determine acceptable behavior within the group. For example, knowing a group's values can help a reader understand a character's or historical figure's motivation or approach to conflict. This knowledge allows the reader to view actions and decisions with less bias or judgment.

AFFECTIVE KNOWLEDGE

In psychology, *theory of mind* is an important social-cognitive skill that involves the ability to think about mental states, both your own and those of others (Cherry, 2023). *Affective knowledge* is related to theory of mind. Studies have shown the important role that theory of mind has on reader comprehension (Dore, Amendum, Michnick Golinkoff, & Hirsh-Pasek, 2018). A reader's ability to tap into their emotions while experiencing text is only achieved when they have knowledge similar to what the character or group of people are experiencing. Therefore, a reader's ability to think about the mental states of others allows them to make connections when authors describe events, characters, or situations with the intent to stir an emotional response. This type of knowledge is more commonly used in fiction, when readers are expected to make text-to-self connections with the characters, thus helping them understand a character's feelings and motives—but it can also be important when reading informational text. A reader who can empathize with historical figures or groups of people will have a deeper understanding of the significance of the event. Affective knowledge is critical in helping readers engage in inferential thinking and deepening their comprehension of text.

The following videos show a progression among lessons of students reading and interpreting historical fiction. The first two videos show the readers interacting with the historical fiction. The third video demonstrates the use of a second text to support students' learning with the first text. You'll read more about the use of text sets further in the chapter. As you watch the videos, see which types of knowledge students are building during these lessons.

INTERMEDIATE LESSON: TEXT INTRODUCTION

INTERMEDIATE LESSON: SETTING A PURPOSE AND MAKING INFERENCES

INTERMEDIATE LESSON: PAIRED TEXT TO BUILD KNOWLEDGE

As you watch these videos, you may notice the types of questions the teacher asks readers about the text. Table 9.2 offers a variety of question stems teachers can use to build the different types of knowledge.

TABLE 9.2: Knowledge-Building Question Stems

Type of Knowledge	Question Stems
Background knowledge: • Episodic • Declarative • Procedural	• What do you already know about [topic]? • Does this remind you of something you've learned previously? How? • What did you learn from reading about [topic]? • How has your understanding changed based on what you read? • Are there still things you wonder or want to learn more about?
Domain knowledge	• What might be confusing in what you are reading? • Are there any words or ideas you would like help understanding? • What do you now understand about [content area]?
Cultural knowledge	• Who are the people being described in the text? • What can you share about what was happening during that time? • How might you describe the setting? • What are some similarities and differences between [group of people or time] and [group of people or time]?
Affective knowledge	• Whose perspective is being shared in the text? • How might different people interpret this text or story differently? • How might [person or group] feel during this part of the text? • How might you be feeling during this part of the text if you were in [person's or group's] shoes?

*Visit **go.SolutionTree.com/literacy** for a free reproducible version of this table.*

The following video shows a conference between a reader and the teacher within the small-group setting. Listen for the teacher's questions to see how the reader built affective knowledge.

INTERMEDIATE LESSON:
SUPPORTING AN INTERMEDIATE READER

Common Strategies to Gauge Readers' Background Knowledge

It is critical to understand the difference between activating background knowledge and knowledge building. Part of the process of knowledge building is knowing our readers, which includes accessing and building upon their prior knowledge. As teachers, we can gauge our students' background knowledge through their interactions with texts, discussions, and vocabulary tasks.

In this section, we explore commonly used strategies that may be repurposed to assess reader background knowledge. As we cover these strategies, we encourage you to view them through the lens of getting to know your readers; this will help you with your instructional decisions. To build on strategies you may already use, we explore three commonly used prereading strategies that you can reframe to assess and categorize students' depth of knowledge.

ANTICIPATION GUIDE

An *anticipation guide* is a prereading strategy commonly used for engagement and activating prior knowledge. This strategy can also help teachers determine what readers know or think they know about a topic. By asking readers to explain their thinking behind their choices, teachers create a window into readers' thinking, allowing them to determine how familiar the readers are with the topic. Teachers can strategically draft the statements in the anticipation guide to capture depth of knowledge. We caution that sometimes these statements provide too much content prior to reading, resulting in less student engagement. In doing so, we inadvertently limit opportunities for readers to grapple with the text to build their own knowledge. The statements you include in the anticipation guide can also intentionally assess the types of knowledge (background knowledge, domain knowledge, cultural knowledge, affective knowledge) readers have about a topic. Figure 9.1 is an example of an anticipation guide.

	True	False	What I Know . . .
Spaghetti models help predict where a hurricane may make landfall.		✓	I don't think you can predict a hurricane. They change where they are going and the weatherman is wrong a lot.
There are many ways to prepare for a hurricane.	✓		My mom and dad have a box in our garage with supplies for when hurricanes come. I also have seen dad cover up our windows and pick up sandbags.
Hurricanes can be devastating and disruptive to communities.	✓		This is very true. During hurricane Ian, we had no power for days! It was so annoying. We also lost trees in my yard and my neighbors did too!
Hurricanes are disturbances that may or may not have strong winds.		✓	They always have strong winds!

FIGURE 9.1: Sample anticipation guide for assessing knowledge.

As you analyze the completed anticipation guide in figure 9.1 (page 173), consider the following questions.

- What types of knowledge is this reader tapping into?
- On a scale of 1 to 5, how would you rate the reader's depth of knowledge? What evidence contributed to your rating?
- What misconceptions may the reader have on the topic?

KWL STRATEGY

The *KWL strategy* (which stands for *Know, Want to Know, Learned*) is often used at the beginning of a unit to activate readers' prior knowledge (see figure 9.2). The *K* and *W* provide insight into a reader's knowledge on a topic and any misconceptions they have. If what readers know is general ideas related to the topic, then a teacher can determine that more depth is needed to fully comprehend the text. Additionally, teachers can analyze the ideas students contribute to the W column by the types of knowledge the readers hold about the topic.

K	W	L
• Hurricanes can be scary because sometimes houses collapse and trees fall on houses. • Hurricanes have an eye in the middle. • Hurricanes are big tornadoes. • Hurricanes usually only hit Florida. • Hurricanes have a lot of rain and wind.	• What causes hurricanes? • Can hurricanes happen in other places? • How do people prepare for hurricanes? • How do we know how strong a hurricane is? • Why do hurricanes have names?	• Hurricanes are giant tropical storms. • Hurricanes have an eye, where the winds are calm and there are no clouds. • In the southern hemisphere, hurricanes rotate clockwise, and in the northern hemisphere, they rotate counterclockwise. • Hurricanes are called cyclones in the Pacific.

FIGURE 9.2: KWL for assessing knowledge.

As you analyze the KWL chart in figure 9.2, consider the following questions.

- What types of knowledge is this reader tapping into?
- On a scale of 1 to 5, how would you rate the reader's depth of knowledge? What evidence contributed to your rating?
- What misconceptions may the reader have on the topic?

WORD SPLASH

A *word splash* is a visual used to activate readers' background knowledge or help them make predictions. Teachers can also use a word splash at the end of a unit to help readers review relationships within a topic. Figure 9.3 is an example of a word splash.

FIGURE 9.3: Sample word splash.

An *affinity diagram* is a visual tool to organize information during a brainstorming session. It is a wonderful way to activate students' prior knowledge and determine what they already know about a topic. Affinity diagrams require readers to organize their ideas into categories. Categories can be student or teacher generated.

In the word-splash-to-affinity-diagram process, teachers provide readers with a word splash of words they will encounter in an upcoming unit. In the word splash in figure 9.3, a teacher displayed words associated with ancient Greece and instructed students to categorize the words utilizing the GRAPES (Geography, Religion, Achievements, People, Economic, Social Structure) acronym. A small-group setting is an ideal context to see and hear how readers make decisions about their categorization. Teachers can use questioning, prompting, and cueing strategies to help readers articulate their developing knowledge. Figure 9.4 shows the transition from a word splash to an affinity diagram.

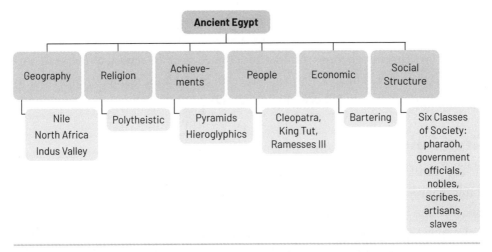

FIGURE 9.4: Sample student affinity diagram for ancient Egypt.

As you analyze the affinity diagram in figure 9.4 (page 175), consider the following questions.

- What types of knowledge is this reader tapping into?
- On a scale of 1 to 5, how would you rate the reader's depth of knowledge? What evidence contributed to your rating?
- What misconceptions may the reader have on the topic?

Although the strategies we provided in this section are used in many classrooms to activate students' prior knowledge, we propose that we can repurpose some of these tried-and-true strategies to help us determine the depth of knowledge a reader brings to the reading experience.

Connections to Whole-Group Topics

During a literacy block, it is common practice to have standards as the focus for instruction during whole-group lessons. Texts, resources, and questions are selected for their ability to help teachers meet the expectations and depth of the standard. As a result, assessments, small-group instruction, and extended practice opportunities are all aligned to the same curriculum standard. Standards-based alignment of instruction deepens readers' understanding of the curriculum benchmarks, and anchoring that instruction in a single topic supports simultaneous knowledge building.

Wexler (2020) stresses the importance of not simply using a book to teach a skill and then moving on to the next text. Wexler (2020) suggests that teachers stay on a topic for days, or even weeks, to deepen students' knowledge of the topic and allow concepts to stick. Just like we intentionally identify instructional focus areas and targeted skills according to curriculum standards, we should be intentional about deepening students' knowledge about topics during whole-group lessons and beyond. Therefore, if we consider topics and concepts as we plan our small-group lessons, we can provide opportunities to leverage texts in ways that help our students deepen their content knowledge. To learn more about making connections to whole-group lessons, revisit chapter 3 (page 49).

Text Sets

The use of text sets is an important instructional decision that enables readers to build knowledge on a topic. *Text sets* are intentionally grouped sets of texts about a specific topic or concept. Text sets can be both print and nonprint. As teachers consider topics for instruction, they may decide to select topics found in content-area standards like social studies, science, or art. Teachers may decide to consider the knowledge demands of a particular anchor novel in language arts and select text sets that help readers make connections to the setting, conflict, or characters in the novel. Text sets enhance the reader's experience by building on what they know and enabling them to connect the dots between content across texts on the same topic. Text sets simultaneously help readers stay engaged, develop content-rich vocabulary, view a topic from varying perspectives, and build knowledge about the world around them.

Zane and the Hurricane (Philbrick, 2014) is an example of an anchor text to use during whole-group instruction. This fictional story follows the events of a twelve-year-old boy as he is unexpectedly separated from his family during Hurricane Katrina. A teacher may choose to use this as an instructional opportunity for knowledge building. Texts related to hurricanes, such as ones on New Orleans and Hurricane Katrina, can be leveraged to deepen students' knowledge and connect to science standards.

Another benefit of using text sets is that they are a natural scaffold for readers who may have limited access to the text due to its readability or their limited knowledge on a topic. Through the strategic sequencing of text, a teacher can provide a scaffold for readers who may not yet be proficient in word recognition: They can provide an accessible text that covers the vocabulary and concepts discussed in a more difficult text in subsequent lessons. Coherence is achieved when the text set is used in all parts of the literacy block and through a variety of literacy activities. Text sets are a powerful way to build on the topics discussed during the literacy block and offer opportunities to connect to discipline-specific content reflected in grade-level standards.

Summary

Building knowledge plays a crucial role in small-group instruction by supporting reading comprehension and enhancing the retention of information. It is essential to provide access to rich, high-quality texts for all students—including those still developing foundational skills—to ensure that every learner can engage in knowledge building. Teachers can incorporate knowledge-building practices such as selecting interdisciplinary texts that connect to students' background knowledge, using content-rich texts that elevate students' understanding, and fostering discussions that integrate literacy with subject-matter learning. These practices help bridge the gap between skill development and comprehension, creating a more holistic approach to literacy instruction.

LAUNCH YOUR REFLECTION

Let's reconnect with Mr. Duncan, who we met at the start of the chapter (page 168). Now that you've read this chapter, consider the following questions.

- What are some ways that Mr. Duncan can assess his students' prior knowledge?
- What are some strategies Mr. Duncan can use to scaffold his students to deepen their knowledge?

RECHARGE YOUR SMALL-GROUP READING INSTRUCTION

The following are some questions you can use to apply the chapter concepts to your own classroom context.

- What is the role of knowledge building in a small-group lesson, and how do I ensure access to text for all students, including those who are building foundational skills?
- What are some examples of knowledge-building practices that I could incorporate into my small-group lessons?

EXPAND YOUR TOOLBOX

To continue your learning, see the "Leading the Learning Action Guide" (page 201) to support you and your colleagues. In the action guide for this chapter, you'll find in-action videos that spotlight teaching strategies as well as differentiated professional learning activities you can try out with your team. Additional tools that support this chapter topic can be accessed online (visit **go.SolutionTree.com/literacy**).

CHAPTER 10

WHAT ARE THE REST OF MY STUDENTS DOING WHILE I'M TEACHING A SMALL GROUP?

Students spend a significant amount of time engaged in literacy learning outside of small-group instruction. Depending on the classroom, this time may be organized as centers or stations, collaborative practice, or independent work. Regardless of the organizational structure, this is valuable time for students to engage in extended practice opportunities and apply their learning through meaningful, authentic literacy tasks. Authentic engagement in collaborative tasks creates opportunities for a community of learners, emphasizing both individual and collective accountability. This chapter helps teachers identify content and tasks for literacy learning to engage the rest of their readers while the teacher gives small-group lessons.

As you read this chapter, consider your own experiences. Reflect on what the rest of the class is doing while you work with small groups. The following questions may also help frame your thinking as you read.

- How do I organize and manage the rest of the class while I meet with small groups?
- What do the tasks and activities look like for the rest of the class?

- How do I keep students accountable for the work they are doing when they aren't with me?

Consider the following example of Ms. Walsh.

MEET THE TEACHER: MS. WALSH

> Ms. Walsh is a beginning teacher. During a recent professional learning session led by the district curriculum team, teachers in the session were asked to share their biggest challenges when planning for small-group instruction. Some of the challenges shared by teachers included access to resources, effective instructional routines, and time. Ms. Walsh quietly listened as each teacher shared their challenge. As the discussion seemed to be ending, Ms. Walsh raised her hand and said, "I just want to know how to manage the rest of my kindergarten class while I am meeting with a small group so that it doesn't feel so chaotic."

Does Ms. Walsh's challenge resonate with you? Have you identified strategies to overcome the challenge shared?

We revisit these ideas and questions at the end of the chapter to identify and plan for engagement strategies that you want to try with your own students.

Considerations for the Rest of the Class

We know that this is a literacy book, but bear with us as we do a math exercise together. Let's look at figure 10.1.

- How much time do you have for your whole literacy block? _____ minutes
- Of that time, how much time is set aside for whole-group instruction? _____ minutes
- Once you subtract your whole-group time, subtract the minutes spent with one small group. _____
- How many minutes are left? _____
- Multiply that number by 180. _____
- This is the number of minutes per school year that students should spend doing literacy tasks on their own or with their peers!

FIGURE 10.1: Time to spend in the literacy block calculation.

We facilitated this math exercise with a room full of principals, district leaders, and K–5 teachers. Regardless of the audience, the response was the same. Both audiences gasped. It was like a metaphorical light bulb went off the moment they learned the final number. For most participants who completed this math activity, the average number of minutes their students spend on their own or with a group of peers during the literacy block ranged from 7,000 to 15,000 minutes per school year, or an average of twenty-five school days! Therefore, when we think about what the rest of our class is doing while we facilitate a small group, we must intentionally organize the time and the tasks to ensure students are engaged.

It is essential to engage students who are not part of the teacher-pulled small group in authentic practice opportunities to reinforce literacy skills in meaningful and applicable contexts. Research indicates that when students engage in activities that closely reflect real-life reading experiences, such as discussing or writing responses to texts, their ability to transfer these skills to independent reading improves significantly (Fisher & Frey, 2021). Authentic practice promotes deeper comprehension, critical thinking, and language development, as students actively construct meaning from texts (Duke, Cervetti, & Wise, 2016). Opportunities that allow for immediate feedback and adjustment also support the development of accurate decoding, reading fluency, and increased reading motivation (Grabe, 2008). By engaging in real-world literacy tasks that include reading, writing, listening, and speaking, students move beyond rote skill practice by applying literacy strategies in diverse contexts, which enhances both short-term learning and long-term reading achievement.

When students engage in independent or collaborative work outside of small-group reading lessons, it is essential to link these activities to prior whole-group or small-group instruction to promote the transfer of these skills to their independent reading. Research emphasizes that tasks connected to previous instruction provide opportunities for meaningful practice, which allows students to apply new skills in varied contexts, strengthening their long-term retention and comprehension (Fisher & Frey, 2021). This connected approach ensures that students are not merely practicing isolated skills but are actively deepening their understanding of previously taught material. In contrast, presenting activities randomly or without connecting them to prior lessons can lead to fragmented learning and missed opportunities for reinforcement (Hattie & Zierer, 2018). When independent work builds on recent instruction, it offers students the time and space to internalize literacy strategies and apply them independently, a key component in developing autonomous readers (Duke et al., 2016). This continuous learning cycle maximizes instructional impact and supports the transfer of skills from guided practice to independent reading.

The Literacy Block

It is important to reframe how we think about our literacy block. Using Fisher and Frey's (2008) GRR instructional framework, let's explore the role and purpose of each phase of instruction as it connects to the literacy block. Focusing on the purpose of each component leads to increased instructional alignment and planning of authentic literacy tasks. Figure 10.2 includes each component of the literacy block and its role within the GRR instructional framework.

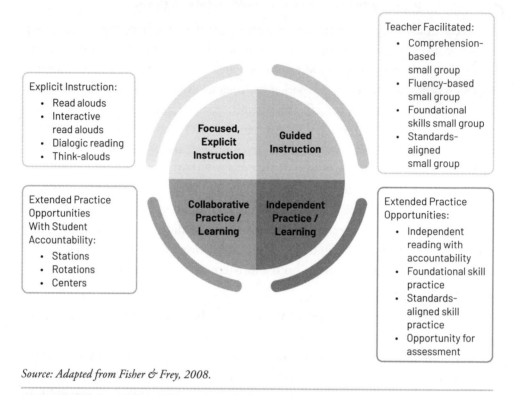

Source: *Adapted from Fisher & Frey, 2008.*

FIGURE 10.2: GRR framework and components of the literacy block.

The following sections detail the connections between the GRR framework and the literacy block.

WHOLE GROUP

A teacher's most explicit instruction takes place during this phase. Fisher and Frey (2008) defined this phase as a *focus lesson*. During whole-group instruction, teachers provide an opportunity for readers to see and hear expert thinking. In this phase, teachers perform think-alouds and work to clear readers' misconceptions. Teachers set the purpose during this phase and make the instructional focus relevant to readers (Fisher & Frey, 2008). The focus of a whole-group lesson is to address the standards and expectations of the curriculum. During this component of the literacy block, the teacher does most of the heavy lifting to illustrate what they expect readers to be able to do as their learning continues.

SMALL GROUP

Small-group instruction is a natural place for guided instruction to occur. Guided instruction during small group has many purposes. Teachers can organize content for small-group instruction by foundational skills, fluency, and comprehension (Conradi Smith et al., 2022). Additionally, teachers can organize by reader readiness. Therefore, they may draw content from the current skills and strategies they discuss during the whole group and differentiate by readers' strengths and needs, which are informed by data. During small-group instruction, the teacher steps out of the shoes of an expert and into the shoes of a facilitator. Their role is to question, prompt, and cue readers as they practice literacy skills and strategies. To learn more about connecting small-group with whole-group instruction and content, revisit chapter 3 (page 49).

EXTENDED PRACTICE OPPORTUNITIES

When Ms. Walsh shared her challenges with planning small-group instruction, she communicated that she needed help to keep the rest of the class organized and on task while she met with a small group. This may have been due to her belief that centers and rotations are physical spaces in the room that students move to. Although teachers can organize collaborative or independent practice in that way, they don't necessarily need to. The idea that centers, rotations, or stations translate to physical locations or spaces may implicitly send the message that they are separate from what is happening in the rest of the block. Therefore, we propose that teachers rename the time away from small group to *extended practice opportunities*. This language focuses on the purpose of the centers, rotations, or stations and facilitates the alignment, authenticity, and depth of instruction. There are several elements to consider when planning for extended practice opportunities, including the following.

- Student grouping
- Authentic, aligned tasks
- Independent or collaborative practice
- Structure (rotations, *must do* versus *may do*, extended time, and so on)
- Teacher considerations and logistics
    + Organization of rotation
    + Pacing
    + Materials
    + Workspace

Consider an example of a teacher who worked on a small-group decoding lesson with her first graders. During the lesson, her readers participated in a phonemic awareness task where they had to identify the medial vowel sound. Later in the lesson, the teacher noticed that there were two students who were struggling to correctly identify the medial sound in single-syllable words with short vowel sounds. The teacher knew that these two students needed more practice. The teacher had students work together to practice identifying medial vowel sounds. The teacher gave students Elkonin boxes, chips, and picture cards that contained objects with short vowel sounds. This activity served as an extended practice opportunity that was specific to the needs of these two students in the small group.

The following video shows how the teacher prepared her students for using the centers—or extended practice opportunities—on their own.

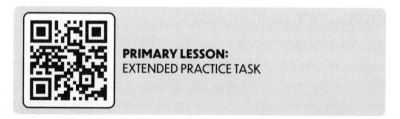

PRIMARY LESSON:
EXTENDED PRACTICE TASK

Authentic, Aligned Tasks With Accountability

Extended practice opportunities are essential for reinforcing literacy skills that were previously taught in whole-group or small-group lessons, but teachers must design these activities with authenticity, alignment, and accountability in mind to maximize their effectiveness. Authentic tasks that mirror real-world reading and writing experiences help students see the relevance of their learning, making it more engaging and meaningful to them. Additionally, ensuring that these practice opportunities and the content of previous whole-group or small-group lessons align is crucial for reinforcing key skills and promoting the transfer of skills to independent reading. Finally, accountability measures, such as clear goals, structured feedback, or peer collaboration, ensure that students remain focused and purposeful in their practice. Together, these elements create a coherent and impactful learning experience that deepens students' comprehension and supports their long-term literacy development.

ALIGNMENT

When planning for extended practice opportunities, the first consideration must be alignment to previous whole-group or small-group instruction. Extended practice opportunities should align with whole-group or small-group instruction based on previously taught skills, or what we call *trailing benchmarks*. If the planned extended opportunity tasks reflect previously learned content, then alignment takes place naturally. One of the biggest frustrations we hear as we work with teachers is they don't know how to design instruction for students who aren't working in small groups. This frustration is a signal that teachers consider this time to be a separate part of instruction. It may also signal that the activities planned are designed to keep readers busy while the teacher works with small groups. This is a red flag. Aligned tasks should not be difficult to plan or create; in fact, planning should be easy because it should come directly from previous instruction! Figures 10.3 and 10.4 provide two examples of how the focus of a lesson can extend through the rest of the literacy block to offer extended practice opportunities. The first example highlights a focus on comprehension (author's point of view), while the second example highlights a focus on foundational skills (digraphs).

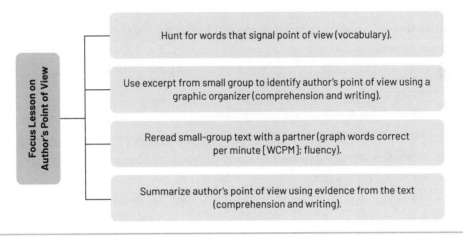

FIGURE 10.3: Whole-group lesson on comprehension through extended practice opportunities.

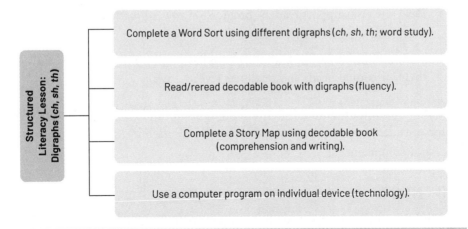

FIGURE 10.4: Small-group lesson on foundational skills through extended practice opportunities.

Alignment ensures that readers can connect new concepts to prior knowledge, thereby helping them deepen their understanding and apply what they've learned in collaborative or independent contexts. When extended practice activities build on previous instruction, readers have the opportunity to practice and refine specific skills in a way that supports their individual learning needs. For example, in a small-group lesson focused on decoding multisyllabic words, the extended practice might involve independent reading tasks that prompt readers to identify and break down complex words within texts or text excerpts. Similarly, after a small-group lesson on summarizing texts, teachers could task readers with rereading an excerpt of the same small-group text and writing brief summaries to help their classmates decide whether they are interested in reading the book.

Additionally, there are opportunities for differentiation if teachers can modify a small-group task for readers to ensure it aligns with their individual needs. Planning for structured alignment prevents readers from feeling disconnected from previous instruction and ensures that practice tasks contribute to coherent progress toward mastery of learning goals. The following questions can help teachers gauge their task alignment.

- Does the task reinforce a specific skill or concept that I taught during a recent whole-group or small-group lesson?
- Is the learning goal of the task clearly linked to the objective of the previous instruction?
- Does the task require readers to apply knowledge or strategies they have already practiced in a familiar context or a similar, slightly varied context?
- Are readers able to make connections between the extended practice task and what they've already learned?
- Does the task support readers' progression toward mastery of a previously taught literacy skill?
- Can I modify the task for different readers to ensure that it aligns with their individual needs and readiness levels?

By ensuring alignment, teachers can design extended practice tasks that not only reinforce students' previous learning but also build upon it, increasing their confidence and competence.

AUTHENTICITY

Extended practice tasks outside of small-group and whole-group lessons should focus on authentic opportunities for readers to read, write, and discuss texts in meaningful ways. Teachers can adapt these tasks to target different learning goals and grade-level expectations—from letter-, word-, or sentence-level work for early readers to passage or full-text reading as appropriate. For example, early readers might work on building words using learned phonics patterns while older readers might engage in writing responses to texts that challenge them to analyze a character's motivation or theme. Discussing texts with peers or writing reflections after independent reading can deepen students' comprehension and provide valuable practice in critical thinking. To reinforce alignment, the text used for these contexts can be the same text that was introduced and read during a previous small-group lesson. Authentic tasks like these give readers a clear purpose, helping them understand how their efforts in the extended practice opportunity contribute to their growth as readers. The following questions can help teachers gauge their task authenticity.

- Does the task involve meaningful reading, writing, or discussion about a text?
- Is the task aligned with a specific literacy goal I previously taught during whole-group or small-group lessons?
- Does the task provide readers with a clear purpose or audience for their work?
- Does the task challenge readers to apply skills in real-world reading or writing contexts?
- Will readers be able to reflect on or discuss how the task is helping them progress toward their reading goals?

Tasks that lack a clear purpose, audience, or connection to prior learning may feel like busy work to readers and fail to support meaningful literacy development. Authentic tasks, however, engage readers in the process of learning by giving them real opportunities to think critically and apply what they've learned.

ACCOUNTABILITY

Extended practice opportunities outside of small-group and whole-group lessons should incorporate accountability measures that motivate readers to stay engaged and reflect on their progress. Accountability measures don't have to require grading, which is a misconception that we often hear from teachers; rather, it can involve a range of strategies that help readers take ownership of their learning. For example, teachers can design tasks where students discuss what they've read with a partner or in small groups, creating a peer-driven environment that naturally holds readers responsible for their participation and comprehension.

Sharing written responses or projects with classmates, or even presenting to an authentic audience such as parents or the school community, gives readers a clear purpose and an incentive to produce thoughtful work. Additionally, using technology to record their reading or writing allows students to revisit their performance, self-assess, and make improvements, fostering their independence and metacognitive awareness. Teachers can also provide rubrics for self-evaluation or peer feedback to encourage readers to critically reflect on their own work or that of their peers. This kind of structured reflection helps readers understand how well they are applying literacy skills and areas where they can grow. Figure 10.5 provides an example that facilitates accountability during extended practice opportunities.

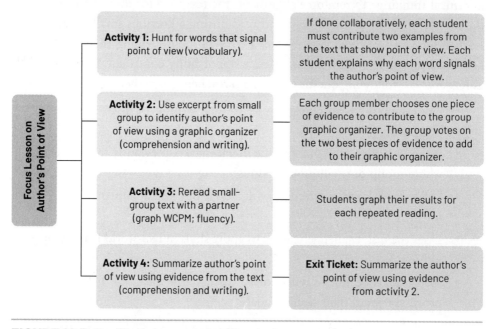

FIGURE 10.5: Facilitating accountability during extended practice opportunities.

Integrating accountability into extended practice tasks not only ensures that readers engage meaningfully with the material but also promotes their long-term skill development by encouraging self-reflection and peer collaboration. The following questions can help teachers gauge their task accountability.

- Does the task provide opportunities for peer discussion or sharing of reading or writing?
- Are readers given the chance to present their work to an authentic audience (classmates, parents, and so on)?
- Can readers use technology to record their reading or writing for self-reflection and improvement?
- Is there a rubric, scoring key, or structured criteria for self-assessment or peer feedback?
- Does the task encourage readers to reflect on their own learning process and identify areas for growth?

By embedding these forms of accountability into extended practice, tasks can move from compliance and completion to fostering a sense of ownership, responsibility, and continuous self-improvement. This approach helps readers see the real-world value of their literacy skills and understand how they contribute to their personal goals and growth.

Student Grouping

Student grouping considerations can be viewed from several lenses. The first decision is based on readiness. Are readers ready to work on a skill from whole group or small group independently, or do they require additional collaborative practice time? Thinking through the lens of the GRR instructional framework, this decision is critical for supporting readers as they acquire new content, skills, or strategies.

Teachers can group students using either homogeneous or heterogeneous approaches. Depending on the focus of this time, they can provide additional scaffolding by pairing readers of different proficiency levels so they can leverage each other's strengths to further extend their learning. Heterogeneous grouping supports tasks aligned with whole-group instruction, whereas homogeneous grouping is appropriate for readers working on specific foundational skills. The following self-check can help teachers plan for grouping.

- Readiness for independent work
  + Are readers ready to practice a skill independently, or do they need additional support through collaborative work?
  + Have readers shown mastery in whole-group or small-group settings, or do they require more guided practice?
- Gradual release of responsibility
  + Is this task designed for independent practice (readers taking full responsibility) or collaborative work (shared responsibility)?
  + Does the task align with the next step in scaffolding, allowing readers to gradually take ownership of their learning?
- Homogeneous grouping (same skill level)
  + Would grouping readers by similar skill levels help them focus on specific areas of need, such as foundational skills or reading similar texts?
  + Are readers working on a specialized skill that requires focused, level-appropriate practice?
- Heterogeneous grouping (mixed skill levels)
  + Would pairing readers with varying proficiency levels help them learn from each other and extend their understanding of a concept?

+ Does the task align with a broad learning goal—such as applying a strategy introduced in whole-group instruction—where peer support might be beneficial?
- Purpose of grouping
  + What is the main focus of this extended practice session—foundational skill reinforcement, strategy application, or collaborative learning?
  + How can grouping enhance the learning experience of each student, either through focused skill work or peer collaboration?
- Flexible grouping
  + Are groups fluid and adjustable based on student progress and changing instructional needs?
  + Can readers switch between independent, paired, or group work depending on the demands of the task or their evolving proficiency?

By considering these factors, teachers can create intentional groupings that best support readers during extended practice, allowing for both skill reinforcement and intentional application of new skills or strategies within text. To learn more about grouping based on data, revisit chapter 2 (page 35).

Structure in Independent Practice

We are often asked how to best structure extended practice opportunities. Our answer is always the same: the structure that best maximizes practice time! Therefore, we will share a few models we have experienced in classrooms, through either observation or our own practice. Keep in mind that these examples are flexible. Teachers can fluidly and flexibly select one model for one unit and utilize a different model for another unit. Teachers may even elect to use a combination of models simultaneously. As you explore the following models, think about your class, your personal preference and comfort level, and the outcomes you hope to achieve each day.

ROTATION MODEL

In a rotation model, either readers physically move from task to task or the materials for each task move to each group. The rotation model is the one we observe most often in schools. However, there are considerations for how to organize and structure this time. One consideration is the number of rotations that need to be achieved. This number can vary from day to day. This consideration allows teachers to prioritize extended practice opportunities for readers. Figure 10.6 provides two sample rotational models that differ in the number of groups and amount of time for each rotation based on a ninety-minute literacy block.

CHAPTER 10: What Are the Rest of My Students Doing While I'm Teaching a Small Group?

Monday Whole Group 9:00–9:30 a.m.	Rotation 1 9:30–9:50 a.m.	Rotation 2 9:50–10:10 a.m.	Rotation 3 10:10–10:30 a.m.
Group 1 ↑	**Teacher Table Activity** Being a Reader lesson	**Independent Activity** Word Sort or identify central idea in <u>Central Idea Graphic Organizer</u> (included)	Technology
Group 2 ↑	Technology	**Teacher Table Activity** Being a Reader lesson or Wonders text lesson; identify central idea in <u>Central Idea Graphic Organizer</u> Benchmarks: 2.2, 2.3 Text: *Animal Families*	**Independent Activity** Word Sort or write about a text from the Teacher Table activity. Continue to work on <u>Central Idea Graphic Organizer</u> by adding details that support the main idea. Benchmarks: 2.2, 2.3 Text: *Animal Families*
Group 3 ↑	**Independent Activity** Read and respond to pages 2–5 independently. <u>Central Idea Graphic Organizer</u> (all questions) Benchmarks: 2.2, 2.3, 3.2 Text: *Animal Families*	Technology	**Teacher Table Activity** <u>Central Idea Graphic Organizer</u> with adjustments—add explanations to justify answers, continuing to next section. Benchmarks: 2.2, 2.3 Text: *Animal Families*

Source: © 2024 by Orange County Public Schools. Used with permission.

FIGURE 10.6: Sample rotational models.

continued ▶

SMALL GROUPS FOR BIG READERS

	Monday Whole Group 9:00–9:30 a.m. →	Rotation 1 9:30–9:45 a.m. →	Rotation 2 9:45–10:00 a.m. →	Rotation 3 10:00–10:15 a.m. →	Rotation 4 10:15–10:30 a.m.
Group 1		**Teacher Table Activity** Being a Reader lesson	**Comprehension Activity** Write the relevant details from the whole-group comprehension text in the Central Idea Graphic Organizer. Benchmarks: 2.2 Text: Whole-group comprehension text from the CRMs	Write to Respond or Word Sort	Technology
Group 2		Technology	**Teacher Table Activity** Being a Reader lesson or Wonders text lesson; identify central idea in Central Idea Graphic Organizer Benchmarks: 2.2, 2.3 Text: *Animal Families*	**Comprehension Activity** Continue to work on Central Idea Graphic Organizer by adding at least one detail that supports the central idea. Benchmarks: 2.2, 2.3 Text: *Animal Families*	**Write to Respond Activity** Word Sort Respond to summarizing question using central idea created in small group. Include one relevant detail. Benchmarks: 2.2, 2.3 Text: *Animal Families*
Group 3		**Write to Respond Activity** Word Sort Respond to summarizing question using central idea created in small group. Include three relevant details. Benchmarks: 2.2, 2.3 Text: *Animal Families*	Technology	**Teacher Table Activity** Being a Reader lesson or Wonders text lesson; identify central idea in Central Idea Graphic Organizer Text: *Animal Families*	**Comprehension Activity** Write about the text from teacher table activity. Continue to work on Central Idea Graphic Organizer by adding details that support the central idea. Text: *Animal Families*
Group 4		**Comprehension Activity** Read and respond to pages 2–5 independently. Central Idea Graphic Organizer (all boxes) Benchmarks: 2.2, 2.3, 3.2 Text: *Animal Families*	**Write to Respond Activity** Respond to summarizing question on foldable; explain the author's purpose. Benchmarks: 3.2, 3.3 Text: *Animal Families*	Technology	**Teacher Table Activity** Central Idea Graphic Organizer with adjustments—add explanations to justify answers, continuing to next section. Benchmarks: 2.2, 2.3 Text: *Animal Families*

Additionally, teachers can decide to be part of the rotation or outside the rotation. An advantage to being outside the rotation is that the teacher is not tied to a certain time frame when meeting with a small group. Some lessons may require twenty minutes, while others may just be a ten-minute session. For example, a teacher may plan for an explicit phonics lesson for one group while they simply check in with another group that is working on a previously taught standards-aligned skill. Removing yourself from the rotations allows for more flexibility. When sharing the *out of the rotation* model, we are often asked how we ensure readers complete all extended practice opportunity activities if they are pulled for a teacher-led group. A suggestion we offer is to have a make-up station. This station can be used to complete missed practice opportunities or to work on tasks that require extended time. Figure 10.7 provides a visual demonstration of what we mean by being *in* the rotation model or *out of* the rotation model.

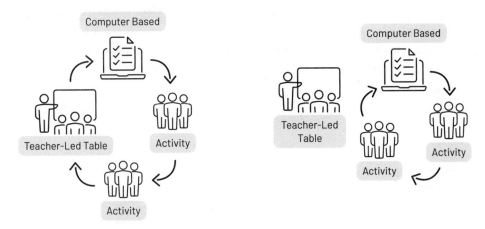

Source: © 2024 by Orange County Public Schools. Used with permission.

FIGURE 10.7: Teacher in the rotation model versus teacher out of the rotation model.

The following are some key features of the rotation model.

- **Task movement:** Readers move between tasks or tasks and materials move to each group.
- **Variable rotations:** The teacher adjusts the number of rotations each day or week based on the goals for extended practice.
- **Inside the rotation:** Readers' rotations include the teacher table for instruction, with fixed time limits for each rotation or station.
- **Outside the rotation:** The teacher works with groups of readers for flexible time frames, allowing deeper instruction where needed and starts and stops to instruction that are variable based on the goals of the group and total time for instruction.

- **Make-up station:** The teacher may include a station for readers to complete missed tasks or extend practice time.
- **Group size and time:** The teacher adapts the rotation length and group size to fit their literacy block, balancing instruction and independent work.

MUST DO, MAY DO MODEL

A *must do, may do* model is an effective way to structure extended practice opportunities. From a motivation and engagement perspective, this model offers readers choices of the tasks they wish to complete. The teacher determines and prioritizes which tasks are essential and then encourages readers to choose from other tasks once they have finished the tasks on the *must do* list. The *may do* list is a great opportunity to add activities that spiral back to prior instruction. An example is a vocabulary activity that provides multiple exposures to select words or independent reading time with accountability. The must do, may do model can also be incorporated into rotations. In a four-rotation model, teachers may choose to designate two rotations to be extended practice opportunities based on small-group work, and they can format the other two rotation activities as a must do, may do. This type of rotation assignment can last days or weeks. Figure 10.8 provides a sample of must do and may do activities.

Whole-Group Instruction: Text Features
Small-Group Instruction: Digraphs *ch, sh, th*

Must Do	May Do
• Complete a Word Sort containing the digraphs *ch, sh, th*. • Reread the decodable book from small group with a partner. • In groups, each member must find two examples of different text features in a nonfiction text.	• Using a self-selected book, conduct a word hunt of words containing the digraphs *ch, sh, th*. • Write a paragraph explaining your favorite part of the book you read in small group. • Choose three words of the week and complete a word map for each word.

FIGURE 10.8: Must do and may do activities example.

Given the options for structuring extended practice opportunities, teachers may choose whichever option or combination of options that work best for them and their readers. The following are some key tips for structuring small-group time.

- **Maximize practice time:** Select a structure that provides readers with the most time to practice.
- **Be flexible:** Choose a structure based on unit goals, students' needs, and your personal teaching style. Models can be mixed or used interchangeably across different units or lessons, as needed.

- **Focus on outcomes:** When planning, think about the learning goals your readers are working toward. Be sure to check in periodically to ensure that the structure you're using for the small-group block is offering the time and practice that readers need to make progress toward the intended learning goals.

The following are some key features of the must do, may do model.

- **Essential tasks (must do):** The teacher identifies critical tasks students must complete.
- **Choice-based tasks (may do):** Once essential tasks are done, students choose from optional, engaging activities.
- **Engagement and motivation:** Readers have autonomy and choice, increasing their engagement.
- **Spiraled instruction:** The teacher uses may do activities to revisit previous skills or provide enrichment (for example, decoding practice, vocabulary work, or purposeful, independent reading).
- **Integration with the rotation model:** The teacher combines must do, may do activities with rotations by designating some rotation time for must do and may do tasks, balancing structure with choice.

Summary

Due to the significant amount of time students spend engaged in literacy learning outside of small-group instruction, the activities, lessons, and tasks they encounter during this time are a critical part of their learning experience. The organization and structure of these extended practice opportunities may include a rotational model; a must do, may do format; or a variation of the two. Regardless of the model selected, teachers must provide students with an opportunity to apply their learning from whole group or small group to authentic literacy tasks. As teachers recharge their small-group reading instruction using the strategies we provided in this chapter, they should reflect on their process. The following reflection is designed to focus your thinking around how to structure extended learning opportunities for your students not engaged in small-group instruction.

LAUNCH YOUR REFLECTION

Let's reconnect with Ms. Walsh, who we met at the start of the chapter (page 180). Now that you've read this chapter, consider the following questions.

- How would you help Ms. Walsh so that her literacy block doesn't feel chaotic?

- What specific strategies could you offer Ms. Walsh to help her students successfully engage in extended practice opportunities?

RECHARGE YOUR SMALL-GROUP READING INSTRUCTION

The following are some questions you can use to apply the chapter concepts to your own classroom context.

- How do I organize and manage the rest of the class while I meet with small groups?
- What do the tasks and activities look like for the rest of the class?
- How do I keep students accountable for the work they are doing when they aren't with me?

EXPAND YOUR TOOLBOX

To continue your learning, see the "Leading the Learning Action Guide" (page 201) to support you and your colleagues. In the action guide for this chapter, you'll find in-action videos that spotlight teaching strategies as well as differentiated professional learning activities you can try out with your team. Additional tools that support this chapter topic can be accessed online (visit **go.SolutionTree.com/literacy**).

EPILOGUE

As you close your journey toward building proficient readers through high-quality small-group instruction, reflect on your learning and how it influences your instructional practice. During your reflection, consider how you will continue to extend your professional learning on small-group literacy instruction for all. As you explored this book, we provided you with innovative frameworks, such as the ABC Reader Profile Framework (chapter 1, page 17). You had opportunities to linger in the *how* of planning for small-group instruction. This included connections to whole-group instruction, practices to support differentiation, and the introduction of literacy routines you can use to translate research into classroom practice. We focused on what role text plays, how to engage readers, and how to respond to readers to strengthen their word recognition, language comprehension, and metacognitive strategies across a variety of texts and contexts. We gave attention to the role of writing in building foundational skills and deepening comprehension of text. Finally, we shared structures, models, and considerations for how to engage all students for impactful practice while you pull a small group.

Extend Your Reflections

As you navigated this book, you may have reflected using the self-assessment and note-taking tool in figure I.2 (page 13). You may have also set a long-term goal with embedded short-term goals and action items (figure I.3, page 14). We would like to provide you with an opportunity to circle back to these tools and invite you to reflect on the following questions. We encourage you to look back on the tools we've provided while you self-assess your journey.

- How have your strengths grown or shifted to a level of deeper understanding?
- Where are there remaining opportunities for growth?
- How might your opportunities for growth have shifted based on your new understandings?
- What wonderings do you still have that you can use as a springboard for extending your learning and practice opportunities after reading this book?
- How will you be (or how have you been) recharging the small-group reading instruction in your classroom?

As we mentioned in the introduction, competence precedes confidence for our students as readers (Hammond, 2015). We hope you feel more competent and confident as you plan and implement small-group reading instruction. As you elevate your professional knowledge and expertise, it is natural for questions to remain and to identify new opportunities to connect and expand your learning.

Expand Your Professional Community and Commitment

We realize that much of your day is spent alone in your classroom with your readers, and at times, our profession may feel isolating, since opportunities to collaborate with colleagues are limited. It is important that we work to reframe our perceptions of working alone. We encourage you to seek out colleagues within your schools and learning communities to reflect, examine reader data, and share practices to build both individual and collective efficacy. Professional colleagues may include grade-level team members, instructional coaches, and principals, each of whom is invested in the success of student reading outcomes.

A powerful tool for teams to consider when working on a particular skill within a small group is lesson study. Within lesson studies, teams collaboratively plan, implement, reflect, and revise lessons that incorporate the elements the team would like to learn more about (Lewis & Hurd, 2011). This allows for a safe environment for teachers to try new instructional strategies and tools. The lesson observation and reflection tools (chapter 6, page 109) can be used during a lesson study to assist you and your colleagues in grounding your observations and reflections for lesson refinement in objective indicators to strengthen instruction.

In the following video, literacy coach Bevan Brown shares how learning at her school site was enhanced through a lesson study focused on small-group reading instruction.

COACH PERSPECTIVE: LESSON STUDY

If you find yourself seeking a learning community outside of your school site, then it might take a little extra looking to find a learning community that fits your needs. As authors, we have each found our own learning communities in various ways. Membership within professional state and national organizations provides opportunities for learning through participation in conferences, subscriptions to professional journals, and networking with other professionals who have similar values and mission-driven goals. If you have not already done so, you may find that you are ready to take the plunge and present at a professional conference to share your journey and the practices you have found to be successful. In addition to professional organizations, a learning community is right at your fingertips in the world of social media. Many experts—including teachers, researchers, and other practitioners—share their thinking, resources, and tools on social media platforms. If you aren't sure where to start looking for an expert to follow on social media, consider asking a colleague!

Additionally, since you heard our voices throughout this book, we hope you consider us to be a part of your professional network. We encourage you to find and follow us on social media (see page ix), share your reflections and ongoing wonderings, and stay connected so we can join you in celebrating your successes with small-group reading instruction. As we shared throughout this book, our own expertise around literacy instruction is strengthened through our work with teachers, and we will continue to seek opportunities to learn from those who are making a difference in the reading lives of students. This includes you.

APPENDIX
LEADING THE LEARNING ACTION GUIDE

This action guide is designed to support you as you lead learning for small-group reading instruction. We wrote this guide to be used in conjunction with the chapters in this book. The videos don't cover all topics within a chapter but serve as a supplement to chapter content. Although we suggest how to use the videos with certain topics, you can use each video in multiple ways and for various purposes. We encourage you to add your perspective and unique lens to focus on the most important aspects for your audience. As you explore these videos, you may decide to enhance your learning through a shared lesson study. In lesson studies, teams collaboratively plan, implement, reflect, and revise lessons that incorporate elements the team would like to learn more about (Lewis & Hurd, 2011). This collaboration fosters a safe environment for teachers to try new instructional strategies and tools. Consider the video of the coach in the epilogue (page 199). This video highlights an effective avenue for leading the learning, which you may wish to consider as you are developing your own action plan for leading learning.

During our work with school leaders, literacy coaches, and teachers, we notice varying beliefs and perspectives of what effective small-group reading instruction looks like. When we ask how we can support schools to enhance this aspect of their reading instruction, a common response is for us to teach lessons in classrooms. To support you as you show what small-group reading instruction could look and sound like, we created a set of videos to share with your audience or with individual teachers. We intended these videos to provide a shared vision for small-group reading instruction. These videos highlight two of the authors as they dive into differentiated reading instruction at a Title I school. Please note, we cannot stress enough that we don't consider these videos to be models without potential for improvement. Rather, we intend for them to serve as shared experiences in which we can reflect with you and highlight our own wonderings based on real instruction in action. The small groups in these videos include students in a particular grade-level band. In collaboration with the school literacy coach, we grouped students based on shared goals. However, student groupings were limited to the students who had permission to participate in the video.

In the following video, Bevan shares some advice for other instructional coaches who are beginning the journey of exploring small groups with their teachers. She shares resources she believes would help coaches along the way.

COACH PERSPECTIVE:
SUPPORTING TEACHERS

As we shared previously, although these videos serve as demonstrations for different reading lenses and purposes, they are not exemplars. Just like all effective teachers, we constantly reflect, noting what went well and what we could have done differently to be more effective. We encourage you and your audience to join in on these conversations and reflections. Note the moments of effective instruction, but also lean into exploring areas that you could have planned or facilitated differently.

In the following sections, you will find guiding questions to support your reflection. As you begin or continue this journey, always keep in mind your *why* for promoting small-group reading instruction.

Julie Calame, a fifth-grade teacher, shares her view of small group as the "heart of reading instruction" in this short clip.

TEACHER PERSPECTIVE:
VALUE OF SMALL GROUP

Since you are an instructional leader and know the professional learning needs of your colleagues the most, we invite you to use these videos and questions in ways that make sense for you. For example, pause the videos to engage in discussions with your audience. Take liberties to engage in additional "teachable moments." Make the videos work for you and your purpose.

In addition to the included videos and guiding questions, you will also find differentiated professional learning implementation activities for each chapter. Educators have unique learning needs and preferences, just like their students. Depending on your professional goals, you can share these implementation activities with your entire audience, use the activities independently, or facilitate learning with teachers (and teams of teachers).

To frame these differentiated learning opportunities, we used the following headings: Get Started, Get Steady, and Get Stronger.

Additionally, in many of the Get Stronger activities, we included considerations for learning walks in which teams of teachers visit one another's classrooms with specific student-focused indicators for observation (Fisher & Frey, 2014). We acknowledge that for learning walks to be successful, teachers must feel supported and safe. Teachers should understand that the learning walk is intended to be an opportunity to make low-inference notes and identify trends by grade or school—not to offer criticism or feedback for individual teachers. You will notice that in each instance where a learning walk is suggested, the indicators are based on what we will see readers saying and doing (as they are reading, writing, and discussing text). We encourage intentional facilitation of learning walks in the beginning, especially if this protocol hasn't been a part of professional practice at your school. Over time and with practice, teachers can engage in learning walks without explicit facilitation.

We hope the differentiated professional learning implementation activities help you consider how to meet teachers where they are and empower them on their own professional learning journeys.

Chapter 1: What Do I Know About My Students as Readers?

The following videos can be used to practice the ABC Reader Profile Framework from chapter 1 (page 17). Teachers can collaborate to complete as much of the matrix as they can as they discover each reader's strengths and learning opportunities from the brief video. It is important to note that when completing the ABC Reader Profile for readers in your school, you will have a variety of data sources to consider to gain an even clearer picture.

Listen to Mikayla as she reads from the text they are working on during small group. In this video, Mikayla also shares about what she just read. A sample ABC Reader Profile for Mikayla is shown in figure 1.2 (page 29). Feel free to use this as you consider Mikayla's strengths as a reader. You may also choose not to use the sample and focus on your audience's interpretation of Mikayla's reading strengths.

INTERMEDIATE READING CONFERENCE: MIKAYLA

Guiding questions:

- Note Mikayla's strengths using the ABC Reader Profile Framework. What did you notice within each category?
- If you were conferring with Mikayla regarding her reading with this book, where might you linger and what next steps might you offer?

Listen to Clara as she reads from the text during small group. In this video, Clara shares what she read.

INTERMEDIATE READING CONFERENCE: CLARA

Guiding questions:

- Note Clara's strengths using the ABC Reader Profile Framework. What did you notice within each category?
- If you were conferring with Clara regarding her reading with this book, where might you linger and what next steps might you offer?

Listen to Seliha as she reads a book at her independent reading level.

PRIMARY READING CONFERENCE: SELIHA

Guiding questions:

- Note Seliha's strengths using the ABC Reader Profile Framework. What did you notice about decoding and fluency?
- If you were conferring with Seliha about her reading, where might you linger and what next steps might you offer?

Listen to Elijah as he reads a nonfiction text and shares about what he read.

PRIMARY READER SNAPSHOT: ELIJAH

Guiding questions:

- Note Elijah's strengths using the ABC Reader Profile Framework. What did you notice about decoding and fluency?
- If you were conferring with Elijah, where might you linger and what next steps might you offer?

Figure A.1 (page 206) shares differentiated professional learning implementation activities to facilitate learning with teachers (and teams of teachers) regarding the content in chapter 1 (page 17). As we mentioned in the opening to this guide, the differentiated learning opportunities are displayed in columns as Get Started, Get Steady, and Get Stronger to help you tailor learning to your teachers' individual needs.

Get Started	Get Steady	Get Stronger
Build data literacy by administering and interpreting reading assessments. Plan for individualized coaching opportunities or team meetings in which a student-centered approach is used to: - Examine each assessment tool to have a deep understanding of what is being assessed, how it is assessed (including assessment conditions), and how to interpret the data - Share examples of a single student's data. Analyze student data to identify asset-based strengths through open-ended discussion, using prompts such as: "What do you notice about this student's strengths?" and "What does this data make you wonder?" After the data discussion, distribute the ABC Reader Profile tool. Prompt teachers (or the single teacher) to identify where this student would fall on the continuum for each area of reading. You may also want to have a vertical copy of curriculum standards accessible during this time to add considerations of grade-level expectations to the discussion about where the student would be placed (and initial implications for instruction based on their placement).	During a collaborative team meeting, engage in discussions about assessment data and an asset-based approach to determining opportunities for instruction. Identify a single student within the grade level as the focal student. Using the process shared in the video observations and notes, invite the reader to engage in text reading with one teacher as other teachers on the team closely observe and take notes using the ABC Reader Profile tool. To debrief these observations, reflect on the following questions. - What do you notice about decoding and fluency? - If you were conferring with Elijah regarding his reading with this book, where might you linger and what next steps might you offer?	Video-record your own interactions with a reader during a conference or text reading from a small-group lesson. Use the ABC Reader Profile Framework based on your observations from your own interactions with the reader. You may also want to note which of the four areas within the ABC Reader Profile Framework you tend to linger in during your interactions.

FIGURE A.1: Differentiated professional learning implementation activities for understanding students as readers.

Chapter 2: How Does Differentiating Small-Group Instruction Promote Access and Equity?

The following videos can be used to focus learning and discussions around access and equity.

PRIMARY LESSON: DECODING

Guiding questions:

- What did you notice in terms of product, access, or process to differentiate instruction?
- How did the teacher keep each student engaged?

PRIMARY READING CONFERENCE: LIAM

Guiding questions:

- What did you notice about Liam's strengths?
- How did the teacher provide access for Liam with both high-frequency words and decodable words?

PRIMARY LESSON: SUPPORTING INDEPENDENT READING–GRADE 1

Guiding questions:

- How was the small-group environment set up so the teacher could conduct conferences with students in the small-group setting?
- What type of feedback did students receive?

Figure A.2 (page 208) shares differentiated professional learning implementation activities to facilitate learning with teachers (and teams of teachers) around access and equity.

Get Started	Get Steady	Get Stronger
Review a class data set based on the reading assessment data that you have available. Use the ABC Reader Profile tool to determine each reader's asset-based strengths in each row on the continuum. Afterward, consider the following questions. • How might you flexibly group students based on the ABC Reader Profile? • What focus area(s) of instruction might you prioritize for each group? • Are there instances where a single reader could benefit from instruction in more than one group? If so, and if you can flexibly group the reader in this way, consider doing so to maximize instructional opportunities. Use the group planning tool to map out the frequency of meetings and focus areas for each group for a two-week period.	Identify three students who are flexibly grouped in three different groups for a given week of small-group instruction. Prompt teachers to track and collect the following over one week of instruction. • Observations from Tier 1 differentiated small-group instruction • Observations from additional intervention or enrichment, if applicable • Student work samples from core whole-group instruction (in response to an on-grade-level task) Consider the following protocol prompts for each reader. • What are the teacher's observations of the reader during differentiated Tier 1 small-group instruction? • Is this reader receiving additional intervention or enrichment? Analyze each reader's work samples from whole-group instruction with the following questions. • Are students demonstrating proficiency or progress toward proficiency? • Have students already demonstrated proficiency or are they in need of additional enrichment opportunities? Consider implications for small-group lessons and extended practice opportunities.	Follow a reader's experience across one school day. Without providing additional instruction, make observations of the reader's engagement across the day. Consider the following questions as you observe. • What opportunities for applied practice of taught skills did the reader have? • In what contexts was the reader successful in meeting lesson learning goals? • What types of scaffolding were provided across lessons? • How did the student engage with text(s) across the day? • What other observations did you notice? Reflect on the following questions. • What did you learn by following this reader across an entire school day? • Where were there opportunities for the reader to practice and build independence that could have been expanded? • What additional questions do you have now? • What big ideas or trends has this experience revealed that would be beneficial to discuss as a grade-level or school team?

FIGURE A.2: Differentiated professional learning implementation activities for access and equity.

Chapter 3: How Do I Connect to Whole-Group Instruction?

The following videos can be used to explore how small group can be connected to whole-group instruction.

Guiding questions:

- How was the skill of ending sounds supported during this small group?
- How can we help our students understand the purpose of knowing different ending sounds?

Guiding questions:

- How was morphology instruction focused on prefixes supported during this small group?
- How can we help our students understand the purpose of knowing different prefixes and address misconceptions as they arise?

Figure A.3 (page 210) shares differentiated professional learning implementation activities to facilitate learning with teachers (and teams of teachers) regarding connecting to whole-group instruction.

Get Started	Get Steady	Get Stronger
Engage in a connect-the-dots activity to look for instructional opportunities to connect whole group and small group. Create a diagram, visual, map, or drawing to show how you will connect the instructional focus of whole group into small-group lessons. Be sure to also note data-informed needs as part of small group as well. • Whole-group focus or benchmark → small-group focus or benchmark If your lesson focus for small group is not directly related to the curriculum standard(s) for whole group, are there nuanced ways where you can integrate some connections? Perhaps this is by genre, a targeted question during text discussion, or a launching point from the small-group lesson to an independent practice activity that connects with the whole-group curriculum standard?	Before you start, analyze reading observations and data for a single student. Select and analyze a grade-level text from whole-group instruction within a single week of instruction. Anticipate what might be challenging for the student by considering the following questions. • What words might be challenging for the student to decode? • What words, phrases, or concepts might be challenging for the student to extract meaning from or build knowledge on? • What elements of the text structure might present comprehension challenges? • Do you anticipate stamina or fluency being an obstacle for the student to read the complete text (or text passage)? • How might you plan for interleaved practice in small-group instruction so that the student can apply the skills they are practicing to more complex text?	Create three lists by engaging in the following instructional focus mapping exercise. 1. Review student proficiency data for the current curriculum standard(s) and benchmark(s). Identify which students need additional support with this standard. 2. Review student proficiency data for the previous or spiraled curriculum standard(s) and benchmark(s), including those that you previously taught that may be recurring and those that you previously taught that may not be recurring. Identify which students need additional support with these standards, organizing your lists and any notes about data-based needs by standard and benchmark. 3. Review current reading assessment data unrelated to curriculum-based measures (such as beginning-of-the-year screening data, middle-of-the-year screening data, and other progress-monitoring tools). Identify which students need additional support on data-informed skills, organizing your lists and any notes about data-based needs by skill. Synthesize the three lists you've created. Plan for how you will provide opportunities for interleaved practice.

FIGURE A.3: Differentiated professional learning implementation activities for connecting to whole-group instruction.

Chapter 4: How Do I Plan for Small-Group Instruction?

The following videos can be used to facilitate discussions around planning for small-group instruction.

PRIMARY LESSON: FOUNDATIONAL SKILL IN A STRUCTURED LITERACY LESSON

Guiding questions:

- What did you notice about the flow and the connection of skills in this small-group lesson?
- Where might writing fit in?

PRINCIPAL PERSPECTIVE: INTENTIONAL PLANNING

Guiding questions:

- How did the principal describe evidence of intentional planning?
- What are important components of small-group instruction that your school would like to plan collaboratively?

PRIMARY LESSON: FOUNDATIONAL SKILLS PHONICS REVIEW

Guiding questions:

- What tools supported student learning?
- What teacher and student behaviors did you notice?

INTERMEDIATE LESSON: MORPHOLOGY

Guiding questions:

- How did the students interact with the content?
- What did you wonder about the examples provided?

PRIMARY LESSON:
FOUNDATIONAL SKILL ROUTINE

Guiding questions:

- When students are stuck on a high-frequency word, what might a teacher do?
- How are high-frequency words different from decodable words?

Figure A.4 shares differentiated professional learning implementation activities to support teachers (and teams of teachers) in planning for small-group instruction.

Get Started	Get Steady	Get Stronger
Before launching small-group instruction for the first time, it may be helpful to visualize how all parts of planning, organizing, and teaching will work together for effective lessons. While it may seem mechanical at first to focus on surface-level materials and organization, having efficient procedures in place will increase the likelihood that small-group instruction as a practice is efficient and sustainable. Engage in learning walks to other classrooms. Plan for a single small-group lesson using a chunking technique. 1. Choose which single routine for a lesson you will focus on. 2. Gather materials. 3. Plan by rehearsing (practice or role-play) as needed to prepare for implementing the routine. 4. Reflect on this routine prior to moving on to the next routine.	Record an instructional routine in action during a small-group lesson. Watch the video of the routine using the instructional routines from chapter 4 (page 65) as a lens for review. If you use this routine again soon, consider the following questions. - What should I do the same way as last time when I implement this routine in future lessons? - What might I do differently? - Where are there opportunities for me to refine my implementation of the routine?	Engage in a learning walk to other classrooms to observe instructional routines in action, using the routines from chapter 4 to capture low-inference notes (what students are saying and doing). Focus on student observations and literacy engagement in response to taught routines (not on the teacher). You might also consider asking if students know how this routine helps them as readers to see if and how they are internalizing the routines as readers.

FIGURE A.4: Differentiated professional learning implementation activities for planning for small-group instruction.

Chapter 5: How Do I Select and Evaluate Text?

The following videos can be used to promote discussions around selecting and evaluating text.

TEACHER PERSPECTIVE:
TEXT SELECTION

Guiding questions:

- How did this teacher select texts for her students?
- What resources support selecting texts?

INTERMEDIATE LESSON:
KEY DETAILS IN NONFICTION

Guiding questions:

- What various roles might the teacher play while students are independently reading?
- What did you notice about the students' interest in the content? How about the genre?

PRIMARY LESSON:
KEY DETAILS IN NONFICTION

Guiding questions:

- What considerations might the teacher have made while selecting this text?
- What expectations did the teacher provide for the students both explicitly and implicitly?

Figure A.5 shares differentiated professional learning implementation activities to facilitate learning with teachers (and teams of teachers) regarding selecting and analyzing text.

Get Started	Get Steady	Get Stronger
Analyze a single text for a small-group lesson using the following questions. • What kind of prior content knowledge is needed? • What might engage my learners in the text? • How interesting is the text? • What is the familiarity with the language structures? • How familiar are students with the characteristics of the genre? • What kind of vocabulary knowledge is needed to understand the text? • What do the readability measures tell us about accessibility of text for the reader? Use each question or consideration as you analyze the text. Record and discuss your analysis and reflections.	Identify and analyze texts for two weeks of instruction for a single group. Consider where you might chunk texts by instructional day, when and how you might revisit texts, and ways in which texts might connect to a subsequent text you plan to use for the same group (assuming the group won't be flexibly changed for the following week of instruction). **Note:** Text does not have to be a full book or passage; it could include letters, words, or sentences for readers, depending on the learning goal.	Before you start, analyze a single text for a small-group lesson using the following questions. • What kind of prior content knowledge is needed? • What might engage my learners in the text? • How interesting is the text? • What is the familiarity with the language structures? • How familiar are students with the characteristics of the genre? • What kind of vocabulary knowledge is needed to understand the text? • What do the readability measures tell us about accessibility of text for the reader? Use each question or consideration as you analyze the text. Record and discuss your analysis and reflections. Observe a lesson in action to see how students engage with the selected text. Consider the following questions. • How did the readers use knowledge to support their comprehension of the text? Where or when would additional knowledge have supported the readers' comprehension? • What did you notice about the readers' word recognition and ability to make meaning at the word and text levels? • Where are there opportunities to revisit the text to strengthen the readers' understanding?

Source: Adapted from CCSSO & NGA, 2010.

FIGURE A.5: Differentiated professional learning implementation activities for selecting and analyzing text.

Chapter 6: How Do I Engage My Readers During Small-Group Instruction?

The following videos can be used to facilitate learning around engaging readers during small-group instruction.

PRIMARY LESSON:
FOUNDATIONAL SKILL ROUTINE

Guiding questions:

- What strategy did the teacher use to support students to learn the high-frequency words?
- How did the teacher ensure that all students in the group participated and engaged in the learning?

PRIMARY LESSON:
PRACTICING FOUNDATIONAL SKILLS

Guiding questions:

- Which strategies did the teacher emphasize to help students with blending and segmenting?
- How did the teacher ensure all students in the group participated and engaged in the learning?

INTERMEDIATE LESSON:
PREVIEWING NONFICTION

Guiding questions:

- How did the students uphold the norms of student-to-student talk?
- What were the students' strengths with navigating nonfiction?

INTERMEDIATE LESSON:
MAKING INFERENCES

Guiding questions:

- What did you wonder about the teacher's actions or choices?
- What was the role of the guiding question during this lesson?

PRIMARY LESSON:
BUILDING LETTER KNOWLEDGE

Guiding questions:

- What did you notice about the teacher's expectations and the teacher-student roles in this video?
- What did you notice and wonder about how the teacher formed the sounds?

PRIMARY LESSON:
FOUNDATIONAL SKILL PRACTICE

Guiding questions:

- What types of physical motions did the teacher use to support blending?
- What did you notice about teacher and student behaviors?

Figure A.6 shares differentiated professional learning implementation activities to facilitate learning with teachers (and teams of teachers) around engaging readers.

Get Started	Get Steady	Get Stronger
Select one of the following reflection tools from chapter 6 based on the lesson goals for one small group: • "Reflection and Observation Tool for Small-Group Instruction With an Emphasis on Building Foundational Skills" (figure 6.1, page 113) • "Reflection and Observation Tool for Small-Group Instruction With an Emphasis on Fluency, Comprehension, and Metacognition" (figure 6.2, page 114) Engage in self-reflection using the selected tool. Determine which indicators you are currently considering and which you may need to intentionally consider when planning.	Video-record at least two small groups with different learning goals. Select the reflection tool(s) that aligns with each lesson. Watch the videos and note which indicators you observe. Where are there strengths in the lesson, according to the tool? Where are there opportunities for potential growth or adjustment? **Extension:** Encourage teachers across the school to video-record, or identify a coach or instructional leader who can capture videos of lessons in action. Create short video clips from lessons to build a schoolwide video library highlighting facilitation strategies and student engagement with literacy tasks in action.	Engage in learning walks using the reflection tool(s) that aligns to the lessons you observed. Note any indicators you observe. If you capture additional notes, ensure that they are low-inference notes (what students are saying and doing only). Discuss trends for the grade—not specific teachers. Any wonderings should be phrased for individual student readers (to keep the environment safe for teachers). **Extension:** Engage in a learning walk across grade levels to determine schoolwide trends.

FIGURE A.6: Differentiated professional learning implementation activities for engaging readers.

Chapter 7: How Do I Monitor and Respond to My Students as Readers?

The following videos can be used to engage in discussions around monitoring and responding to students as readers.

INTERMEDIATE LESSON: METACOGNITION

Guiding questions:

- What was the teacher's purpose in asking students this question?
- What were some of the strategies emphasized by the teacher?

PRIMARY LESSON:
SUPPORTING INDEPENDENT
READING–GRADE 2

Guiding questions:

- What structures might need to be in place to allow the teacher to conference with each student?
- What teacher moves did you notice within each conference?

PRIMARY READER SNAPSHOT: ELIJAH

Guiding questions:

- What did the teacher do to help the student persevere during the reading?
- How did the teacher close the conference?

PRIMARY LESSON:
FOUNDATIONAL SKILL ROUTINE FOR
HIGH-FREQUENCY WORDS

Guiding questions:

- What did you notice about the teacher's support?
- Notice that the teacher was mouthing the words. What might you suggest?

**INTERMEDIATE READING
CONFERENCE:** CHASE

Guiding questions:

- What did you notice or wonder about this conference?
- What was the teacher's focus during this conference?

INTERMEDIATE LESSON:
SUPPORTING INDEPENDENT READING

Guiding questions:

- How did the teacher involve the student in the focus of the conference?
- How might the teacher select what feedback they provide?

Figure A.7 shares differentiated professional learning implementation activities to facilitate learning with teachers (and teams of teachers) around monitoring and responding to students as readers.

Get Started	Get Steady	Get Stronger
Revisit the Get Started activity from chapter 5 on anticipating readers' needs (figure A.5, page 214). Review tables 7.1 (page 142), 7.2 (page 144), and 7.3 (page 145) to anticipate prompts that might be helpful to support readers at anticipated points of need during text reading. Consider printing the tables, laminating them, and putting them on a ring to make them accessible from the teacher table for on-the-spot use during a lesson.	Record a small-group lesson that includes an instructional routine from chapter 4 (page 65) in action. Watch the video using tables 7.1 (page 142), 7.2 (page 144), and 7.3 (page 145) as lenses for observation. Consider the following questions. - If you do this lesson again, how might you prompt students in the same ways? - What might you do differently? **Note:** This activity is similar to the activity in the Get Steady section for chapter 4 (figure A.4, page 212). **Extension:** Ask readers what they can do if they get stuck to glean insight into which strategies they've internalized and which ones they need to practice further.	Engage in a learning walk to observe readers immersed with text during small-group lessons. (Be sure to carefully plan the right times to visit classrooms.) Use tables 7.1 (page 142), 7.2 (page 144), and 7.3 (page 145) from chapter 7 as lenses for observation. Discuss trends for the grade—not specific teachers. Any wonderings should be phrased for individual student readers (to keep the learning environment safe for teachers). **Note:** This activity is similar to the Get Stronger activity from chapter 6 (figure A.6, page 217). **Extension:** Engage in a learning walk across grade levels to determine schoolwide trends. Consider questions such as the following. - Are we helping students engage in productive struggle (without rescuing them)? - Are we prompting students in ways that will support them in internalizing the prompts for future use (and not just for the reading of this text)?

FIGURE A.7: Differentiated professional learning implementation activities for monitoring and responding to students as readers.

Chapter 8: How Does Writing Connect to My Small-Group Instruction?

The following videos can be used to think about how writing connects to small-group instruction.

PRIMARY LESSON: ENCODING

Guiding questions:

- How might the teacher have selected the focus for the guided spelling?
- What opportunities did the teacher provide for each student to engage them in the learning?

PRIMARY LESSON: BUILDING FOUNDATIONAL SKILLS

Guiding questions:

- How did the tools the teacher used support student learning?
- How did the phonemic awareness activity in this lesson serve as a precursor for future encoding practice?

PRIMARY LESSON: PREPARING FOR EXTENDED PRACTICE

Guiding questions:

- How did the teacher introduce this center?
- How did this center support students in word building?

Figure A.8 shares differentiated professional learning implementation activities to facilitate learning with teachers (and teams of teachers) regarding the connection between writing and small-group instruction.

Get Started	Get Steady	Get Stronger
Plan for writing opportunities. Identify a single small-group lesson to consider opportunities to plan for writing instruction. Consider the following questions. • How might I include writing in this lesson? • How might I introduce writing as a springboard for extended practice opportunities beyond the lesson?	Analyze writing samples from your class. Use the examples from chapter 8 (figures 8.4 [page 154], 8.5 [page 155], 8.6 [page 155], 8.11 [page 162], and 8.13 [page 164] as a guide to collect writing samples from your class in which readers apply their encoding skills or writing in response to text. Consider the following questions. • How do your students' writing samples show evidence of their progress toward the reading learning goal? • What opportunities for reading instruction do these samples present? What about opportunities for writing instruction? **Extension:** Analyze writing samples across your team. Each teacher should bring three varied writing samples from their classroom in which readers have applied their encoding skills or writing in response to text. Use the preceding prompts to engage in collaborative discussion about the writing samples.	Engage in a learning walk across grade levels to determine schoolwide trends. Consider the following questions. • Are we seeing evidence that writing instruction is connected to reading (during lessons, as artifacts in the classroom)? • What do we notice about the strengths and opportunities in the writing samples we see? Discuss trends for the school—not specific teachers. Any wonderings should be phrased for individual student readers (to keep the learning environment safe for teachers).

FIGURE A.8: Differentiated professional learning implementation activities for connecting writing and small-group instruction.

Chapter 9: How Do I Build My Readers' Knowledge?

The following videos can be used to initiate discussions around building students' disciplinary knowledge.

INTERMEDIATE LESSON:
TEXT INTRODUCTION

Guiding questions:

- How did the teacher help build the context and background of the story?
- How did the teacher ask the students to engage in the text?

INTERMEDIATE LESSON:
SETTING A PURPOSE AND MAKING INFERENCES

Guiding questions:

- What was the role of the guiding question throughout the lesson?
- What did you notice about student discourse and its role in students' understanding of the story?

INTERMEDIATE LESSON:
PAIRED TEXT TO BUILD KNOWLEDGE

Guiding questions:

- What might have helped support student learning further in this lesson?
- What type of knowledge were the teacher's questions prompting students to develop?

PRIMARY LESSON:
TEXT-BASED DISCUSSION

Guiding questions:

- What did you notice about the teacher and student roles?
- What type of knowledge were the teacher's questions prompting students to develop?

INTERMEDIATE LESSON: SUPPORTING AN INTERMEDIATE READER

Guiding questions:

- How did the teacher support the student's understanding and connection to the text?
- How can the teacher or student determine if a text is good for the student?

Figure A.9 shares differentiated professional learning implementation activities to facilitate learning with teachers (and teams of teachers) around knowledge building through text.

Get Started	Get Steady	Get Stronger
Analyze a single text for small-group instruction and consider where students have opportunities to build knowledge that will deepen their comprehension of the text. Plan for one of the strategies from chapter 9 to assess and build knowledge (figures 9.1–9.4, pages 173–175). **Extension:** Consider printing and laminating the question stems from table 9.2 (page 172) that prompt for building different types of knowledge to use as instructional prompt cards during small-group instruction.	Build a text set for a series of small-group lessons in which readers have an opportunity to build knowledge. Use the following considerations as you select texts to include. • How have you included a variety of genres in your text set that will support readers to build different types of knowledge on a topic? • How have you selected text that offers potential instructional scaffolds for complexity?	Engage in a learning walk to interact one-on-one with readers. Visit classrooms at targeted times, during which you'll have an opportunity to talk to students about the texts they're reading. Use the prompts from table 9.2 to support your discussions with readers. Discuss trends for the grade—not specific teachers. Any wonderings should be phrased for individual student readers (to keep the learning environment safe for teachers).

FIGURE A.9: Differentiated professional learning implementation activities for knowledge building through text.

Chapter 10: What Are the Rest of My Students Doing While I'm Teaching a Small Group?

The following videos can be used to explore what the rest of the students are doing while the teacher is teaching a small group.

TEACHER PERSPECTIVE:
PLANNING EXTENDED PRACTICE OPPORTUNITIES

Guiding questions:

- What were some of the activities this teacher used for centers?
- How did this teacher ensure students understood how to participate in each center?

PRIMARY LESSON:
EXTENDED PRACTICE TASK

Guiding questions:

- What did you notice or wonder about the game?
- How might the teacher know when the students are ready to play the game independently?

Figure A.10 shares differentiated professional learning implementation activities to facilitate learning with teachers (and teams of teachers) around what the rest of the class might be doing while the teacher is working with a small group of students.

Get Started	Get Steady	Get Stronger
Visualize how students will engage in extended practice opportunities outside of the pulled small group. For example, will you use a rotational model; a must do, may do model; or another type of organizational structure? How will you organize and manage materials to ensure student self-regulation and independence? Revisit and expand upon the Get Started activity from chapter 3 (figure A.3, page 210). Identify independent extended practice opportunities that connect to whole group and small group. Brainstorm a list first, and then select your preferred activities with intention. Use figure 10.3 (page 185) as you consider your selections.	Engage in a give-one-get-one sharing activity. Each teacher on the team should bring the materials and a student work sample for one extended practice opportunity to share with colleagues. **Extension:** Repeat this activity across the school during a faculty meeting. Look for vertical progressions of activities. Use the ABC Reader Profile Framework to align opportunities along the continuums of each area of reading.	Engage in a class audit of extended practice opportunities. For one day, refrain from pulling one small group for a lesson, and instead, use the time to silently observe students as they engage in extended practice opportunities. Try to stay at the teacher table and refrain from giving directions or offering immediate corrective feedback. The goal of this activity is to audit (get a closer look) how students are engaging and self-regulating during this independent time. Consider the following questions. - In what ways are students self-regulating their own behavior and demonstrating independence to meet the learning goals of this independent or collaborative time? - Are there any procedures or logistics that you could refine to increase the likelihood of student success? If your observations warrant adjustments in expectations, student engagement, or other areas, consider holding a class meeting after completing the audit to share your observations and establish clear goals for the students' next opportunity for extended practice (that day or the following day). Following the instructional block to practice, hold another class meeting to reflect on what went well. Invite students to share their ideas about what they might do differently the next day to increase the likelihood for individual and class success toward the learning goals and expectations.

FIGURE A.10: Differentiated professional learning implementation activities for engaging students not in small group.

Summary

As you rewatch the first video and watch the second, consider the outcomes you wish to achieve with your professional learning audience. When you step back and consider the big picture of this learning, how do you hope it impacts teachers and students? Reflect on the following.

- What are your hopes for your professional learning audience?
- What misconceptions of small-group instruction might your audience hold?

COACH PERSPECTIVE:
VISUALIZING INSTRUCTION

PRINCIPAL PERSPECTIVE:
VISUALIZING INSTRUCTION

REFERENCES AND RESOURCES

Achieve the Core. (n.d.). *Text set project: Building knowledge and vocabulary.* Accessed at https://achievethecore.org/page/2784/text-set-project-building-knowledge-and-vocabulary on June 16, 2024.

Al Otaiba, S., McMaster, K., Wanzek, J., & Zaru, M. W. (2023). What we know and need to know about literacy interventions for elementary students with reading difficulties and disabilities, including dyslexia. *Reading Research Quarterly, 58*(2), 313–332.

Amira Learning. (n.d.). *Amira Reading suite.* Accessed at https://amiralearning.com/amira-reading on January 21, 2025.

Arego, R. (2016). *Winter fun* (M. Leggitt, Illus.). Center for the Collaborative Classroom.

Austin, C. R., & Boucher, A. N. (2022). Integrating word-meaning instruction within word-reading instruction. *Intervention in School and Clinic, 58*(1), 21–30. https://doi.org/10.1177/10534512211047592

Ball, D. L., & Cohen, D. K. (1996). Reform by the book: What is—or might be—the role of curriculum materials in teacher learning and instructional reform? *Educational Researcher, 25*(9), 6–14.

Beck, I. L., McKeown, M. G., & Kucan, L. (2002). *Bringing words to life: Robust vocabulary instruction*. Guilford Press.

Belluck, P. (2016, April 30). What is Alzheimer's disease? *The New York Times*. Accessed at www.nytimes.com/2016/05/02/science/what-is-alzheimers-disease.html on June 16, 2024.

Bennett, L. (2014). *The battle against pests*. McGraw-Hill Education.

Blintt, J. (2020, October 20). *The importance of a diverse classroom library* [Blog post]. Accessed at www.literacyworldwide.org/blog/literacy-now/2020/10/20/the-importance-of-a-diverse-classroom-library on June 16, 2024.

Bondie, R. S., Dahnke, C., & Zusho, A. (2019). How does changing "one-size-fits-all" to differentiated instruction affect teaching? *Review of Research in Education, 43*(1), 336–362.

Boyer, N., & Ehri, L. C. (2011). Contribution of phonemic segmentation instruction with letters and articulation pictures to word reading and spelling in beginners. *Scientific Studies of Reading, 15*(5), 440–470. https://doi.org/10.1080/10888438.2010.520778

Brown, J. D. (2009). *Language curriculum development: Mistakes were made, problems faced, and lesson learned*. Accessed at www.hawaii.edu/sls/wp-content/uploads/2014/08/3-Brown.pdf on December 4, 2024.

Caravolas, M., Lervåg, A., Mikulajová, M., Defior, S., Seidlová-Málková, G., & Hulme, C. (2019). A cross-linguistic, longitudinal study of the foundations of decoding and reading comprehension ability. *Scientific Studies of Reading, 23*(5), 386–402. https://doi.org/10.1080/10888438.2019.1580284

CAST. (2024). *Universal Design for Learning guidelines 3.0*. Accessed at http://udlguidelines.cast.org on June 16, 2024.

Center for the Collaborative Classroom. (n.d.a). *Elements of effective implementation tool: Being a Reader*. Author.

Center for the Collaborative Classroom. (n.d.b). *Instructional cues and feedback BAR document*. Author.

Center for the Collaborative Classroom. (2021a). Generating independent thinking. In *Being a Reader: Small-group reading, set 10* (2nd ed.). Author.

Center for the Collaborative Classroom. (2021b). Week 4, day 1. In *Being a Reader: Small-group reading, set 2* (2nd ed.). Author.

Center for the Collaborative Classroom. (2023). *Being a Reader: Teacher's manual, grade 3* (2nd ed.). Author.

Cervetti, G. N., Wright, T. S., & Hwang, H. (2016). Conceptual coherence, comprehension, and vocabulary acquisition: A knowledge effect? *Reading and Writing: An Interdisciplinary Journal, 29*(4), 761–779. https://doi.org/10.1007/s11145-016-9628-x

Chambrè, S. J., Ehri, L. C., & Ness, M. (2020). Phonological decoding enhances orthographic facilitation of vocabulary learning in first graders. *Reading and Writing: An Interdisciplinary Journal, 33*(5), 1133–1162.

Cherry, K. (2023, April 4). *How the theory of mind helps us understand others.* Accessed at www.verywellmind.com/theory-of-mind-4176826 on June 16, 2024.

Christison, M., Krulatz, A., & Sevinç, Y. (2021). Supporting teachers of multilingual young learners: Multilingual Approach to Diversity in Education (MADE). In J. Rokita-Jaśkow & A. Wolanin (Eds.), *Facing diversity in child foreign language education* (pp. 271–289). Springer.

Coleman, T. E., & Money, A. G. (2020). Student-centered digital game–based learning: A conceptual framework and survey of the state of the art. *Higher Education, 79*(3), 415–457. https://doi.org/10.1007/s10734-019-00417-0

Colorado Encyclopedia. (n.d.). *Cripple Creek.* Accessed at https://coloradoencyclopedia.org/article/cripple-creek on June 16, 2024.

Conradi Smith, K., Amendum, S. J., & Williams, T. W. (2022). Maximizing small-group reading instruction. *The Reading Teacher, 76*(3), 348–356. https://doi.org/10.1002/trtr.2146

CORE. (2008). CORE Phonics Survey—Record form [Measurement instrument]. In *Assessing reading: Multiple measures for kindergarten through twelfth grade* (2nd ed., pp. 41–52). Arena Press.

Curriculum Associates. (2011). *i-Ready Diagnostic* [Measurement instrument]. Accessed at www.curriculumassociates.com/programs/i-ready-assessment/diagnostic on October 11, 2024.

Danneberg, J. (2009). *Family reminders* (J. Shelley, Illus.). Charlesbridge.

Davis, P. (2021). *Floating in the deep end: How caregivers can see beyond Alzheimer's.* Liveright.

Dixon, J. K., Brooks, L. A., & Carli, M. R. (2019). *Making sense of mathematics for teaching the small group.* Solution Tree Press.

Dore, R. A., Amendum, S. J., Michnick Golinkoff, R., & Hirsh-Pasek, K. (2018). Theory of mind: A hidden factor in reading comprehension? *Educational Psychology Review*, *30*(3), 1067–1089. https://doi.org/10.1007/s10648-018-9443-9

Duke, N. K. (2020, November). When young readers get stuck. *Educational Leadership*, *78*(3), 26–33.

Duke, N. K., & Cartwright, K. B. (2021). The science of reading progresses: Communicating advances beyond the simple view of reading. *Reading Research Quarterly*, *56*(S1), S25–S44.

Duke, N. K., Cervetti, G. N., & Wise, C. N. (2016). The Teacher and the Classroom. *Journal of Education*, *196*(3), 35–43.

Duke, N. K., Ward, A., & Klingelhofer, R. (2020). *Listening to reading–Watching while writing protocol (LTR-WWWP)*. Accessed at www.nellkduke.org/listening-to-reading-protocol on September 4, 2024.

Duke, N. K., Ward, A., & Pearson, P. D. (2021). The science of reading comprehension instruction. *The Reading Teacher*, *74*(6), 663–672. https://doi.org/10.1002/trtr.1993

Ehri, L. C. (1995). Phases of development in learning to read words by sight. *Journal of Research in Reading*, *18*(2), 116–125.

Ehri, L. C. (2014). Orthographic mapping in the acquisition of sight word reading, spelling memory, and vocabulary learning. *Scientific Studies of Reading*, *18*(1), 5–21. https://doi.org/10.1080/10888438.2013.819356

Ehri, L. C. (2020). The science of learning to read words: A case for systematic phonics instruction. *Reading Research Quarterly*, *55*(S1), S45–S60.

Elkonin, D. B. (1963). The psychology of mastering the elements of reading. In B. Simon & J. Simon (Eds.), *Educational psychology in the U.S.S.R.* (pp. 165–179). Routledge.

Fien, H., Chard, D. J., & Baker, S. K. (2021). Can the evidence revolution and multi-tiered systems of support improve education equity and reading achievement? *Reading Research Quarterly*, *56*(S1), S105–S118.

Fisher, D., & Frey, N. (2008). *Better learning through structured teaching: A framework for the gradual release of responsibility*. ASCD.

Fisher, D., & Frey, N. (2014, January). Using teacher learning walks to improve instruction. *Principal Leadership.* Accessed at www.scsk12.org/memo/files/files/learning%20walk2.pdf on October 25, 2024.

Fisher, D., & Frey, N. (2021). *Better learning through structured teaching: A framework for the gradual release of responsibility* (3rd ed.). ASCD.

Fisher, D., & Frey, N. (2022). *Past successes, new ideas.* International Literacy Association.

Fitzgerald, J., & Spiegel, D. L. (1983). Enhancing children's reading comprehension through instruction in narrative structure. *Journal of Reading Behavior, 15*(2), 1–17.

Flint, A. S., & Jaggers, W. (2021). You matter here: The impact of asset-based pedagogies on learning. *Theory Into Practice, 60*(3), 254–264.

Florida Center for Reading Research. (n.d.). *Fluent phrasing.* Accessed at https://fcrr.org/sites/g/files/upcbnu2836/files/media/PDFs/student_center_activities/23_fluency_phrases/23_f012_fluent_phrasing.pdf on December 4, 2024.

Förster, N., & Souvignier, E. (2014). Learning progress assessment and goal setting: Effects on reading achievement, reading motivation and reading self-concept. *Learning and Instruction, 32,* 91–100. https://doi.org/10.1016/j.learninstruc.2014.02.002

Frey, N., & Fisher, D. (2011, January). Guiding learning: Questions, prompts, and cues. *Principal Leadership.* Accessed at https://ofd.med.utoronto.ca/sites/default/files/assets/resource/document/guided-learning-questions-prompts-and-cues.pdf on October 25, 2024.

Gersten, R., Newman-Gonchar, R., Haymond, K. S., & Dimino, J. (2017, April). *What is the evidence base to support reading interventions for improving student outcomes in grades 1–3?* U.S. Department of Education. Accessed at https://files.eric.ed.gov/fulltext/ED573686.pdf on October 25, 2024.

Gibbons, G. (2020). *Sea turtles* (2nd ed.). Holiday House.

Gonzalez-Frey, S. M., & Ehri, L. C. (2021). Connected phonation is more effective than segmented phonation for teaching beginning readers to decode unfamiliar words. *Scientific Studies of Reading, 25*(3), 272–285.

Gough, P. B., & Tunmer, W. E. (1986). Decoding, reading, and reading disability. *Remedial and Special Education, 7*(1), 6–10.

Grabe, W. (2008). *Reading in a second language: Moving from theory to practice*. Cambridge: Cambridge University Press.

Graham, S., Bollinger, A., Booth Olson, C., D'Aoust, C., MacArthur, C., McCutchen, D., et al. (2012). *Teaching elementary school students to be effective writers: A practice guide* (NCEE 2012-4058) [Report]. Accessed at https://ies.ed.gov/ncee/wwc/Docs/practiceguide/writing_pg_062612.pdf on October 25, 2024.

Graham, S., & Hebert, M. (2010). *Writing to read: Evidence for how writing can improve reading* [Report]. Alliance for Excellent Education. Accessed at https://acuresearchbank.acu.edu.au/download/13ef501c229bbc1e5fbfacfdb49ae4840396b026642edd5601d829e5a0d75e05/562446/66819_downloaded_stream_54.pdf on June 16, 2024.

Graham, S., Liu, X., Aitken, A., Ng, C., Bartlett, B., Harris, K. R., et al. (2018). Effectiveness of literacy programs balancing reading and writing instruction: A meta-analysis. *Reading Research Quarterly, 53*(3), 279–304. https://doi.org/10.1002/rrq.194

Gregory, G., Kaufeldt, M., & Mattos, M. (2016). *Best practices at Tier 1: Daily differentiation for effective instruction, elementary*. Solution Tree Press.

Grimes, K. J., & Stevens, D. D. (2009). Glass, bug, mud. *Phi Delta Kappan, 90*(9), 677–680.

Guthrie, J. T., Wigfield, A., Barbosa, P., Perencevich, K. C., Taboada, A., Davis, M. H., et al. (2004). Increasing reading comprehension and engagement through concept-oriented reading instruction. *Journal of Educational Psychology, 96*(3), 403–423. https://doi.org/10.1037/0022-0663.96.3.403

Haelermans, C. (2022). The effects of group differentiation by students' learning strategies. *Instructional Science, 50*, 223–250. https://doi.org/10.1007/s11251-021-09575-0

Hammond, J. (Ed.). (2001). *Scaffolding: Teaching and learning in language and literacy education*. Primary English Teaching Association.

Hammond, Z. (2015). *Culturally responsive teaching and the brain: Promoting authentic engagement and rigor among culturally and linguistically diverse students*. Corwin Press.

Hatcher, P. J., Hulme, C., & Snowling, M. J. (2004). Explicit phoneme training combined with phonic reading instruction helps young children at risk of reading failure. *Journal of Child Psychology and Psychiatry, 45*(2), 338–358. https://doi.org/10.1111/j.1469-7610.2004.00225.x

Hattie, J. (2009). *Visible learning: A synthesis of over 800 meta-analyses relating to achievement.* Routledge.

Hattie, J. (2012). *Visible learning for teachers: Maximizing impact on learning.* Routledge.

Hattie, J., & Zierer, K. (2018). *Ten mindframes for visible learning: Teaching for success.* Routledge.

Hattie, J., & Zierer, K. (2025). *Ten mindframes for visible learning: Teaching for success* (2nd ed.). Routledge.

Helfer, A. (2016). *Sharks!* Center for the Collaborative Classroom.

Hickman, P. (2005). *Turtle rescue: Changing the future for endangered wildlife.* Firefly Books.

Hwang, H., & Duke, N. K. (2020). Content counts and motivation matters: Reading comprehension in third-grade students who are English learners. *AERA Open, 6*(1), 1–17.

International Literacy Association. (2020). *Teaching writing to improve reading skills* [Research advisory]. Author. Accessed at www.literacyworldwide.org/docs/default-source/where-we-stand/ila-teaching-writing-to-improve-reading-skills.pdf on June 16, 2024.

International Literacy Association. (n.d.). *Literacy glossary.* Accessed at www.literacyworldwide.org/get-resources/literacy-glossary on June 16, 2024.

IRIS Center (n.d.). *What is differentiated instruction?* Accessed at https://iris.peabody.vanderbilt.edu/module/di/cresource/q1/p02/ on December 1, 2024.

Jackson, D. (2021). *Leveraging MTSS to ensure equitable outcomes.* Center on Multi-Tiered System of Supports at American Institutes for Research.

Jenkins, J. R., Schiller, E., Blackorby, J., Thayer, S. K., & Tilly, W. D. (2013). Responsiveness to intervention in reading: Architecture and practices. *Learning Disability Quarterly, 36*(1), 36–46.

J4P4N. (2021, October 9). *Cat's cradle.* Accessed at https://openclipart.org/detail/333646/cats-cradle on June 16, 2024.

Keesey, S., Konrad, M., & Joseph, L. M. (2015). Word boxes improve phonemic awareness, letter–sound correspondences, and spelling skills of at-risk kindergartners. *Remedial and Special Education, 36*(3), 167–180. https://doi.org/10.1177/0741932514543927

Kilpatrick, D. A. (2016). *Phonological Awareness Screening Test (PAST)* [Measurement instrument]. Accessed at https://masp.wildapricot.org/resources/Documents/PAST%202016.pdf on June 16, 2024.

Kintz, C. (2016). *Sunny days, starry nights.* Center for the Collaborative Classroom.

Kise, J. A. G. (2007). *Differentiation through personality types: A framework for instruction, assessment, and classroom management.* Corwin Press.

Kise, J. A. G. (2021). *Doable differentiation: 12 strategies to meet the needs of all learners.* Solution Tree Press.

Kramer, S. V., Sonju, B., Mattos, M., & Buffum, A. (2021). *Best practices at Tier 2: Supplemental interventions for additional student support, elementary.* Solution Tree Press.

Kuhn, M. R. (2014, May 7). *What's really wrong with round robin reading?* [Blog post]. Accessed at www.literacyworldwide.org/blog/literacy-now/2014/05/07/what's-really-wrong-with-round-robin-reading- on August 29, 2024.

Kuhn, M. R. (2020). Whole class or small group fluency instruction: A tutorial of four effective approaches. *Education Sciences, 10*(5), Article 145. https://doi.org/10.3390/educsci10050145

Ladson-Billings, G. (2009). *The dreamkeepers: Successful teachers of African American children* (2nd ed.). Jossey-Bass.

Lastiri, L. (2022, June 21). *What are the levels of comprehension?* Accessed at https://irisreading.com/what-are-the-levels-of-comprehension on October 10, 2024.

Lee, H. S., & Ha, H. (2019). Metacognitive judgments of prior material facilitate the learning of new material: The forward effect of metacognitive judgments in inductive learning. *Journal of Educational Psychology, 111*(7), 1189–1201. https://doi.org/10.1037/edu0000339

Lee, S. H., & Tsai, S.-F. (2017). Experimental intervention research on students with specific poor comprehension: A systematic review of treatment outcomes. *Reading and Writing: An Interdisciplinary Journal, 30*(4), 917–943.

Lemons, C. J., Vaughn, S., Wexler, J., Kearns, D. M., & Sinclair, A. C. (2018). Envisioning an improved continuum of special education services for students with learning disabilities: Considering intervention intensity. *Learning Disabilities Research and Practice, 33*(3), 131–143.

Lemov, D. (2015). *Teach like a champion 2.0: 62 techniques that put students on the path to college* (2nd ed.). Jossey-Bass.

Leonard, K. M., Coyne, M. D., Oldham, A. C., Burns, D., & Gillis, M. B. (2019). Implementing MTSS in beginning reading: Tools and systems to support schools and teachers. *Learning Disabilities Research and Practice, 34*(2), 110–117.

Lervåg, A., Hulme, C., & Melby-Lervåg, M. (2018). Unpicking the developmental relationship between oral language skills and reading comprehension: It's simple, but complex. *Child Development, 89*(5), 1821–1838. https://doi.org/10.1111/cdev.12861

Lewis, C. C., & Hurd, J. (2011). *Lesson study step by step: How teacher learning communities improve instruction*. Heinemann.

Lindsey, J. B. (2022). *Reading above the fray: Reliable, research-based routines for developing decoding skills*. Scholastic.

Little, M. E., Slanda, D. D., & Cramer, E. D. (2025). *The educator's guide to action research: Practical connections for implementation of data-driven decision-making*. Rowman & Littlefield.

Loftus, M., & Sappington, L. (Hosts). (2023, May 26). Wild about Wexler: Take 2! [Audio podcast episode]. In *Melissa & Lori Love Literacy*. Accessed at https://literacypodcast.com/podcast?podcast =Buzzsprout-12689920 on October 28, 2024.

Mackie, M. (2014). *Life in a tide pool*. McGraw-Hill Education.

Maeker, P., & Heller, J. (2023). *Literacy in a PLC at Work: Guiding teams to get going and get better in grades K–6 reading*. Solution Tree Press.

Markle, S. (2020). *Volcanoes*. McGraw-Hill.

Martin, K. (2019, May 19). *Three professional learning practices that honor the expertise of educators* [Blog post]. Accessed at https://katielmartin.com/2019/05/19/3-professional-learning-practices-that-honor-the-expertise-of-educators on June 16, 2024.

Mattos, M., Buffum, A., Malone, J., Cruz, L. F., Dimich, N., & Schuhl, S. (2025). *Taking action: A handbook for RTI at Work* (2nd ed.). Solution Tree Press.

McCarthey, S. J., Hoffman, J. V., Christian, C., Corman, L., Elliott, B., Matherne, D., et al. (1994). Engaging the new basal readers. *Reading Research and Instruction, 33*(3), 233–256. https://doi.org/10.1080/19388079409558157

Meneses, A., Uccelli, P., Santelices, M. V., Ruiz, M., Acevedo, D., & Figueroa, J. (2018). Academic language as a predictor of reading comprehension in monolingual Spanish-speaking readers: Evidence from Chilean early adolescents. *Reading Research Quarterly, 53*(2), 223–247. https://doi.org/10.1002/rrq.192

Miciak, J., Roberts, G., Taylor, W. P., Solis, M., Ahmed, Y., Vaughn, S., et al. (2018). The effects of one versus two years of intensive reading intervention implemented with late elementary struggling readers. *Learning Disabilities Research and Practice, 33*(1), 24–36. https://doi.org/10.1111/ldrp.12159

Mokhtari, K., & Reichard, C. A. (2002). Assessing students' metacognitive awareness of reading strategies. *Journal of Educational Psychology, 94*(2), 249–259. https://doi.org/10.1037/0022-0663.94.2.249

Møller, H. L., Obi Mortensen, J., & Elbro, C. (2022). Effects of integrated spelling in phonics instruction for at-risk children in kindergarten. *Reading and Writing Quarterly, 38*(1), 67–82. https://doi.org/10.1080/10573569.2021.1907638

Nation, K., Angell, P., & Castles, A. (2007). Orthographic learning via self-teaching in children learning to read English: Effects of exposure, durability, and context. *Journal of Experimental Child Psychology, 96*(1), 71–84. https://doi.org/10.1016/j.jecp.2006.06.004

National Governors Association Center for Best Practices & Council of Chief State School Officers. (2010). *Common Core State Standards for English language arts and literacy in history/social studies, science, and technical subjects.* Authors. Accessed at https://learning.ccsso.org/wp-content/uploads/2022/11/ADA-Compliant-ELA-Standards.pdf on June 16, 2024.

National Reading Panel. (2000). *National Reading Panel: Teaching children to read—An evidence-based assessment of the scientific research literature on reading and its implications for reading instruction* [Report]. Author. Accessed at www.nichd.nih.gov/sites/default/files/publications/pubs/nrp/Documents/report.pdf on October 25, 2024.

Neitzel, J., Franzmeier, N., Rubinski, A., Dichgans, M., Brendel, M., Malik, R., et al. (2021). KL-VS heterozygosity is associated with lower amyloid-dependent tau accumulation and memory impairment in Alzheimer's disease. *Nature Communications, 12*(1), Article 3825.

Nelson, P. T., Dickson, D. W., Trojanowski, J. Q., Jack, C. R., Boyle, P. A., Arfanakis, K., et al. (2019). Limbic-predominant age-related TDP-43 encephalopathy (LATE): Consensus working group report. *Brain, 142*(6), 1503–1527. https://doi.org/10.1093/brain/awz099

Onyishi, C. N., & Sefotho, M. M. (2020). Teachers' perspectives on the use of differentiated instruction in inclusive classrooms: Implication for teacher education. *International Journal of Higher Education, 9*(6), 136–150.

OpenAI. (2024a). *ChatGPT* (Feb 2 version) [Large language model]. Accessed at https://chatgpt.com on October 28, 2024.

OpenAI. (2024b). *Copilot* (May 16 version) [Large language model]. Accessed at https://copilot.microsoft.com on October 28, 2024.

OpenAI. (2024c). *Copilot* (May 16 version) [Large language model]. Accessed at https://copilot.microsoft.com on October 28, 2024.

OpenAI. (2024d). *Copilot* (May 16 version) [Large language model]. Accessed at https://copilot.microsoft.com on October 28, 2024.

OpenAI. (2024e). *Copilot* (May 21 version) [Large language model]. Accessed at https://copilot.microsoft.com on October 28, 2024.

OpenAI. (2024f). *Copilot* (May 21 version) [Large language model]. Accessed at https://copilot.microsoft.com on October 28, 2024.

OpenAI. (2024g). *Copilot* (May 21 version) [Large language model]. Accessed at https://copilot.microsoft.com on October 28, 2024.

OpenAI. (2024h). *Copilot* (May 22 version) [Large language model]. Accessed at https://copilot.microsoft.com on October 28, 2024.

Orange County Public Schools. (n.d.). *B.E.S.T-aligned questions*. Accessed at https://drive.google.com/file/d/166ziwXBLUZ3KhT5gVsJFBuNcOIv-xccP/view on June 16, 2024.

Orange County Public Schools. (2024). *Elementary ELA diving into small-group instruction.* Accessed at https://drive.google.com/file/d/1174-rI2WN4O_e_HpxbucGYYlwHpJfg-y/view?usp=sharing on June 16, 2024.

Paris, S. G. (2005). Reinterpreting the development of reading skills. *Reading Research Quarterly, 40*(2), 184–202.

Park, V., & Datnow, A. (2017). Ability grouping and differentiated instruction in an era of data-driven decision making. *American Journal of Education, 123*(2), 281–306.

Pearson, P. D., & Gallagher, M. C. (1983). The instruction of reading comprehension. *Contemporary Educational Psychology, 8*(3), 317–344. https://doi.org/10.1016/0361-476X(83)90019-X

Perritano, J. (2021). *Games around the world.* Children's Press.

Philbrick, R. (2014). *Zane and the hurricane: A story of Katrina.* Blue Sky Press.

Phillips, B. M., Kim, Y.-S. G., Lonigan, C. J., Connor, C. M., Clancy, J., & Al Otaiba, S. (2021). Supporting language and literacy development with intensive small-group interventions: An early childhood efficacy study. *Early Childhood Research Quarterly, 57*(1), 75–88.

Piasta, S. B., & Wagner, R. K. (2010). Developing early literacy skills: A meta-analysis of alphabet learning and instruction. *Reading Research Quarterly, 45*(1), 8–38. https://doi.org/10.1598/RRQ.45.1.2

Pierantoni, R. (2017, February 15). *How classroom predictability and student trust enhance student learning* [Blog post]. Accessed at https://njalternateroute.rutgers.edu/blog/how-classroom-predictability-student-trust-enhance-student-learning on June 16, 2024.

Pulley Sayre, A. (2010). *Turtle, turtle, watch out!* (A. Patterson, Illus.). Charlesbridge.

Pyle, N., Vasquez, A. C., Lignugaris-Kraft, B., Gillam, S. L., Reutzel, D. R., Olszewski, A., et al. (2017). Effects of expository text structure interventions on comprehension: A meta-analysis. *Reading Research Quarterly, 52*(4), 469–501.

Reading Rockets. (n.d.a). *Phonics instruction: The value of a multi-sensory approach.* Accessed at www.readingrockets.org/topics/curriculum-and-instruction/articles/phonics-instruction-value-multi-sensory-approach on June 16, 2024.

Reading Rockets. (n.d.b). *What is evidence-based instruction?* Accessed at www.readingrockets.org/classroom/evidence-based-instruction/what-is-evidence-based-instruction on September 1, 2024.

ReadWorks. (n.d.). *Jellyfish take over!* Accessed at www.readworks.org/article/Jellyfish-Take-Over!/53cbdde9-2a23-4a22-85bb-1b2f8c0d5b70#!articleTab:content on June 16, 2024.

Reis, S. M., McCoach, D. B., Little, C. A., Muller, L. M., & Kaniskan, R. B. (2011). The effects of differentiated instruction and enrichment pedagogy on reading achievement in five elementary schools. *American Educational Research Journal, 48*(2), 462–501.

Remillard, J. (2016, October). How to partner with your curriculum. *Educational Leadership, 74*(2), 34–38.

Remillard, J. (2018). Mapping the relationship between written and enacted curriculum: Examining teachers' decision making. In G. Kaiser, H. Forgasz, M. Graven, A. Kuzniak, E. Simmt, & B. Xu (Eds.), *Invited lectures from the 13th International Congress on Mathematical Education: ICME-13 monographs* (pp. 483–500). Springer. https://doi.org/10.1007/978-3-319-72170-5_27

Remillard, J., & Heck, D. J. (2014). Conceptualizing the curriculum enactment process in mathematics education. *ZDM, 46*(5), 705–718. https://doi.org/10.1007/s11858-014-0600-4

Rogers, P., Smith, W. R., Buffum, A., & Mattos, M. (2020). *Best practices at Tier 3: Intensive interventions for remediation, elementary.* Solution Tree Press.

Roth, W.-M., & Lee, S. (2002). Scientific literacy as collective praxis. *Public Understanding of Science, 11*(1), 33–56.

Samman, E., & Santos, M. E. (2009). Agency and empowerment: A review of concepts, indicators and empirical evidence. *OPHI Research in Progress 10a.* Accessed at https://ophi.org.uk/sites/default/files/OPHI-RP10a.pdf on October 25, 2024.

Sawchuk, S. (2023, January 17). *How does writing fit into the "science of reading"?* Accessed at www.edweek.org/teaching-learning/how-does-writing-fit-into-the-science-of-reading/2023/01 on June 16, 2024.

Scarborough, H. S. (2001). Connecting early language and literacy to later reading (dis)abilities: Evidence, theory, and practice. In S. B. Neuman & D. K. Dickinson (Eds.), *Handbook of early literacy research* (Vol. 1, pp. 97–110). Guilford Press.

Schmidt, S. (2020, February 25). *Day 1 discussion: Productive struggle with complex text with Anita Kerr!* [Forum]. Accessed at https://community.lincs.ed.gov/group/25/discussion/day-1-discussion-productive-struggle-complex-text-anita-kerr on June 16, 2024.

Shamir, A., & Korat, O. (2015). Educational electronic books for supporting emergent literacy of kindergarteners at-risk for reading difficulties—What do we know so far? *Computers in the Schools, 32*(2), 105–121.

Shanahan, C. (2009). Disciplinary comprehension. In S. E. Israel & G. G. Duffy (Eds.), *Handbook of research on reading comprehension* (pp. 240–260). Routledge.

Shanahan, T. (2019, July 30). *Is round robin reading really that bad?* [Blog post]. Accessed at www.readingrockets.org/blogs/shanahan-on-literacy/round-robin-reading-really-bad on June 16, 2024.

Shanahan, T. (2020, May 16). *What about tracing and other multi-sensory teaching approaches?* [Blog post]. Accessed at www.shanahanonliteracy.com/blog/what-about-tracing-and-other-multi-sensory-teaching-approaches on June 16, 2024.

Shanahan, T., Callison, K., Carriere, C., Duke, N. K., Pearson, P. D., Schatschneider, C., et al. (2010). *Improving reading comprehension in kindergarten through 3rd grade: A practice guide* (NCEE 2010-4038) [Report]. Accessed at https://files.eric.ed.gov/fulltext/ED512029.pdf on June 16, 2024.

Simple world map. (2011, August 31). *In Wikimedia Commons.* Accessed at https://commons.wikimedia.org/wiki/File:Simple_world_map.svg on June 16, 2024.

Slanda, D. D., Pike, L. M., Herbert, L., Wells, E. B., & Pelt, C. (2022). Dismantling disproportionality in special education through antiracist practices. In T. M. Mealy & H. Bennett (Eds.), *Equity in the classroom: Essays on curricular and pedagogical approaches to empowering all students* (pp. 218–264). McFarland.

TNTP. (2022, June). *Instructional coherence: A key to high-quality learning acceleration for all students.* Author. Accessed at https://tntp.org/wp-content/uploads/Tools/instructional-coherence.pdf on October 28, 2024.

Tomlinson, C. A. (2001). *How to differentiate instruction in mixed-ability classrooms* (2nd ed.). ASCD.

Tomlinson, C. A., & Jarvis, J. M. (2009). Differentiation: Making curriculum work for all students through responsive planning & instruction. In J. S. Renzulli, E. J. Gubbins, K. S. McMillen, R. D. Eckert, & C. A. Little (Eds.), *Systems and models for developing programs for the gifted and talented* (2nd ed., pp. 599–628). Routledge.

Torppa, M, Georgiou, G. K.; Lerkkanen, M.-K., Niemi, P., Poikkeus, A.-M., & Nurmi, J.-E. (2016). Examining the simple view of reading in a transparent orthography: A longitudinal study from kindergarten to grade 3. *Merrill-Palmer Quarterly, 62*(2), 179–206.

Toste, J. R., Capin, P., Williams, K. J., Kearns, D. M., & Vaughn, S. (2023). *Word connections: A multisyllabic word reading program* (2nd ed.) [MOOC]. Figshare. https://doi.org/10.6084/m9.figshare.c.6259368

Toste, J. R., Didion, L., Peng, P., Filderman, M. J., & McClelland, A. M. (2020). A meta-analytic review of the relations between motivation and reading achievement for K–12 students. *Review of Educational Research, 90*(3), 420–456. https://doi.org/10.3102/0034654320919352

University of Florida Literacy Institute. (n.d.). *What is UFLI Foundations?* Accessed at https://ufli.education.ufl.edu/foundations on June 16, 2024.

University of Oregon. (n.d.). *Dynamic Indicators of Basic Early Literacy Skills* (DIBELS; 8th ed.) [Measurement instrument]. Accessed at https://dibels.uoregon.edu on June 16, 2024.

Vail-Smith, S. (Host). (2021, May 28). Science of reading AND learning: Interview with Mrs. Zaretta Hammond [Audio podcast episode]. In *Alabama Literacy Network.* Accessed at https://literacyalabama.podbean.com/e/science-of-reading-learning-interview-with-mrs-zaretta-hammond on June 16, 2024.

Valencia, R. R. (2010). *Dismantling contemporary deficit thinking: Educational thought and practice.* Routledge.

Wanzek, J., Vaughn, S., Scammacca, N., Gatlin, B., Walker, M. A., & Capin, P. (2016). Meta-analyses of the effects of Tier 2 type reading interventions in grades K–3. *Educational Psychology Review, 28*(3), 551–576.

Washburne, C. W. (1953, December). Adjusting the program to the child. *Educational Leadership, 11*(3), 138–147.

Weisberg, P., & Savard, C. F. (1993). Teaching preschoolers to read: Don't stop between the sounds when segmenting words. *Education and Treatment of Children, 16*(1), 1–18.

Wexler, N. (2020). Building knowledge: What an elementary school curriculum should do. *American Educator, 44*(2), 18–21.

White, S., Sabatini, J., Park, B. J., Chen, J., Bernstein, J., & Li, M. (2021, April). *The 2018 NAEP Oral Reading Fluency Study* (NCES 2021-025). U.S. Department of Education. Accessed at https://nces.ed.gov/nationsreportcard/subject/studies/orf/2021025_orf_study.pdf on October 28, 2024.

Wiesner, D. (1990). *Hurricane*. Clarion Books.

Wint, K. M., Opara, I., Gordon, R., & Brooms, D. R. (2022). Countering educational disparities among Black boys and Black adolescent boys from pre-K to high school: A life course-intersectional perspective. *The Urban Review, 54*(2), 183–206.

Ziebell, N., & Clarke, D. (2018). Curriculum alignment: Performance types in the intended, enacted, and assessed curriculum in primary mathematics and science classrooms. *Studia Paedagogica, 23*(2), 175–203.

INDEX

A

ability grouping vs. differentation, 41
access and equity, 5
    differentiating, 35-48
    differentiating small-group discussion
        promotes, 7, 13
accountability, 187–189
    facilitating, 188
    questions to gauge, 188
action and expression, 38–39
active self-regulation, 23, 25, 27
Active View of Reading model (Duke & Cartwright), 20–24, 98, 102–103
adding domains, 43
affective knowledge, 169, 171–172
alignment, 184–186
    coherence from whole to small group, 59–62
    examples, 185
    sample literacy blocks, 59–61
all means all, 5, 7, 17
alliteration, 150
alphabetic approach, 23, 81
    connecting to writing, 150
    defined, 20
Amendum, S. J., 67
Amira Reading (Istation), 40
analysis, 4
anticipation guide, 173–174
    sample, 173
applying learning through written expression, 158
Arego, R., 140
argumentative text, 56
    writing, 151
artificial intelligence (AI) for text creation, 105–106
asking questions, 115
assessments, 40
asset-based approach
    defined, 19
    flexible grouping, 42
Asset-Based Continuum (ABC) Reader Profile Framework, 7, 25–28, 197
    expand your toolbox, 148
    in action, 31–32
    leveraging observation as opportunities, 147
    monitoring and responding to students, 141
    observational reading data build a reader profile, 28–30
    planning for small-group instruction, 65–66, 68–70
    profile tool, 141–142
    promps for comprehension, self-monitoring, and metacognition, 145
    prompts for decoding and word recognition, 142–143
    prompts for fluency and bridging processes, 144
    reader observation tool, 141
    recharge your instruction, 148
    reflections, 148
    sample observation tool, 146
    sample reader profile, 155–156
audience, 151
authentic, aligned tasks with accountability, 9, 58, 100–101183–184
    accountability, 187
    alignment, 184–186
    authenticity, 181, 186–187
awareness of task, 151

B

background knowledge, 23, 169–170, 172
The Battle Against Pests (Bennett), 102–104
Bennett, L., 104
big readers
    defined, 4

243

blending, 89
Blevins, W., 152
Blintt, J., 106
blocked practice, 52
Bondie, R. S., 37
book study with colleagues, 12–13
"boss figure," 53
bridging processes, 21–22, 26, 29
    prompts for, 144
Brown, J. D., 111–112
building readers' knowledge, 9, 13, 167–168
    connections to whole-group topics, 176
    expand your toolbox, 178
    guiding questions, 222–223
    implementation activities, 223
    Leading the Learning Action Guide, 221–223
    recharging your instruction, 178
    reflections, 178
    role of knowledge building in literacy instruction, 168–172
    strategies to gauge, 172–176
    text sets, 176–177
    videos, 171–172, 222–223

C

Calame, J., 202–203
Cartwright, K. B., 102
Cartwright, K. B., 20–24
Center for the Collaborative Classroom, 118–119, 140–141
Cervetti, G. N., 168–169
characterization, 151
choice-based tasks, 195
choosing curriculum sources, 71–72
choral reading, 90
class work during small groups, 9, 179–180
    authentic, aligned tasks with accountability, 184–189
    considerations for the rest of the class, 180–181
    expand your toolbox, 196
    guiding questions, 224
    implementation activities, 225
    Leading the Learning Action Guide, 224–225, 224
    the literacy block, 181–184
    recharge your instruction, 196
    reflections, 195–196
    structure in independent practice, 190–195
    student grouping, 189–190
    videos, 184, 224
cohesiveness, 151
Coleman, D., 53
collaborative learning, 55–56, 133–134
collaborative team discussions, 31
Common Core State Standards (CCSS), 94, 102
communication tool, 32
compreaction, 90
comprehension, 22–23, 25, 27, 30
    planning for small-group instruction, 76, 85, 90
    prompts for, 145
    routine for, 85, 145
    writing to enhance, 158
connecting to whole-group instruction, 7, 12–13, 49–51, 176
    alignment and coherence, 59–62
    gradual release model, 55–57
    guiding questions, 209
    implementation activities, 210
    interleaved practice, 52–55
    knowledge of curriculum standards, 57–58
    launch your reflection, 62–63
    Leading the Learning Action Guide, 209–210
    recharge your instruction, 63
    videos, 51–52, 209
considerations for the rest of the class, 180–181
    time to spend in the literary block calculation, 180
constrained skills, 23
content
    defined, 38
content-specific knowledge, 158
    defined, 22
core instruction within tiered supports, 4–5
CORE Literacy Library, 71
CORE Phonics Survey (CORE Literacy Library), 71
creating a personal response and reaction to a text, 158
creating a story, 158
creating mood, 151
cueing, 115–116
cultural knowledge, 169–172
    connecting to writing, 151
    defined, 22
culturally responsive practice
    flexible grouping, 42
Culturally Responsive Teaching and the Brain (Hammond), 1
curiosity, 4–5
Curriculum Associates, 40
curriculum
    enacted vs. operational, 111
    knowledge of standards, 57–58
    standards, 49
curriculum-based measures of assessment, 40
CVC words, 122–125

D

Dahnke, C., 37
data sources, 24–25
data to form groups, 11
Datnow, A., 41
declarative knowledge, 169
    defined, 170
decodable text, 100
Decoding Prompts, 148
decoding, 4, 25–26, 29, 153, 168
    connecting to writing, 150
    defined, 21
    lesson snapshot, 122–126
    prompts for, 142–143
deficit-based approach
    defined, 19
designing equity-centered, differentiated literacy blocks, 37–38
    domains of differentiation across grade-evel text, 38
determining data-informed focus areas, 67–70
    defined, 37
differentiated reading instruction, 36–37
    equity-centered, differentiated literacy blocks, 37–38
    flexible grouping, 41–42
    using data, 40–41

within Universal Design for Learning, 38–39
differentiated small-group instruction, 11
    expand your toolbox, 48
    guiding questions, 207
    implementation activities, 208
    in the classroom, 43
    Leading the Learning Action Guide, 207–208
    promotes access and equity, 7, 13, 35–36
    reading, 36–43
    recharge your instruction, 48
    reflection, 47
    videos, 39–40, 45, 207
    within MTSS, 43–47
digital text concepts, 90
Dimono, J., 1–2
direct explanations, 115–116
directionality, 150
discipline-specific writing, 151
district-purchased and -adopted screener and diagnostic assessments, 40
diverse learning characteristics, 36
domain knowledge, 169–170, 172
drafting, 151
Duke, N. K., 20–24, 40, 102, 137, 140
Dynamic Indicators of Basic Early Literacy Skills (DIBELS; University of Oregon), 40

E

echo reading, 90
    with phrase-cued text, 128–129
economy of language, 116–117
Education Week, 152
elaboration, 151
Elkonin boxes, 125, 184
    template, 92
embedded writing, 12
enacted curriculum, 111
encoding, 150, 153–154
encouraging unique thought about a text, 158
engagement, 38–39, 195
    connecting to writing, 151
    decoding lesson snapshot, 122–126
    defined, 23
    making inferences lesson snapshot, 130–135
    phonemic awareness lesson snapshot, 119–122
    prosody lesson snapshot, 126–130
    strategies in action, 119
    strategies, 12
    teacher facilitation and, 110–119
engaging readers, 8, 13, 109–110, 197
    engagement strategies in action, 119–135
    expand your toolbox, 136
    guiding questions, 215–216
    implementation activities, 217
    Leading the Learning Action Guide, 215–217
    recharge your instruction, 136
    reflections, 135
    teacher facilitation and student engagement, 110–119
    videos, 122, 126, 134, 215–216
enriching discussions, 46
enrichment, 46
episodic knowledge, 169
    defined, 170
equity, 35–48
equity-centered literacy blocks, 37–38
essential tasks, 195

establishing norms for student-to-student engagement, 117–118
evaluating outcomes, 43
evidence-based practices and programs, 6, 8, 44, 51
examples. See samples and examples
executive function skills
    connecting to writing, 151
    defined, 23
expand your toolbox, 10
    building readers' knowledge, 178
    class work during small groups, 196
    connecting to whole group–instruction, 63
    connecting writing to small–group instruction, 165
    differentiated instruction, 48
    engaging readers, 136
    monitoring and responding to students, 148
    planning for small-group instruction, 92
    selecting and evaluating text, 107
    students as readers, 33
expanding your professional community and commitment, 198–199
    video, 199
explicit instruction
    defined, 89
expressive reading, 4
extended learning opportunities, 60–61
Extended Practice Opportunities Considerations, 196
extended practice opportunities
    literacy block, 183–184
Extended Practice Reflection and Observation Tool, 196
extending your reflections, 198

F

facilitating new understanding and connections, 158
Fisher D., 55, 167, 181–184
five-day assisted learning template, 76
fix-up strategies, 138
    teaching, 140
flexibility, 194
flexible grouping, 12, 41–42, 190
    defined, 41
    sample tool, 42
    vs. ability grouping, 41
Floating in the Deep End (Davis), 96, 98
fluency, 25–26, 29, 150
    defined, 21
    prompts for, 144
    routine, 84–85, 90
focus lesson, 182
focused instruction, 55–56
focusing on outcomes, 195
fostering explicitness and literal comprehension, 158
fostering independence, 140
foundational skills, 51
framing reading opportunities, 73–78
Frey, N., 55, 167, 181–184

G

genre, 151
Gersten, R., 1–2
goals. See learning goals
grade-level text
    differentiation with, 38
gradual release model, 55–57, 130
    components, 56–57

planning for, 189
Graham, S., 158
grammar, 151
graphemes, 150
graphophonological-semantic cognitive flexibility
    connecting to writing, 151
    defined, 22
Gregory, G., 41
group size and time, 194
grouping decision, 31
GRR framework (Fisher & Frey), 181–182, 189
    components, 182
guided instruction, 55–56, 183
guiding questions, 10
    building readers' knowledge, 222–223
    class work during small groups, 224
    connecting to whole-group instruction, 209
    differentiating small-group instruction promotes access and equity, 207
    engaging readers, 215–216
    monitoring and responding to students, 217–219
    planning for small–group instruction, 211–212
    selecting and evaluating text, 213
    what do I know about my students as readers? 204–205
    writing connects to small-group instruction, 220
Guth, G., 126

H

Hammond, Z., 1
Haymond, K. S., 1–2
Hebert, M., 158
Heck, D. J., 111
heterogeneous grouping, 41–42, 189–190
Hickman, P., 104
high-frequency words, 150, 153
high-quality literacy instruction, 1–3
high-stakes testing, 41
homogeneous grouping, 41–42, 189
Hurricane (Wiesner), 170
Hwang, HJ, 168–169

I

identifying learning goals, 71
implementation activities, 203
    building readers' knowledge, 223
    class work during small groups, 223
    connecting to whole-group instruction, 210
    differentiating small-group instruction promotes access and equity, 208
    engaging readers, 217
    monitoring and responding to students, 291
    planning for small-group instruction, 212
    selecting and evaluating text, 214
    what do I know about my students as readers? 206
    writing connects to small-group instruction, 221
independent learning, 55, 57
independent or collaborative practice, 183
individual readers, 31
Individualized Daily Reading Conference Record (Center for the Collaborative Classroom), 140–141
inside the rotation, 193
instructional approaches, 58
instructional coherence. See connecting to whole–group instruction
instructional focus area, 25
instructional opportunities by text, 98
instructional organization, 11
instructional pacing, 118–119
instructional routines, 11, 72–86
    alphabet instruction, 81
    comprehension instruction, 85
    fluency, 84–85
    introducing sound-spelling relationships, 82
    morphology instruction, 84
    phonemic awareness instruction, 80
    reading a decodable text, 83
intentional planning, 67
    determining data-informed focus areas, 67–70
    identifying learning goals, 71
    sample ABC Reader Profile, 69–70
    selecting curriculum resources, 71–72
interleaved practice, 52–55
    examples, 54
    text-attack process poster, 55
    vs. blocked practice, 52
International Literacy Association (ILA), 152, 158
    blog, 106
intervention, 58 (see also multitiered system of supports) providing, 45–46
introducing sound-spelling relationships, 82
i-Ready Diagnostic (Curriculum Associates), 40
Istation, 40

J

Jarvis, J. M., 37
"Jellyfish Take Over!" 160

K

Kaufeldt, M., 41
Keller, H., 104, 130–134
Kennedy, A. 168
Kilpatrick, D. A., 40
Kintz, C., 126–129
Klingelhofer, R., 40
knowledge as Velcro, 169
knowledge building, 103–105
knowledge of curriculum standards, 57–58
    instructional approaches, 58
Knowledge-Building Question Stems, 172, 178
KWL strategy, 174

L

language features, 8
language structure
    connecting to writing, 151
    defined, 22
launch your reflection
    building readers' knowledge, 178
    class work during small groups, 195–196
    connecting to whole-group instruction, 62–63
    connecting writing to small-group instruction, 165
    differentiated instruction, 47
    engaging readers, 135
    monitoring and responding to students, 148
    planning for small–group instruction, 91
    selecting and evaluating text, 107
    students as readers, 32

Index

Leading the Learning Action Guide, 9–10, 48, 61, 92, 107, 136, 148, 165, 178, 196, 201–225
    building readers' knowledge, 221–223
    class work during small groups, 224–225
    connecting to whole-group instruction, 209–210
    differentiating small-group instruction promotes access and equity, 207–208
    engaging readers, 215–217
    monitoring and responding to students, 217–219
    planning for small-group instruction, 211–212
    selecting and evaluating text, 213–214
    videos, 202–202, 226
    what do I know about my students as readers? 204–206
    writing connects to small-group instruction, 220–221
learner diversity, 36–37
learning goals, 12
    ABC Reader Profile, 31
    choosing curriculum goals that support, 71–72
    determining, 66, 58, 71, 151
Lemov, D., 116
lesson observation and reflection tool (Center for the Collaborative Classroom), 113–114
lesson snapshots
    decoding, 122–126
    making inferences, 130–135
    phonemic awareness, 119–122
    prosody, 126–130
lesson structures, 72–73
    five-day assisted learning template, 76
    lesson template for comprehension skills, 78
    lesson template for foundational skills based on structured literacy, 77
    lesson template menu, 75
    to frame reading opportunities, 73–78
lesson study, 198–199
lesson templates
    for comprehension skills, 78
    for foundational skills based on structured literacy, 77
    menu, 75
letter formation, 76, 150
letter ID activity, 76
letter names-sounds, 89
leveraging observation as opportunities, 147
Listening to Reading—Watching While Writing Protocol (LTR-WWWP; Duke et al.), 40, 140
literacy blocks, 37–38, 181–182
    extended practice opportunities, 183–184
    first grade, 59–60
    fourth and fifth grade, 60–61
    GRR framework and components, 182
    small group, 183
    time to spend in, 180
    whole group, 182
literary devices, 151

M

make-up station, 194
making a claim, 158
making inferences
    graphic organizer, 136
    lesson snapshot, 130–135

Mattos, M., 41
maximizing practice time, 194
memoirs, 151
metacognitive skills, 30, 46
    prompts for, 145
monitoring and responding to students, 8, 12–13, 137–142
    ABC Reader Profile Framework reader observation tool, 141
    expand your toolbox, 148
    guiding questions, 217–219
    implementation activities, 219
    Leading the Learning Action Guide, 217–219
    leveraging observation as opportunities, 147
    recharge your instruction, 148
    reflections, 148
    responding on the spot, 142–146
    videos, 140, 146, 217–218
morphological awareness
    connecting to writing, 151
    defined, 22
    instruction, 84, 90, 98
motivation, 90–91, 195
    connecting to writing, 151
    defined, 23
multilingual students, 47
multitiered system of supports (MTSS), 4–5
    differentiated instruction in, 35, 43–45
    enrichment, 46
    intervention, 45–46
    multilingual students, 47
    students with disabilities, 46
must do, may do model, 194–195
    example, 194
    integrating with the rotation model, 195

N

narrative writing, 151
Newman-Gonchar, R., 1–2

O

observational notes from instruction, 40
observational reading data build a reader profile, 28
open-access informal reading assessments, 40
operational curriculum, 111
organization of rotation, 183
organizing and planning, 12–13, 151
organizing, managing, and preparing materials, 86–88
    sample logistics, 87–88
orthographic mapping, 89, 125, 150–151, 153
out of rotation model, 193

P

paired reading, 90, 130
paragraph structure, 151
parent/caregiver communication, 32
Paris, S. G., 23
Park, V., 41
pedagogy of compliance, 5
Philbrick, R., 177
phonemes, 150
phonemic awareness, 76, 168
    lesson snapshot, 119–122
    routine for instruction, 80, 89
    warm-up, 153

phonics knowledge, 23, 89
    connecting to writing, 150
    defined, 20
Phonological Awareness Screening Test (PAST; Kilpatrick), 40
phonological awareness, 23
    connecting to writing, 150
    defined, 20
phrase-cued text, 127–129
placemat consensus, 56
planning for small-group instruction, 8, 13, 65–66, 151
    expand your toolbox, 92
    guiding questions, 211–212
    implementation activities, 212
    intentional, 67–72
    launch your reflection, 91
    Leading the Learning Action Guide, 211–212
    lesson structures and instructional routines, 72–86
    organizing, managing, and preparing materials, 86–88
    recharge your instruction, 91–92
    teacher content knowledge, 89–91
    videos, 67, 86, 211–212
point of view, 151
print concepts, 90
    connecting to directionality, spacing, and punctuation, 150
    defined, 21
print-rich environment, 46
procedural knowledge, 169
    defined, 170
process
    defined, 38
product
    defined, 38
promoting synthesis and integration of information, 158
Prompting Cue Cards for Responding to Readers, 148
prompting, 155
    for comprehension, self-monitoring, and metacognition, 145
    for decoding and word recognition, 142–143
    for fluency and bridging processes, 144
prosody
    lesson snapshot, 126–130
    reading phrase-cued text, 127–128
providing intervention, 45–46
punctuation, 150–151
purpose, 151
purpose for reading, 56
purpose of grouping, 190

Q

question stems. See Knowledge-Building Question Stems
questioning, 4
questions. See also guiding questions
    gauging accountability, 188
    gauging alignment, 186
    gauging authenticity, 187
    planning for grouping, 189–190
    to self-assess your journey, 198

R

RAFT strategy, 160

Rammilard, J. T., 111
reader's theater, 90
readers' knowledge, 90
reading a decodable text, 83
reading and writing connection, 150–151
Reading and Writing Integration Planning Tool, 165
reading cups, 124–125
reading fluency. See fluency
reading research translations to practice, 89
reading-specific background knowledge
    connecting to writing, 151
    defined, 22
recharge your instruction
    building readers' knowledge, 178
    class work during small groups, 196
    connecting to whole-group instruction, 63
    connecting writing to small-group instruction, 165
    differentiated instruction, 48
    engaging readers, 136
    monitoring and responding to students, 148
    planning for small-group instruction, 91–92
    selecting and evaluating text, 107
    students as readers, 33
recognition of words by sight. See word sight recognition
refine and adjust, 43
reflecting and adjusting, 140
reflection, 4, 10, 13–15
    tool, 14
refocusing the roles of students and teacher, 112–115
    reflection and observation tool, 113–114
reliable assessment data, 11
representation, 38–39
    in texts, 106
responding to readers on the spot, 142
    prompts for comprehension, self-monitoring, and metacognition, 145
    prompts for decoding and word recognition, 142–143
    prompts for fluency and bridging processes, 144
    sample reader observation tool, 146
revising, 151
rhyming, 150
role of knowledge building in literacy instruction, 168–169
    affective knowledge, 169, 171–172
    background knowledge, 169–170, 172
    cultural knowledge, 169–172
    domain knowledge, 169–170, 172
    types of knowledge, 169
roles. See refocusing the roles of students and teacher
rotation model, 190–194
    organization, 183
    samples, 191–192
    teacher in and out, 193
round-robin reading, 139
routines. See also instructional routines
    for comprehension instruction, 158
    for introducing sound-spelling relationships, 153

S

Samman, E., 106
samples and examples
    ABC Reader Profile, 69–70, 155–157
    alignment, 185
    anticipation guide, 173
    connected reading and writing task, 160

decodable text, 100
how text features contribute to meaning and the author's purpose, 164
identifying the central idea, 162
identifying the central idea—text excerpt, 162
informational text about games from around the world, 164
informational text, 101
interleaved practice, 54–55
KWL for assessing knowledge, 174
KWL strategy, 174
logistics, 87–88
must do, must do model, 194
reader observation tool, 146
rotational model, 191–192
student affinity diagram, 175
student word list, 154–157
text consideration, 102–103
tool to organize flexible learning, 42
types of text, 95–97
word splash, 175
writer-generated narrative story, 155
writer-generated note, 155
Santos, M. E., 106
scaffolding, 102–103, 139
example text, 104–105
examples, 115–117
strategic, 115–116
selecting and evaluating text, 8, 13, 93–94
artificial intelligence for text creation, 105–106
expand your toolbox, 107
guiding questions, 213
implementation activities, 214
launch your reflections, 107
Leading the Learning Action Guide, 213–214
recharge your instruction, 107
representation in texts, 106
text accesibility, 103–105
text alignment to lesson purpose, 99–101
text considerations, 102–103
text definition, 94
text selection, 95–99
videos, 99, 105, 213
selecting curriculum resources, 71–72
self-assessment
of small-group reading practices, 13
teacher, 198
self-monitoring, 139
prompts for, 145
self-reflection, 30
self-regulation, 90–91
sentence elaboration, 151
sentence structure, 151
shared learning experiences, 6
sheet music, 111–112
sight words, 168
sight words, 20–21, 103–105, 168
prompts for, 142–143
writing to support, 152–154
small group
literacy block, 183
"Small-Group Reading Implementation Quick-Guide," 10–12
Small-group reading instruction, 1–2
Smith, K. C., 67
sound-spelling relationships, 82

routine for introducing, 153
spacing, 150
spelling, 150
inventory, 154
spiraled instruction, 195
start slowly, 43
strategies to gauge readers' background knowledge, 172–173
anticipation guide, 173–174
KWL strategy, 174
word splash, 174
strategy use, 151
structure, 183
in independent practice, 190
must do, may do model, 194–195
rotation model, 190–194
student facilitation, 125–126
student grouping, 183, 189–190
student ownership, 12
student reader profiles, 24–25
student reflection, 31
students as readers, 3–4
ABC Reader Profile Framework, 25–32
Active View of Reading model, 20–24
asset-based lens, 19
data sources and student reader profiles, 24–25
expand your toolbox, 33
guiding questions, 204–205
implementation activities, 206
Leading the Learning Action Guide, 204–206
recharge your instruction, 33
reflection, 32
videos, 18, 28, 204–205
what do you know about them? 7, 13, 17–18, 204–206
students with disabilities, 46
student-to-student engagement, 117–119
summarizing text, 4, 158, 151
Sunny Days, Starry Nights (Kintz), 126–129
syllable instruction, 90
syntax, 8, 151
systematic instruction
defined, 89

T

taking notes, 158
task movement, 193
Teach Like a Champion 2.0 (Lemov), 116
teacher content knowledge, 89–91
teacher facilitation and student engagement, 110–112
economy of language, 116–117
establishing norms for student-to-student engagement, 117–118
instructional pacing, 118–119
prosody lesson snapshot, 126–127
refocusing roles, 112–115
stragetic scaffolding, 115–116
Teacher Reflection Tool, 14
"Teaching Elementary School Students to Be Effective Writers" (WWC), 151
Team Data Meeting Reflection Questions, 32
sample, 32
tensions, 151
text accessibility, 103
knowledge building, 104–105
word recognition, 104–105
text alignment to lesson purpose, 99–101

sample decodable text, 100
sample informational text, 101
text selection decision-making tool, 99
text considerations, 12, 102–103
sample, 102–103
text definition, 94
range of text types, 94
text selection, 11, 95–99
decision-making tool, 99
instructional opportunities by text, 98
text examples, 95–97
text sets, 176–177
text structure, 8, 151
defined, 56
text type, 151
theme, 151
theory of mind
connecting to writing, 151, 171
defined, 23
Tier 1 instruction, 4–5, 40, 44, 52
Tier 2 instruction, 4–5, 46, 52
Tier 3 instruction, 44–45
Tier 3 words, 170
timing and frequency, 11
Tomlinson, C. A., 37
tone, 151
transition words, 151
Turtle Rescue (Hickman), 104
types of knowledge, 169
affective, 169, 171–172
background, 169–170, 172
cultural, 169–172
domain, 169–170, 172

U

unconstrained skills, 23
Universal Design for Learning
defined, 38
differentiating within, 38–39
Implementation Rubric, 48
Lesson Plan Template, 48
strategies, 44
University of Oregon, 40
using data, 40–41, 43

V

variable rotations, 193
verbal reasoning
connecting to writing, 151
defined, 22
vertical team discussions, 31
videos and artifacts as shared learning experiences, 6
videos, 10
building readers' knowledge, 171–172
class work during small groups, 184
connecting to whole-group instruction, 51–52
connecting writing to small-group instruction, 154
differentiating instruction, 39–40, 45
engaging readers, 122, 126, 134
expanding your professional community and commitment, 199
monitoring and responding to students, 140, 146
planning for small-group instruction, 67, 86

selecting and evaluating text, 99, 105
students as readers, 18
Visual Drill Card for Alphabet Instruction, 92
Visual Model of the Curriculum Policy, Design, and Enactment System (Ramillard & Heck), 111
visualization, 4
vocabulary knowledge, 23, 76, 90
connecting to writing, 150
defined, 21
writing with a focus on building, 158
voice, 106

W

Ward, A., 40
Wexler, N., 169, 176
What Works Clearing House (WWC), 151–154, 158
whole group work, 182
Wiesner, D., 170
Williams, T. W., 67
Winter Fun (Arego), 140
word choice, 150–151
word recognition, 20–21, 103–105, 168
defined, 21
prompts for, 142–143
writing to support, 152–154
word splash, 174–176
sample, 175
student affinity diagram, 175
Wright, T. S., 168–169
write to respond, 57
writing, 9, 13
embedded, 12
writing connecting to small-group instruction, 149–150
expand your toolbox, 165
guiding questions, 220
implementation activities, 221
instruction in small-group lessons, 152
launch your reflection, 165
Leading the Learning Action Guide, 220–221
opportunities in and beyond the small-group lesson, 158–161
reading and writing connection, 150–151
recharge your instruction, 165
routine for introducing sound-spelling relationships, 153
samples for understanding reader comprehension, 161–164
samples for understanding word recognition skills, 154–157
to enhance reading comprehension, 158
to support word recognition, 152–154
video, 154, 220
written responses to text-dependent questions, 158

Z

Zane and the Hurricane (Philbrick), 177
Zusho, A., 37

Literacy in a PLC at Work
Paula Maeker and Jacqueline Heller

Rely on this essential guide to provide equitable literacy outcomes for every student. Learn practical strategies for utilizing data as collaborative teams to answer the four critical questions of learning, and access templates and protocols to improve literacy for all.

BKG046

Making Sense of Mathematics for Teaching the Small Group
Juli K. Dixon, Lisa A. Brooks and Melissa R. Carli

Make sense of effective characteristics of K–5 small-group instruction in mathematics. Connect new understandings to classroom practice through the use of authentic classroom video of pulled small groups in action. Use the TQE (Tasks, Questions, Evidence) Process to plan time effectively for small-group instruction.

BKF832

It's Possible!
Pati Montgomery and Angela Hanlin

Based on research regarding how to improve outcomes for students and highly effective schools, leaders, including principals, now have a reliable guide to ensure universal literacy instruction while supporting their teachers and increasing reading proficiency for all students.

BKG161

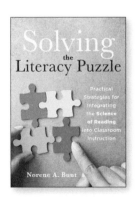

Solving the Literacy Puzzle
Norene A. Bunt

Using graphic organizers, assessments, and reflection questions, educators can unpack five core components of literacy instruction within the science of reading framework. This comprehensive guide prepares teachers to confidently implement effective literacy instruction in their classrooms.

BKG158

Solution Tree | Press

a division of Solution Tree

Visit SolutionTree.com or call 800.733.6786 to order.

Quality team learning **from authors you trust**

Global PD Teams is the first-ever **online professional development resource designed to support your entire faculty on your learning journey.** This convenient tool offers daily access to videos, mini-courses, eBooks, articles, and more packed with insights and research-backed strategies you can use immediately.

GET STARTED
SolutionTree.com/**GlobalPDTeams**
800.733.6786